It's Different When You Manage

It's Different When You Manage

Raymond J. Winters

LexingtonBooks
D.C. Heath and Company
Lexington, Massachusetts
Toronto

Library of Congress Cataloging in Publication Data

Winters, Raymond J.
  It's different when you manage.

  Bibliography: p.
  Includes index.
  1. Management. I. Title.
HD31.W565   1983   658   83-47500
ISBN 0-669-06679-6

To my wife, Marie

Contents

Figures and Tables

Figures

Tables

Preface

Contemporary managers function in an increasingly complex and changing business environment. To gain insight into managerial effectiveness it is necessary to carefully dissect the techniques used by effective managers into pieces for study: This book does so.

My aim is to help you, the reader, better understand the practices and techniques used by effective managers and to show you how to use them to improve managerial effectiveness. Therefore I offer some insights for improving interpersonal relationships in the organization. Effective managers are continually confronted with the challenge of managing conflict and handling change, making financial decisions and solving problems. Hence, a spectrum of managerial approaches are discussed.

Managers cannot avoid making decisions; for even a decision to remain passive implies a decision. Sometimes doing nothing is the best course of action, but even to wisely reach this conclusion you need opinions, facts, experiences, and judgments. Doubt and concern enter into every significant decision-making situation, but with more accurate and complete information at hand you can make less-ambiguous decisions. Your decisions will be better as well as made with more confidence and self-assurance. This book examines the process for choosing between alternatives while giving due consideration to the risks.

The changing business world requires that managers know how to perceive the needs of the marketplace. It demands that you build the organization and apply good leadership strategies effectively. However, good plans and programs are not enough: They must be successfully implemented. The keys to this are effective communication and motivation. In order for an organization to function with strength of purpose and harmonious accord, all members must work together to accomplish the company's objectives. This means that all reactions by people in the organization must be meaningful, positive responses to managerial actions. Motivation is mirrored in behavior; experienced managers learn how to read behavior and implement change accordingly. Each individual has different needs and the test for a manager is being able to marry these so that the group can work together to accomplish the organization's goals, which might be different than the member's goals. A successful manager helps his or her people to perform better on the job while providing the opportunity and environment for satisfying the individual's needs.

Today's rapid technological developments require that all management resources be used in the most productive manner possible. Managers must be technically competent in order to support their staff. When a manager lacks technical knowledge and expertise about the equipment, processes, and facilities used in the company, his or her credibility with staff members and higher-level managers is dangerously weakened. An investment in education improves a manager's effectiveness and presents a good return to the company.

However, technical competence is not enough, for getting the job done requires competence in interpersonal relationships as well. The contemporary higher-level manager must establish an organization and create an environment where all of his or her managers can function more effectively. This means that managers must be aware of the need to establish nontraditional frameworks for perceiving the changing roles of authority and levels of responsibility often needed to handle current sociological and technological problems. Effective managers begin with clear mission statements and then see that they are translated into goals and objectives for the functional departments. When this has been done, priorities can be assigned and tasks ranked for allocation of resources. The performance of the managers responsible for the tasks can then be measured against expectations. When possible, managers can work together on resolving mutual problems; this often results in better solutions and cross-education.

It is important that the strengths of all managers be unified. This generally does not evolve without the benefit of a democratic managerial style. Contemporary managers are less authoritarian and more democratic than those of yesterday. However, many organizations are still not meeting their goals, and thus human relationships are not improving sufficiently.

This book represents my thoughts on these ideas and many more areas of managerial concern. These comments spring from many observations based on over thirty years in managerial positions with major international companies and over twenty-five years of teaching management at the graduate level at leading universities. If the reader benefits from even a few of my ideas, my efforts have been worthwhile.

1 Effective Motivation

In today's highly competitive economy, a company's only long-term advantage lies in its human resources. People are the company's most valuable asset. Technological developments, more-efficient production methods, reduced material and labor costs, and the development of new domestic and foreign markets are all short-run advantages. Therefore a company must rely primarily on its human resources for survival and growth. What the employee brings to the job are skills, initiatives, and the willingness to work hard. A manager must assess these and build upon the self-motivating strengths of a person to raise performance level: This is a manager's most-difficult function.

Competence and Achievement

An employee shows competence when he or she demonstrates control over the working environment. Most people have a strong desire to handle their environment in a manner that is most personally satisfying and permits the opportunity to make things happen. It is difficult to separate competency and expectancy, for an employee has a strong sense of competency if she or he has been successful in the past and thus will develop a high level of goals and objectives to be attained. An employee with a track record of more failures than successes, however, might have low-level expectations and lack self-motivation. This kind of employee will let the business environment control them and will offer little effort to change conditions. Effective managers know that through a series of successful experiences an employee's sense of competence can be made stronger. This becomes a self-fulfilling prophecy for success. A manager must provide the opportunities that permit an employee to challenge and master difficult situations. Each person will assess the possibility of success or failure; and if the person is a risk taker, he or she will be more motivated to attempt a task even if the possible outcome is not controlled. A big score is made if the employee wins, and if he or she loses it can be rationalized away because of the non-controllable forces and factors. On the other hand, an employee with a low-risk profile takes few chances and becomes very conservative. Managers must recognize that most achievement-motivated employees walk the middle of the road as they want their skills and talents to be properly employed

1

in order for them to influence the outcome of the course of events. This is a mark of aggressive realism, a much-sought-after quality. Motivating this type of person is easier than you might expect for they get great satisfaction out of accomplishments and a smart manager provides feedback by which the employee can measure the degree of success. Also, recognition among one's peers further feeds the need for measurement of performance. The achievement-motivated people are the ones who help a company grow rapidly and they provide the foundation upon which all strong organizations operate. If we know all of this, then why don't we have more highly motivated employees in business today?

Why Motivational Approaches Fail

Have the common motivational approaches used over the past half a century failed? The answer is yes, for it is often said that a given person is just not putting forth the effort required by the job, or productivity is low and the quality of the goods and services produced does not meet established standards. The common motivational approaches have failed for the following reasons:

1. Managers either do not recognize or accept the fact that if an employee has a low level of motivation his or her performance will suffer as much, if not more, than if he or she lacked the necessary skills, abilities, talents, and resources to do the job.
2. Managers tend to blame low-level performance on lack of job training, education, or experience and try to provide more of the same. Often a manager does not realize that the employee needs no more of these but instead has learned that by working at levels as low as one-quarter of ability they can still keep their job. Most of these employees with proper motivation could perform at well over three-quarters of their ability. (See figure 1-1.)
3. Managers do not understand that if an employee's needs and aspirations are properly addressed, both the person and the organization will be more productive and grow.

Achieving Higher Motivational Levels

Why are managers not more successful in helping employees to move to higher levels in the motivational range? First, managers have many functions to perform. Motivation is but one and most managers are better at performing such functions as organizing, planning, and controlling. Because they feel

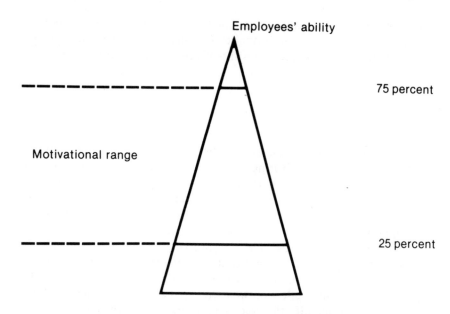

Figure 1-1. Motivation and Performance

more comfortable with these functions, they focus on them rather than on motivating their employees. Second, most managers, in addition to not knowing how to motivate their employees, do not give it a high-priority position in the daily performance of their job. Third, few managers have a realistic perspective of what level the employee is at in the motivational range. This is often because they do not attempt to measure it. Why not? Because, few managers appreciate the importance of motivation in increasing productivity, do not know how to measure the change in productivity should it be brought about, and are not sure how to change an employee's behavior through motivation in order to improve productivity. Motivation can be measured through the willingness of the employee to accept new and challenging assignments, striving for higher levels of authority and responsibility and increased professionalism in all that they do. Fourth, many managers often overestimate or discount the abilities, skills, and talents of an employee and thereby set performance levels too high or too low. If goals and objectives have not been set at an attainable level for an employee, then little challenge for success might be present or excessive pressures might arise, and either of these might result in less rather than more productivity. Fifth, some managers have preconceived evaluations—often subjective—about an employee that discourage the manager from attempting to motivate the employee to higher levels. There can be the tendency to sell the employee short. The feeling that the employee can really do very little more than he or she is already doing and that the efforts put into greater motivation of this person will really bear little reward to the person, the manager, or the organization.

The Need To Excel

Some employees have a strong drive to be successful in their work and they carry an internal self-motivating force that constantly urges them to perform at ever-increasing levels. However, other employees are content with their status in life and in the organization and might not care to expend any more effort than is needed to hold the job. When you as a manager look at your employees, how can you evaluate the intensity of this internal drive?

This can best be done by carefully observing the employee's behavioral patterns. If you have the opportunity to observe these outside of the business environment, you have more valuable information. Without this opportunity, you must reflect on what you see happening on the job. First, you should try to identify the goals and aspirations of the employee. Are they realistic, too high, or too low? Does the business environment provide the opportunity for the attainment of these goals? If the answer is yes, then the employee can perhaps be motivated through the understanding that success is highly probable and within his or her reach. If the answer is no and the environment restrains the person from reaching desired goals, can the environment be changed or must the employee's levels of aspiration be redirected to new disciplines, new positions, or even opportunities outside the present organization? The highly self-motivated individual often places monetary rewards at a level significantly below the self-satisfaction that he or she gets in having done a job well. Public praise and recognition is a prize that this employee dearly loves to receive, yet many managers are not aware of this type of person or otherwise fail to give adequate recognition to the accomplishments. To the highly self-motivated person, praise for a job well done is a reward in itself. A manager must give the degree of recognition in keeping with the accomplishments. Showing adequate recognition in public to those with records of accomplishment is a greater motivator and to all those who are aware of the praise. However, insufficient recognition can be worse than no recognition at all. Reputations of being unappreciative and cheap are very hard for managers to live down. The news spreads within and outside the organization with amazing speed. The impact can be a highly negative motivator and produce a decline in both an employee's morale and output capacity. Remember, the high achiever—whom most managers wish they had more of—measures himself or herself not only against his or her peers but also against the expectations that can be successfully achieved. They track and monitor their progress and growth, so a manager should provide them with the feedback and data necessary to perform this task. A good manager always asks, "What am I doing to give high visibility to the high achievers?"

The Importance Of Feedback

If feedback is so important to the high achiever, then isn't it even more important to the person who needs motivation? After all, how can you motivate low-performance-level people to a higher level if they are not aware of what they are contributing as measured against what you expect them to contribute? An effective manager lets each employee know exactly where he or she stands at all times. If the results are good, give praise; if the results are fair or poor, explain why and help the employee correct the situation. Capitalize on the employee's strengths, but also help him or her to recognize weaknesses and embark on a course of action that will turn these into strengths. Some managers feel that giving praise to an employee will go to his or her head. They fear the employee will get overconfident, ask the manager for a raise, and if the raise is not forthcoming, reduce both effort and output. The Machiavellian concept seems to be employed; keep them guessing, put the pressure on, and you can get increased productivity from the person. Never give praise, keep the person insecure, and he or she will work harder and harder for you. This is not only sheer nonsense, but highly destructive to the employee, the organization, and the growth of the company. The number of people who do not see through this style of management is minute. It is not a sound, constructive approach for developing and retaining people who must become the company's most valuable resource. A judicious use of the carrot-and-the-stick approach can be effective, but the sole use of the stick is foolish. Why some companies and managers still insist on trying to motivate by fear is perplexing since it has never been productive in the long-run.

Highly Motivated People Advance

A highly motivated employee spends a considerable amount of time figuring out how the job can be done better and how other employees can contribute more. The manager should encourage these peoples' suggestions and involve them in helping other employees. A highly self-motivated person can be moved about the organization in order to be in close contact with other employees who need motivation. These employees will observe and learn, and it can become contagious. Everyone learns from example and experience;

when a highly motivated person gains recognition and promotion, the recipe for success is quickly seen and appreciated. Those with a very low level of ambition do not recognize the road to success and remain unconcerned with changing work habits. A manager should advance his or her high achievers rapidly for the company that follows this policy will grow faster than competitors. The highly motivated person often expects other people to fit the same mold. This might cause a problem in the organization if these individuals exert undue pressures on those who perform at low levels and appear content with that status. The highly motivated, high achiever often climbs the executive ladder at a fast pace because he or she gets the job done. Often they have little compassion for those employees who have lower-level productivity. Of course, your position as a manager requires you to motivate the less-productive employees; however, to maintain a cooperative tone in the organization it is important to help the high achievers to become sensitive and empathetic to those working at a lower-productivity level. This does not mean that they condone such performance but instead that they realize that they have special traits, abilities, characteristics, and drives that other employees do not have and must be given a reasonable chance to reach the mark. If the high achievers are to be promoted to higher levels they too must learn to show less frustration and more patience in developing people into wanting to achieve higher-level performance.

What happens to an employee's motivation when he or she gets a new manager? Let's look at an employee who is operating at a high percentage of his or her performance-ability level. In most cases the employee is comfortable in the current position, feels that the job tasks are well under control, and is not unduly affected by anxiety or stress. Should the current manager be replaced by one who has less concern for the employee, the work environment might become less congenial and within a short period of time the employee's productivity might decline if he or she feels that efforts are not being recognized. This performance decline might be either intentional or unintentional. Unless the new manager becomes more convinced that the employee is truly the most valuable resource of the company, the work environment might become even more disorganized with greater amounts of freedom from pressures, greater amounts of relaxation, and perhaps even more benefits and higher salaries accompanied by less loyalty and performance. Many managers find it comfortable to blame the decline in productivity in the organization to a declining work ethic among younger employees. This is a poor excuse for far too many younger employees work much harder than they should, owing in part to the tremendous competitive pressures that they have faced from high school right through the college or university that they attended. Every new manager should sit down at the earliest convenient time with each person and understand what his or her goals and interests are and how these can be joined to the objectives of the organization. A manager's primary responsibility is to help an employee grow, mature, and improve his or her abilities, and increase the desire to reach the rewards of the high-achieving employee. An employee's new manager has the commitment not only to sustain a high level of motivation and performance but also to raise it to higher levels.

What Is Employee Maturity?

Employee maturity is a condition where the best blend of motivation and ability combine to help an employee rise to the highest level of willingness and capacity to accept responsibility. It is also when an employee is not willing or is not able to accept responsibility that we have employee immaturity. Within these two levels are ranges where a person might be willing to accept responsibility but is unable to do so without help in improving his or her skills. A manager must focus on training and education in this situation to move the employee to a higher level of maturity. Ability, rather than motivation, is the primary problem. Another range between the two extremes of maturity is where the employee is not willing to accept responsibility but is able to do it with the skills he or she already has. A manager must now focus on the primary problem of motivation rather than ability. Building higher levels of skill is always much easier than increasing a person's self-motivating forces for the latter requires the employee to perceive respect and have a good inner feeling. Personal maturity grows when a person develops self confidence that has resulted from handling difficult tasks and building a record of successful accomplishments. Wise managers help an employee to build a record that fosters pride in what he or she has contributed to the organization. Recognition promotes pride, pride improves motivation, motivation and ability increase productivity, and the mature employee engenders successful accomplishments and grows with the company. Each person must hold before him- or herself goals and objectives that he or she see as being attainable in order to improve self-motivation. If a manager sets a goal too high, an employee will perceive it as impossible to achieve and not be motivated. It might even cause dismotivation which might feed on itself should other goals be seen as also not achievable. A wise manager sets goals that are high enough to cause an employee to reach yet at a level that the employee perceives to be attainable.

Excessive Goals for Middle Managers

In recent years many stories have surfaced about excessive goals being set by management in an effort to force greater amounts of motivational efforts within the organization. Some of these stories are true, but others have been grossly exaggerated. Where the stories are true, it appears that the excessive goals have been applied more to the middle-management levels than to the nonmanagement employees. It is quite necessary for higher-level management to establish goals that are a challenge to middle management. Pressure on middle managers often causes them to be more productive in the use of their resources; however, sometimes a pressure-cooker atmosphere is established. Unrealistic goals that result in failure on the part of the manager are often not seen to be the cause of the failure and the quick dismissal of a manager can result in the organization losing a valuable person. The loss of this manager to your company might become a valuable gain to another company, perhaps your competitor. What brings about this dangerous practice of setting excessive goals for middle managers? It starts with higher-level management setting their aims at high levels that will make them look good to the officers and board of directors. The tendency is to measure results in numbers (that is, revenue, sales, percent of market, and so forth) and to achieve these numbers that are increased annually the pressure is put on middle managers to achieve these high goals and to use whatever practices might be necessary, even if they prove harmful in the long-run. The measurement is based on the short-run and only this kind of performance seems to matter to higher-level management. What can happen? Sales figures can be overstated and returned sales not properly recorded. Inventories and invoices can be misstated and monies either hidden or not properly accounted for in a timely manner. Sometimes suppliers are paid in advance and the overpayments of the cash are returned later, resulting in deceptive expense charges and misleading accounting.

There is tremendous pressure to make the numbers look good and to keep performance high regardless of the price that is being paid either now or in the future. A major company recently went so far in this direction that it had to delay an annual meeting in order to buy the necessary time to present an acceptable picture to the stockholders. The opinion of the outside auditors was withheld until the impact on earnings of such pressures and tactics (estimated to be an overstatement in excess of $8 million) could be identified and corrected. Although it often is good to use a reasonable amount of pressure to motivate middle management, if the goals are too high and unreasonable, the threat of punishment for not meeting the goals can have serious consequences and result in the loss of many good managers. If middle managers perceive that they are going to be marked as unsuccessful if goals are not met, they are likely to try to find ways to shortcut or bypass the rules, regulations, procedures, and practices of the company; if unethical or improper steps are ways of meeting the goals there is a strong temptation to risk this approach. Higher-level management often causes the middle manager to take the risk and play bet your job by promising rewards based solely on performance and accomplishment. However, in most companies there is less of the carrot dangling to achieve the goals and more of the whip-snapping approach. Has management forgotten that sugar draws more flies than vinegar? Managers at all levels—and nonmanagement employees—will rise to a challenge and a reward more than to a threat, particularly if they have self-confidence and self-assurance. Intimidation is never effective in the long-run. Why do managers hide behind it?

When the pressure to perform reaches the point where middle managers, or any level of managers or employees, are willing to overlook the rules, look the other way, or compromise their conduct, integrity, and personal honor, then management has created a real monster and the company might pay a very high price for these actions. How serious can all of this become? It is not just a matter of poor morale, conflict, and contention among managers and employees, but it can result in lawsuits by vendors, suppliers, and stockholders. Such unreasonable pressures can result in an unaccepable product with defects or failures that result in product-liability suits. When this happens, then the decisions of management can become very expensive for what little benefits might have been attained. Bring on criminal charges and governmental investigations and you have paid a high price for setting excessive goals for middle managers. Bring on union problems and you will be even more sorry for attempting excessive motivation.

A manager is in a difficult position when excessive motivation becomes the way of running the business. Frequently, he or she has little voice in setting the goals for the organization; they are set by higher-level managers. The normal approach is for a manager to set goals and objectives together with his or her employees. When higher-level management begins to set the goals and objectives for the managers without consulting the manager, they often become unreasonable and not able to be accomplished with the given resources. Middle managers grow and move ahead, in most cases, only if they satisfy their immediate manager and help develop an impressive record. Without union protection, and often little job security, a middle manager often feels that his or her job is on the line. The strategy adopted then is rather than to fight those goals and objectives to go along with the excessive demands and use whatever techniques might help in meeting the targets. Should you play bet your job? Each manager at some time is faced with this decision. Each manager must decide for himself or herself. I have always found it better to fight than run for you must live with yourself and only you can set for yourself the code of conduct that you can live with. If the company's standards of business conduct are not compatible with yours, then you must make some decisions quickly. You harm youself and your career if you try to bend the rules and play the game that you are not comfortable with and cannot support. The outcome might be a no-win situation. You should not compromise your standards and moral values.

What Are Your Moral Responsibilities?

If production is falling and as a manager your facilities or department might be eliminated, should you falsify records to prevent this from happening? The answer is **no**. Yet this is done by some managers who feel the pressures. In one company where this happened the manager was eventually fired and the firm had to restate their earnings downward for a few years. Who was the winner? No one. It is not uncommon for a manager to be under pressure to increase the performance of his or her organization annually; however, constant unrealistic pressure is short-sighted. Excessive motivation is rarely effective in the long-run.

One of the major automobile manufacturers found that excessive pressure to increase profits caused many problems. The company was under pressure by the government to meet the government's emission standards. The records of the test results were incorrectly managed in order to produce the numbers that would meet the standards. Later when these records were found unacceptable, the company agreed to pay $7 million in civil and criminal penalties to settle the charges. Excessive and improper motivation can be very costly.

Most of the pressures for producing the numbers come to middle managers from higher-level managers. True, some middle managers try to outperform their peers to gain higher visibility, but when they do this they often still set attainable goals. The problem is that the middle manager is never asked what he or she can do; rather, they are given the numbers, and told to go and make them. If the numbers are not attainable, a manager must say so and articulate the reasons to his or her boss. Perhaps the numbers are unreasonable and when assigned were not perceived as such; therefore direct communication is a must and a manager has an obligation and moral responsibility to say "I can't make these, and let me tell you why . . ."

An additional example of violation of moral responsibilities and conduct for good business actions was another major automobile company that was found to have installed a hidden control box to override the speed of the assembly line and therefore increase production. Of course this was a serious violation of the union contract. How did middle management explain their actions in not revealing this condition? They said that they couldn't keep missing their targets on production, and as their managers were putting pressures on them they had no choice but to go along. It was even reported that they tried to have this higher-level management pressure removed but were turned down. It appeared that top management knew that the assembly lines were being sped up but expected middle management to cooperate and not to spill the beans. The middle managers shirked their moral obligations to say what was on their minds and went along with what was expected of them. Did it cost the company? Yes, the union went to court, proved the speedup of the assembly line, and won $1 million. Excessive motivation combined with managers not taking a moral stand was not a wise practice.

Managers Set Motivational Levels

You as a manager have a very responsible position for you must motivate your employees wisely without creating an environment that condones any form of unethical behavior. You must be honest with the company, your employees, and yourself. Focus on the latter and the other two will fall in place. Don't just ask if the results were achieved, but ask how they were achieved. If you are in any way asking your employees to cut corners and use even minor unethical tactics to meet unrealistic goals, you had better get your act together. Otherwise, everyone suffers.

What can you do to see that your managers or employees do not engage in illegal or unethical behavior? First, make sure that unrealistic goals and excessive pressures are not to blame for causing anyone to attempt to cut corners or attempt any form of unethical behavior or conduct. How can you monitor this when it can be far-reaching within the organization? You don't do it all yourself; you place the responsibility on all people in the organization to speak up and make their views known. Communication must flow up as well as down, so cultivate an environment that encourages such a flow. Second, you should have a complete and detailed written code of conduct that every employee in the company is required to read once each year. They then should be required to sign off that they have read them, understand them, and agree to abide by them. Failure to do so should carry the penalty of dismissal from the company. These codes of conduct should be very explicit and cover all significant areas of the company's activities (that is, marketing practices, accepting gifts, moonlighting and using company resources, competition, public statements and activities, and so forth). Third, it is important that all levels of management take an active role in establishing the goals, objectives, and motivational forces and directions. Define what is going to be measured, why it is being measured, how it is going to be measured, and how the numbers will be evaluated.

Self-Motivation

Why is it that so few people today give a second thought to self-motivation? Perhaps it is because the world is spinning so fast that just keeping up with the day-to-day tasks is challenge enough. It also might be that most people seek easy and quick solutions to everyday problems and focusing inward takes time, concern, and the willingness to accept change. If you are about to change your level of self-motivation then you had best be prepared to spend a lot of time on this program and realize that you are embarking on a long-term commitment. No one turns himself or herself around very quickly nor is it done without some acceptance of weaknesses and the willingness to get to work and do things differently. Why is it such a difficult program? Because few people can help you. You alone can set new directions for yourself and accomplish them with zeal and fervor.

A person may have a strong desire to improve him- or herself and this self-motivation is commendable; however, motivation is tied in very closely with the environment in which we live and our intimate personal values. Going back and changing the environment in which you were raised is impossible and the effects that it had on you are already in place. The best that a person can do is to look at these, evaluate the elements carefully and choose how, when, and where weak points can be strengthened. You must sit down and do an in-depth study of what your values really are, how they got there, whether you accept them, and whether you are going to change them. It is only when you truly know what is important to you and where you want to go in life that you can even begin to establish a direction and level of self-motivation. Do you sell yourself short? Don't—reach for confidence and you will gain it. Your self-image often directs you into playing the role and making it self-fulfilling. See yourself with a low self-image and you will shirk responsibility and growth. Picture yourself with a high self-image and you will seek a far-greater role in personal life and business. It is the person who feels inferior who escapes the very challenges that can make him or her master personal destiny. It is easy to run and hide, but it takes courage to get out and attempt to accomplish something even if it does mean a risk of failure. The old adage that a turtle gets someplace by sticking out its neck is worth remembering.

See yourself as a winner and you will succeed. A manager must try to make each employee picture himself or herself as a person who has the ability and capability to achieve something of importance. Only if a person perceives this will he or she attempt to accomplish the task. Faith leads to success and success leads to confidence which then creates greater success. If you believe that you can do something, you can. Perhaps not the first time, but you can do it if you don't quit. The more confidence a person has within him- or herself the greater likelihood that he or she will be successful. A manager must instill a high level of self-confidence in every employee who reports to him or her. This is not just a nice goal; it is a responsibility. Higher-level management must evaluate a manager on how effectively he or she achieves this responsibility because positive attitudes are the most forceful growth tools for any organization. If a person is to be successful he or she must have the attitude that he or she is capable of achieving something important. Ralph Waldo Emerson said, "Nothing great was ever achieved without enthusiasm." If you or your employees have self-motivation then little change is required. The difficult task is to get the person who has a fear of doing something different to try and get out from under the security blanket. This often requires a change in how a person thinks, talks, and acts. The first step in the right direction is to speak in terms of "I can do it" or "I will do it" for self-confidence encourages self-motivation. Not only can you as a manager help your employees speak and think in a more enthusiastic manner, but an attempt should be made to help an employee to visualize constructive changes and successful outcomes. If a person can picture himself or herself attaining an objective, then there is a high probability that enough self-motivation will be generated that the results will be accomplished.

Motivation Requires a Purpose

Many people are insufficiently motivated because they do not really know what they want in life and have set no targets to aim for or directions to head in with a planned program of steps to be taken. How can a manager get this type of person to take the first step and do some goal setting? One of the best approaches is to have an employee reflect on what position they want to hold five years from now and where he or she sees him- or herself in the organization. The best that a manager can do in this respect is to be the catalyst that gets the thinking process working. Direction for self-motivation must always come from within a person and no manager can tell an employee what is the best program of personal action. Unless this employee sees something of significant importance that he or she is willing to work hard to attain, then he or she will be little motivated to build an action program and follow it diligently. You can help your employees to consider the following four steps: First, goals cannot be clearly identified and considered over a period of time (for evaluation, measurement, or modification) unless they are written down. To make this an effective process the goals must be identified as to whether they are short-run or long-run in nature. A short-run goal might be to get promoted to the next level in the organization within the next two years, whereas the long-run goal might be to become a manager in the organization within the next four years. As a manager you can play an effective role in helping the employee to outline realistic goals. Second, a person must prioritize his or her goals. What is important and which goals should be accomplished first? Trying to do many things in a short period of time is rarely efficient or effective. Practice and experience in the basics is often a prerequisite to the more-advanced skills.

You would not participate in a hockey game until you learned how to skate; likewise, if your long-run goal is to become the chief financial officer you had better learn a lot about finance and capital budgeting. Third, an action program must be established and this also is put in writing. Each goal is clearly identified along with the steps necessary to attain it in the time span allocated. This action program must be complete in all possible detail and potential problems should be identified along with ways in which they can be handled. Alternative goals should be listed as well as the conditions that might require motivation to be redirected. Fourth, a time table must be constructed that outlines a reasonable schedule for accomplishing each goal. Unless a targeted completion date is established in advance, the initial thrust of self-motivation can falter. There is always the risk that a person will delay striving for his or her goals, but the greater risk is that enthusiasm will die early before results reinforce the initial desire to become a high achiever. The latter problem can be countered by setting short-run goals that are small in scope and can be completed and measured.

Effective Motivation Requires Commitment

Many managers and those people working for them start off in a position with a high degree of motivation, run into some setbacks, failures, or frustrations and immediately sign-off. How unfortunate this is when often careful planning and much dedicated effort went into trying to accomplish the goals that were so carefully established. We all suffer discouragement and at times it can seem like an impossible mountain. The secret is to never quit. Most football games are won in the last two minutes and many races in the last few seconds. Once you have embarked on a course you must be dedicated and stick with it until the end. When the trail gets steeper, you must climb harder. If you are committed to a goal, then you are going to achieve it within a reasonable time. Think long and hard before you remove that responsibility that you established and agreed to accept. You have a pledge to yourself to succeed and the last person that you can let down is you.

Improving Employee Motivation

In almost all cases, improving employee motivation and commitment is with a lot of hard work. It is very difficult to motivate people and it is much harder—if not sometimes almost impossible—if the individual sees no real need to become a higher achiever. Each person has goals that are directly beneficial to him or herself but often are not compatible with the organization's goals. It is not easy for a manager to unite these goals so that the employee will turn his or her energies in the direction so that both he or she and the company benefit. Part of the problem is that an employee has basically short-term goals in that he or she is interested in higher salary, promotion, and better working conditions; and the company has long-term goals such as profit improvement, growth of the business, and technological development of new products.

A manager needs to help an employee realize that if he or she puts his or her efforts into helping the company meet its goals along the way the employee's goals and needs will also be met. In Japan the continuance of lifetime employment is contingent on the growth of the company; hence, all parties have a vested interest in the success of the business. The difficult task for a manager is to gain the trust of the employee. A greater commitment by an employee will benefit the employee in addition to the company. A strong bond of trust and confidence needs to be developed and a manager can do this only by specifically demonstrating a direct connection. In addition to identifying the elements in this connection, a manager must point out what steps can be measured and evaluated by the employee to convince them to continue to direct their efforts and loyalty in the best interests of the company. A very clear picture must be presented to overcome any distrust that an employee is carrying over from past years under different managers or in other jobs held in other companies. As these experiences were outside of your control, you as a manager are not responsible; however, the business of making each person who works for you a dedicated, loyal, and committed employee is your responsibility. Higher-level management will measure you on how well you succeed in these efforts.

Your first step in this direction is to ensure that you have no assumptions concerning the employee that can in any way affect your efforts to motivate that person. It is easy to harbor an assumption such as: "John is lazy" or "Mary is not well organized" and these thoughts tend to become influential forces in how you motivate and manage these people. It is going to take time, perhaps years, for any negative feelings carried over by an employee from previous work experiences to dissipate and it should come as no shock to a manager that gaining commitment and loyalty is a long and difficult task. Don't set your goals too high, either, for you will find that some employees will never be 100 percent devoted to the company and its goals. You may have the best of intentions to gain a high level of employee commitment and motivation; however, some employees harbor fears of being exploited and will not give you the full trust that you desire. Some employees resent any attempts to manage and motivate them and you will need to set some realistic expectations for them. Set your expectations too high and the pressures in trying to achieve them will cause you frustration and disappointment and might even harden the employee's feelings further about being exploited and used by you and the company.

Methods used in the past to motivate employees and achieve commitment seem to be ineffective today. Many books have been written and countless seminars held in an effort to improve productivity by developing committed and dedicated employees. Many managers have spent large amounts of money on sensitivity-training programs, encounter sessions, morale surveys, and extensive job-enlargement efforts. Fringe benefits provided by many companies grow at increasingly faster rates each year, yet the return on the investment seems very small. It is difficult to see any major gains in productivity; costs seem harder to control whereas gaining larger shares of foreign markets becomes more elusive each year. Employees seem to be less enthusiastic in accepting the rapid technological developments brought about by our highly competitive free-enterprise system. Because of this, managers must constantly reach out for new approaches in effectively motivating employees. Each employee has different drives and needs that must be met if he or she is to become a more productive person. Identify these and focus in on appealing to them. What does the person want? Is it higher salary, greater challenges in the job, more security, a larger office, the need for a title, or the need to feel recognized and important? Some employees will not take risks because they feel that you, the manager, will not tolerate the smallest mistake and he or she will not gamble on being put in the penalty box for a period of time. Are employees going to become self-motivated if you have created this impression? When this happens, who is at fault: the employee or you? Motivation can be improved by your becoming a little more forgiving and perhaps creating an environment in which the employee feels less threatened and not too closely supervised. Learning and growing does not take place without some experience gained by making mistakes. You as a manager have made them; why can't your employees?

Some employees' need to have their skills and abilities put to maximum use feeds their self-motivation and commitment. They want to feel that their job is important, that they are important, and that they are properly involved and contributing to the growth and success of the business. In order to evaluate their status, they want to know what is going on in the company. You have a responsibility in managing this type of person to see that they get adequate feedback and insight as to these matters that are important to them. Often you will find that such employees believe in the policies and practices of the company and have a high degree of loyalty. They want a manager they can look up to with respect and who is empathetic to their needs and feelings. An insensitive manager will quickly create a less-dedicated employee. Some managers not only are poor at motivating employees, but they excel in demotivating individuals as well as whole groups of people. A motivating force for the employees who sincerely desire to contribute to the organization is to give them new and challenging assignments that push them to excel and gain further recognition while helping the company to further its growth.

Another way for a manager to build more motivation into his or her organization is to develop team spirit and competitiveness between groups. Give each team a set of high goals to strive for and measure them against their record of completion and against the track record of other groups. A person who is not very self-motivating can be caught up in the striving of the group toward an objective and peer pressure can be quite great if the employee is not pulling his or her own weight. A recognition and award to the team for outstanding accomplishment gives added visibility to the team members and reinforces the value for additional efforts and dedication. Some people are not overly concerned with individual accomplishments as they feel that they will go unnoticed; hence the efforts are really not worth the prize. However, being part of a winning team is prestigious and an award is perceived as being more likely to be granted and worth the efforts expended. A person might let him- or herself down and not feel responsible to anyone, but this is more difficult to do when part of a group activity. A person perceives the respect that a manager has for them as being greater when the extra recognition of the team's contribution is added to what the individual employee has performed. You will find that giving employees the opportunities to have greater responsibilities is a strong motivating force and if you want both the employees and organization to grow, accompany it with adequate recognition of the accomplishments produced. The team approach can be an acceptable way for a person who is not self-motivated to be pushed into higher levels of performance without feeling that you are singling him or her out from the group. If the latter is perceived then the employee develops more feelings of hostility and becomes even less dedicated and committed to tasks.

It is always difficult to manage a less-than-fully motivated employee for a decision must be made as to the nature of the action to be taken. There is a tendency to come down hard on the employee and give a veiled threat of demotion that might lead to firing. This is better as a final course of action rather than an initial step in endeavoring to gain more commitment and performance. Once the strong stand is taken a manager leaves him- or herself with few other options and a potentially good employee might be lost too quickly by not giving him or her enough time to increase his or her dedication. The correct first step is to lay out a program for the employee whereby he or she sees exactly what is expected and in what period of time. Build such a program in stages with each stage requiring greater commitment and further demonstration of higher levels of performance. Growth during such a program must be visible and measurable and feedback regarding how you see the employee's progress given back to the employee.

Passive or Active Role?

All individuals are different; however, the development processes that take place within people are relatively standard. Generally a person grows from a

passive state as a child into a more active state as an adult. As this growth
takes place a person tends to be less dependent on other people and becomes
more independent and self-sufficient. Barring personality problems, the
development of a mature person proceeds in this direction. However, some
people, because of their environment and circumstances, have not followed
the path from the passive role as a younger person to the more-active and
independent role as an adult. Managers often find that such an employee is
unable to identify a real sense of direction in life or work and might even
not be able to accurately determine his or her real role as passive or independent. If the employee clearly wants to fullfill a passive role in the organization, then any motivation techniques that appeal to this posture might be
effective for you, the manager. Security, benefits, and protection from sudden changes will provide the stability that this person seeks, and a manager
must realize that there are some people who are not going to become highly
motivated regardless of how hard the manager works with them. This does
not mean that a manager totally gives up on them. It does mean that a
manager must give adequate time to other employees who can and want to
be motivated. Employees who want to play strong and active independent
roles are capable of much self-direction and you will find that only minor
motivational nudges are necessary, and these perhaps quite infrequently.

The employee who remains passive is going to look more to you for
leadership, direction, and support. You must help them to learn to think for
themselves and to develop the necessary courage to act on their own. This
takes time and it is brought about by carefully going through stages of ever-
increasing responsibility and authority. Show the employee how a decision
was reached and encourage him or her to make the next one under your
preestablished procedures. You must help them yet not be overprotective. A
protective manager might be replaced by a manager who is far from protective and past practices, policies, and procedures will offer little safety to the
passive employee. You really do this type of employee an injustice if you
allow him or her to continue a pattern of working habits that will not
prepare them for possible harsh and abrupt changes in future employee-
manager relationships that might lie outside of your control.

Motivate employees by giving them meaningful assignments where they
will achieve recognition and respect by their peers. You can also help an
employee to grow into a more meaningful person by encouraging him or her
to enjoy deeper and wider interests both on and off the job. If an employee
is a good speaker, encourage him or her to give presentations not only
within the company but in public groups. Not only will the employee reach
higher levels of self-confidence but the company will also benefit through
the resulting public relations and contribution to social needs. It is quite
possible that with such help and encouragement you can help to turn an
employee from a passive degree of loyalty to one of active commitment

and dedication to the organization. The following are some approaches for you to consider. First, use the carrot more than the stick. There is a tendency to take the posture of the strong leader and to prod employees into higher levels of productivity by subtle fears and threats. In the majority of cases this is not going to work and the manager is either going to have to back down or take an action that he or she might not really want. Younger employees today do not take very well to intimidation, for they are quite independent and perhaps need you and the position a lot less than you and the company need them. Waving a punishment stick doesn't even work in the home with children; why then do some managers think it will work with mature young employees? Employees are far more productive when they want to do something and feel good about doing it rather than feeling threatened. Second, focus on the employee achieving small short-run goals rather than long-run company goals. Small goals are more easily attainable and measurable and if they are short-run in nature the results can be quickly observed. Furthermore, the satisfaction of accomplishment is more visible and more sustaining to future efforts. The short-run goals for an employee should be built into the annual-performance plan and when the employee has had a hand in building that plan he or she will be motivated to achieve the goals. There are no surprises and the methods of measuring and evaluating progress have been determined and agreed upon in writing. Third, help each employee to set goals that are not only realistic but attainable given their skills and experience. Be definitive in what is to be expected. One manager set as a motivational performance goal for an employee: "You will get rave reviews about your work." What is a rave review? Who is to give them? When? How? Is this an objective and measurable standard or purely subjective comments? Do you think this manager was wisely motivating or was this manager trying to set a condition where he or she could say "See you didn't get rave reviews, therefore your performance was unsatisfactory" and put the employee in the penalty box? How do you think an employee would perceive such a goal? Why do some managers insist on playing such games and then ask why they don't have loyal, committed, motivated, and dedicated employees? It is this very poor management of people that so seriously impacts the further growth of productivity in the nation today. A very realistic question that each manager must ask of him- or herself is "Am I most wisely developing and maximizing the use of my greatest asset the employees?" Most employees want to use their skills and abilities in doing things that will bring credit to themselves and the organization. Good managers find ways for this to be done.

Motivational Factors That Affect Productivity

Since one of the primary purposes of increasing motivation is to improve productivity, it is necessary first to identify some of the important factors that affect productivity. Only when a manager recognizes these factors can he or she understand how to motivate an employee. Each of the following actions fall within the range of tasks performed by managers and therefore are under the manager's control and can become measurable items in the performance evaluation of the manager. First, productivity almost always improves when better planning is performed. Planning is not the sole responsibility of the manager for it was found in the previously referenced Hawthorne experiments that when managers involve the employees in planning more positive cooperation ensued and productivity improved. Employees must be motivated to develop short-term plans as well as long-range plans and all of these should mesh in a coordinated and cohesive manner with the long-range plans of the company. Plans are put in writing, reviewed, and approved and become the action programs that direct work motivation and effective utilization of employees. Second, a penalty-free environment and open democracy in the group is necessary to encourage employees to participate and share in the decision-making processes. It has been found many times that broadening the responsibilities of employees is not only beneficial to the employees but is a gain for the company. Managers must give people the opportunity to grow and mature on the job in order to motivate them and direct more of their abilities toward achieving the goals of the organization. Generally employees do not want to accept greater responsibility in making decisions for they feel that it is the manager's job and that is what the manager is getting paid for. "Why should we do the manager's work?" is the statement often heard. The fear of the extra work and problems that getting involved in decision making might bring causes many employees to avoid the process. Third, managers must build into the work environment opportunities for an employee to do more exciting and challenging work. Create an environment where an employee can be creative and initiate some measures on their own to make the tasks more interesting and less demanding. Giving the employee the opportunity to meet his or her own motivational needs and to meet the manager's expectations in performing these will help the employee to mature and grow. As a result, his or her abilities increase and he or she becomes even more capable of handling more difficult assignments and raising his or her level of productivity. Managers must recognize, however, that there is a significant difference in changing the work environment through job enlargement and job enrichment. The former often adds only a mixture of different tasks that may not be meaningful to the employee and often are not related to producing a more satisfying job. In fact, a hodge-podge of added duties often makes a job less satisfying. The secret in job enrichment is that greater motivation arises because the nature and scope of the work has been changed, more responsibility and challenge has been added, and the employee definitely perceives his or her position as being upgraded in the eyes of management and peers. Fourth, examine the qualifications of the person you have put on the job to make sure that he or she is not over-qualified. Very little will be gained by utilizing job enrichment to motivate an employee when he or she is already overqualified for the job. One company hired only the top 10 percent of high school graduating classes for work in their mail rooms. These young people had abilities far in excess of the demands of the work and job enrichment would hardly ever go far enough to satisfy the esteem and self-actualization needs of these young people. Overhiring results in poor morale and a high rate of turnover. Absenteeism, tardiness, boredom, and many other symptoms are often dis-counted and disharmony in the organization increases.

Fifth, what you as a manager expect of your employees and how you treat them will in a large measure determine their level of performance, pro-ductivity, and career progress. You might want to motivate through incen-tive programs that reward employees who contribute more, not just by work-ing harder but also by working smarter. Give employees more training and help them to improve their technical skills as well as their business acumen. Improve channels of communication and provide an environment where employees feel free to discuss new ways of doing old jobs. Sixth, one motivating technique used today is for a manager to motivate employees through the use of a variable wage program. A given percentage of salaries are withheld—usually only a few percent—and then at the end of the year if the company has not made an established profit level the company retains some or perhaps all of the salary monies that were set aside. This becomes a motivator for the employees to work smarter and harder to help the com-pany meet the established profit and growth goals. In addition, another part of the program provides a bonus payment—usually of a few percent of salary—to the employees when the profit target is significantly exceeded and this becomes an added motivator. Also, part of the program can consist of distributing stock of the company to the employees through a profit-sharing plan. The motivation here is for the employee to produce more profits for the company which will help him or her to benefit from holding the stock. Only a small amount of salaries are withheld from employees if the profit goals are not met; however, usually this is more than offset in the long-run by the rewards of the bonus and stock benefits which result from exceeding the profit target. There can be many variations to a motivational program of this nature and each requires study before being implemented.

Internal Environment

An employee's behavior reflects externally the nature of his or her internal environment. A study of an employee's behavior leads to an identification, through such clues as lack of aggressiveness, insecurity, and so forth, of his or her drives and an evaluation of these lead to a better understanding of the person's value goals and needs. The importance of knowing an employee's aspirations is to better understand what he or she is working to achieve. If behavior indicates a need for recognition and/or promotion, these values must be appealed to with programs that will help the employee to accomplish them. Another employee might be striving for challenging work; hence, a motivational program addressing that must be offered to him or her. Other employees' behavior might indicate a high value on securing salary increases without the added pressures that might arise from promotion or more-challenging work. A manager must put in place a program to motivate each employee based on what he or she values and needs. You cannot take a program that motivates one employee and use it to try to motivate a person who has far-different goals.

Managers must be aware of the internal environment of values and goals that an employee has identified for him- or herself. Your chances of changing these are very small. What you must do is know what causes an employee to behave in a given manner and how you can externally motivate him or her to become a higher achiever and become a more dedicated, loyal, committed, and productive employee. Your greatest assistance can come from changes that you can effect in the work environment, organizational structure, and peer relationships and interactions. Try to assign the employee to tasks that complement his or her particular needs (for example, security, challenge, high visibility, and so forth). Position the employee in the organizational structure in a way that will encourage greater participation and a higher level of contribution. See that the employee receives proper peer recognition and support. Assign challenging goals and recognize and reward the achieving of them in a manner that says thanks for the effort. The management of many companies often make foolish mistakes in this area. One major company recruited MBA graduates and the cream of the crop of their own staffs for a special nine-month full-time training program to qualify them for executive or internal consulting positions that carried an almost limitless job potential.

Upon completion of this rigorous program the graduates were given a raise amounting to only a few dollars per week before taxes. This was not motivational; it was insulting. Yet management never could understand why the dynamic graduates recruited from outside the company never stayed more than a few years. When, as a manager, you encourage a high level of dedication and performance, then you had best reward it well. News travels fast.

Many managers think only in terms of monetary rewards for the high achievers. Indeed, this is very important. You can add further recognition, however, by allowing the employee who has performed at outstanding levels to attend educational seminars.

Some employees are very conscious of their physical work environment and a motivator to them might be a fresh coat of paint, some new pictures on the wall, and some flowers on a desk. Most employees take pride in their working environment and this can be a strong motivational force. One company, known for having tremendous esprit de corps and intensive motivational drive among its employees, always had a few beautiful baskets of fresh flowers in highly visible locations. Everyone who entered those offices immediately had their spirits uplifted. The external environment most definitely affected the mood of each person's internal environment. The cost of the flowers was small compared to the vast benefits of improved employee morale and motivation and the feeling it presented to visiting customers and business people.

Building Confidence

A manager should endeavor to see how an employee perceives his or her abilities. Often this is shown in how the employee interacts with their peers. Is the employee shy and quiet or aggressive and vocal? In the former case, the employee may lack confidence and need encouragement. However, even the latter case can be a cover-up for insecurity and a strong need for the employee to keep proving him or herself by trying to make others look and feel insecure, thereby building up their own ego. Managers, even at very high levels, often demonstrate these same traits. The ego-insecure employee rarely has the authority to inflict much hardship on other people, but this is not true of middle managers who try to motivate with force or intimidation to make him- or herself appear strong. As a manager you have some control over helping an employee build successively higher levels of confidence with ever-more-demanding assignments accompanied by encouragement and praise on completion.

If the internal forces that motivate an employee are difficult to identify, they are even harder to change. Some alteration might be required if the individual's goals differ significantly from those of the group. All that you as a manager can do is to provide motivating directions, programs, and incentives for an employee. Even extensive educational programs will result in little productivity improvements if the employees do not want to grow and become high achievers. The benefits need to be sold up front and then the programs offered to those who really care.

The internal environment in which each employee evaluates job-related events has a foundation that rests on home and social forces and experiences that have set his or her personality long before you become this person's manager. If the employee had parents who were permissive in most matters, it might be difficult to manage this person using rigid disciplinary techniques. Such an employee is better managed by letting him or her become more involved in planning and controlling more of the day-to-day work activities given the goals of the group. It is important then that a manager learn to know and understand his or her employees to better recognize what channels of expression exist and to what degree, if any, they might be modified. A manager learns these things best by communicating extensively in an informal manner and observing behavioral patterns. If possible, the good and bad experiences in the life of the employee are worth knowing. As their manager you can then use motivational approaches that are closest to the good experiences. For example, if it is apparent that an employee has enjoyed trips and travel, perhaps a trip or assignment away from the area would be an incentive. On the other hand, an employee who has a fear of flying and does not like to be away from home might find a trip or assignment away from the area a disincentive for greater commitment, loyalty, dedication, or improved productivity. Some employees have established strong family roots in a geographical location and relocation might be the wrong move for them and the organization. However, other employees can adjust quickly to new people and surroundings, and relocating them might be a very positive motivator. An employee in New York City who has his or her heart in San Francisco might become much more committed to the job if given an opportunity to live and work in that area.

Areas Of Motivation

Employees are motivated in three areas and each affects behavior differently. The first is the area of the internal forces, which are the factors that develop from childhood experiences and the personality traits of the individual. Levels of being introverted or extroverted are built over many years. Although a manager can help an employee identify these levels and handle them, it is difficult to make a major change. Tasks must be assigned that are compatible with the employee's personality. It is difficult to motivate a highly introverted person into becoming a super salesperson and it is difficult to motivate a highly extroverted person to become a programmer. This is because selling requires much interaction with people whereas programming requires far less. A manager who recognizes and understands how the internal forces work in an employee is better able to predict how the person will act in given situations and can assign work that will be less stressful and more productive to the organization. The second area are the external forces; these are actions and environmental conditions that you as the manager can control. As they are visible to the employee, you are measured by how well they help each person to meet his or her own personal goals and needs as well as those of the organization. You can motivate an employee through job titles, salary levels, and increased amounts of authority and responsibility. These external forces can be carefully orchestrated in a well-planned career-path program. As the employee expects you to act in his or her behalf you need to sit down and plan with each person what is to be done and how it will be measured. Build on strengths and correct weaknesses. Tasks must be clearly related to the needs of the organization to achieve a high level of commitment.

The third area where you can take motivational steps is in organizational style. A style is set with the purpose of synergistically molding the strengths of everyone in the organization in the most productive and acceptable manner possible. If you show that you do not trust your people and do not have confidence in their ability to effectively make decisions and implement them, then you have discounted their talents and they will not respect you. Should you try to intimidate or coerce your employees you are encouraging them to informally organize and oppose your authority. To increase cooperation and initiative you should delegate as much of the planning and decision making as possible to your people and reward good performance and wisely punish poor judgment. The associations that develop in an organization can be improved when you as a manager provide good upward and downward channels of communication. With good communication, many people involved in the decision-making process, a high degree of mutual trust and confidence, and responsibility for control of the work in the hands of the employees you will be employing a style that encourages a high level of self-motivation in your staff.

Employees want you to be a successful manager and they want to be proud of the organization. The manager who has a sincere interest in the growth of each of his or her employees aids organizational and personal growth. Do not be too quick to identify each action observed in an employee with a specific motivator. For example, people will go to the same restaurant for many different reasons. Some go for the good food whereas others go because the prices are reasonable. Some restaurants offer neither, but may be the place to be seen. Some people go to a restaurant because the atmosphere is nice, because it is nearby, it has a good reputation, or they have gone there as a custom for years. To be a successful restauranteur you must consider all of these motivating forces and appeal to as many as possible. To ignore any one of these motives, could reduce your business revenues. Effective managers must also observe the motivational needs of their employees and provide the means for them to achieve their goals. An employee who talks constantly might be reflecting his or her insecurity and trying to talk him or herself into getting greater, higher-level recognition and importance in the group. The need to attract attention might be seen in the practice of name dropping or exaggerating experiences. As a manager you should try to help this person feel less insecure; this can be done by assigning some confidence-building tasks. An employee who is also aggressive in acting to get attention might be led into situations that cannot be mastered; failure will then lead to even greater damage to self-confidence.

Sometimes behavior reveals the existence of conflicting motives. An employee might express the desire to take on greater responsibility in order to gain promotion, yet he or she lacks a strong commitment and dedication to success. Because of the lack of self-confidence the fear of failure before their peers causes them to back off in even the smallest of conflict situations. Sometimes there is the fear that if they succeed their peers will be jealous and the friendship built over many years will be threatened. It is important to make this person realize that by taking the assignment they are not losing friends but gaining new ones in different parts of the company. In fact, the opportunities and recognition might improve the bonds of friendship.

Motives change because the needs and goals of an employee alter as the result of new experiences in changing environments. As motives change the motivational approaches must also evolve. The employee whose children are through college and has paid off the mortgage might have a lesser need for the large salary increase associated with high-level-risk assignments. A greater value might be placed on title than money. Management often does things in reverse. The young employee often needs a high salary with frequent increases to meet the expense of buying a home and raising a family. Yet he or she is often given a title instead. However, the older employee who places a higher value on position and title rather than money often in the later years receives significant salary increases instead; this is not what he or she really wants or perhaps needs. Why do managers try to motivate employees by often giving exactly what is not wanted or needed? Effective motivation focuses on the employees' needs. If you don't know what the needs of each person are then how can you motivate to them? You expect your manager to understand your needs, goals, and values and your employees expect you to know theirs.

The payoff on carefully conceived motivational programs comes when employees willingly accept greater responsibilities that reinforce self-growth and the success of the organization. Each employee has his or her sights set on personal targets as well as the organizational targets. Help them to achieve the correct goals. An employee might incorrectly perceive what steps to take in order to grow in and with the organization. An employee, for example, who is an outstanding salesperson might perceive that the way to the top in the company is through finance and by going off in this direction find that he or she does not have the necessary skills and thus becomes less valuable to the organization. The temptation to change occurs when we go back and look at the career paths followed by others in the past to reach the highest positions in business. In the 1940s most executives rose from manufacturing, during the 1950s from marketing, during the 1960s from finance, during the 1970s from legal, and during the 1980s from engineering due to the emphasis given to technological developments. You and your employees will climb to the top by doing what you do best. Managers know how important perception is in communication; however, it is also very important in motivating people. How you perceive the abilities, skills, and talents of a person will go a great way in determining what motivational approaches you use. High-level performance rarely arises without intelligent motivation programs.

Inward Drive

Motivation is an internal drive that results from a stimuli that causes a person to act in a self-serving manner. External stimuli such as pep talks are not effective motivators unless a person perceives them to be beneficial. A manager using any form of manipulative approach will be less successful in generating a high level of motivation than one who tries to understand the inward drives of a person. You should get employees to do what you want for the organization while showing that it also helps their personal goals and needs. The following are some items that people see as motivators. Which of these items are motivators to your employees? One way to find out is to reproduce this list and distribute it to each person in your organization. Ask each person to select the six items that motivate him or her the most. After you have summarized the results you can build a profile of your organization and develop some long-range motivational programs.

Understanding what is expected of me

Steady employment

A good program of employee benefits

Working for a manager whom I can respect

Higher-than-average pay

Knowing that my skills are wisely used

Challenging work and opportunities

Good working environment

Opportunity for rapid promotion

Recognition and praise

A high level of accomplishment to attain

A feeling of belonging

Good vacation and pension program

Freedom to be creative

A good performance-evaluation program

Close supervision

Personal respect

Conditions that permit quality work

Opportunity for growth and self-development

Being a part of the decision-making process

Not too much pressure

Good two-way communication

A high level of esprit de corps in the organization

Opportunity to travel and/or relocate geographically

Acceptance of mistakes

Inward drives that result in higher levels of motivation can with proper planning be channeled into higher-level productivity. This can be done by identifying the factors that affect productivity and relating them to the value beliefs of the individual so that he or she feels a need to move in that direction. Some examples follow.

1. Better planning is a factor that affects productivity. Many employees have a real need to be part of a planning process before they can feel committed to the assignment; therefore involve them early in the process of goal setting. Formulate programs for accomplishing these goals.
2. More and better training can improve productivity. Do you ask each employee what training he or she needs or do you decide a program for them? Most people have a desire to increase their knowledge, improve skills, and excel on the job. Give an employee the opportunity to outline in writing what he or she needs in the way of education and training and then jointly develop a program that addresses these needs. This should be an annual program, reviewed and updated semi-annually.
3. Both job enlargement and improved working conditions are factors that affect productivity. Most employees want to learn new skills and be assigned challenging tasks, provided they see reward and recognition for their efforts. Ask what new tasks and job assignments an employee

would like. Ask employees whether working conditions need to be improved and get suggestions from them. All of the suggestions that you receive might not be practical, but you should at least ask for them and evaluate them carefully. Far too many managers ask for suggestions and as soon as the employee speaks up they jump all over him or her with reasons why they won't work.

4. A greater degree of participation by employees in the decision-making process can be a significant contributor to improving productivity. Do you encourage it or do you discount the ability of your employees to make effective decisions? Most people place a high value on their abilities to make decisions. Why don't you?

5. More effective incentive programs can significantly affect productivity. Most employees work too hard rather than not hard enough. Do you realize this? In most situations your employees will set goals for themselves that are far higher than you might expect. Your biggest problem might be how you can scale them down without dismotivating the person.

The preceding are just a handful of factors that affect productivity. These must be combined with the following additional items in motivational approaches that produce lasting effectiveness.

Better communication both interpersonal and organizational

Higher standards of quality and dedication to excellence

Better utilization of technological developments

More efficient use of capital and cash flow in the firm

Greater opportunities for advancement and learning new skills

A higher-quality working life; more satisfaction with your position both on and off the job

Increased market growth and penetration with the understanding that as the firm grows so does the employee

Each employee has a self-image and perception of what can be accomplished. Both of these can be raised; that is your primary mission as a manager. With a perceived low self-image a person cannot accept a large role of responsibility for he or she will feel inadequate and this might result in failures. However, with an enlarged self-image a person can take responsibility too lightly, and this can also result in failures. To be effective a person must maintain a proper balance between self-image and responsibility. However, the inward drives of a person are unique in many other respects.

Each person has a value system of beliefs built up from childhood; these are not easily changed. They are based on experiences, environment, habits, needs, attitudes, opinions, fears, associations, emotions, and conditioning. This value system, although establishing the inward drive to accomplish the needs defined by the person, also throws up defense mechanisms. Effective managers probe the defense mechanisms to uncover repressed expressions of needs and build motivational programs to address them.

Why is it important for a manager to try to identify the elements and forces that might change a person's behavior? This is so because all behavior is motivated and some kinds of behavior are profitable to the organization whereas others are costly. If an employee is absent or tardy frequently, uncooperative, lazy, or careless on the job the organization pays a price. However, the employee who is cooperative, works hard, accepts responsibility readily, and keeps growing in knowledge and skill makes a valuable contribution to the organization. Behavior is affected by motivation and you as a manager have the ability to set motivational forces in motion. Don't force an employee to comply with your wishes; rather, show how he or she can achieve their needs while also meeting the needs of the organization.

Is the effort worth the results? You will arrive at an affirmative answer very quickly as soon as you price out what turnover, poor quality, and low productivity costs the organization. These costs can be quite visible but there can be a much larger invisible set of costs. This is the cost of the employees who do not resign their positions but retire on the job. The loss of dedication, commitment, and loyalty negatively impacts the effectiveness of the organization and the revenues from the sale of the company's products and services begin a rapid descent. The loss in revenue and competitive posture can in time bring the most successful company into a position where it is fighting for its very survival.

A business can and often does fail because of improperly motivated employees and the resulting ineffective decision implementation. Managers also fail, not because they have a weakness in their technical skills, but rather because they cannot properly motivate people to work for the common goals of the organization. Develop your own style in motivating people. Many managers use an intimidation approach and get results—but not without the creation of some levels of conflict and hostility. Some employees don't get mad, they just get even. Motivational rewards do not always have to be in terms of higher salary levels. You can motivate and reward employees with a much nicer physical environment.

Research Findings

The major findings when collectively analyzed focus in on three basic premises that managers must consider and effectively apply within the organization. They are simple points and as such are often overlooked. First, most employees have a sincere desire to use as much of their skills and abilities as possible on the job. Many managers err in that they do not fully understand how extensive these skills and abilities are in an individual. This occurs because a manager often simply doesn't take the necessary time to recognize an employee's true potential. Unless you work at identifying what employees can do and then discuss it, you can never know their true potential. When you give an employee superficial attention and recognition you cannot truly understand what drives them to higher levels of achievement. Help each employee to identify their unique skills and talents and endeavor to enlarge his or her job in a manner that will let the employee strive for greater accomplishments.

Next most managers either do not build a profile of the skills of his or her employees, or they do so unwisely. Look beyond the scope of your department and find where the employee can grow and contribute to the success of the company. It takes a manager with a high degree of security and self-confidence to unselfishly transfer one of his or her best employees to another functional department in the company. Managers must realize that they are measured on how successfully they develop their employees and move them to greater levels of responsibility within the company. Higher-level management should look very carefully at the manager who over a period of time has not moved some of his or her employees into better positions within the company. Many managers use the skills of a person to the maximum to help them look good to higher-level management rather than thinking about how these skills and abilities can help the company in other parts of the organization. Managers lock in people to protect their positions rather than to help the company to grow. In many organizations people transfer out to better jobs only because of their extensive efforts to grow, and they overcome the blocking of the move done by their managers. Is it happening in your organization? How many have moved to bigger and better jobs in the past two years? Did they move because the manager helped them or did they do it by themselves in the face of risks and intimidation?

Third, managers are challenged to organize and structure work in such a manner that it satisfies the needs of the employee as well as the needs of the organization. How do you know if you are doing a good job in this respect? You can get the answer by conducting job reviews with each employee. Give them the chance to tell you what they are doing, how they can do it better, and what else they can do for the organization. A lot can be gained by asking an employee, "How can we improve our organization and the tasks that we are performing?"

The Breakfast Meeting as a Motivational Force

Employees can be highly motivated through an inexpensive approach. In many organizations the pressures of the work assignments do not allow sufficient time for meetings and if they are held after the end of the work day they are often perceived by employees as another way of getting extra hours of effort without compensation. A carefully planned and orchestrated breakfast meeting does not create these negative feelings. Like all good things, these meetings should not be overdone or they lose their effectiveness. More than two in a given year will decrease the value of this approach in the organization. These breakfast meetings should begin about one hour before the start of the work day. It is best to use a nearby hotel or motel dining room if possible as it adds an air of importance that might not be gained by using on-site dining facilities. When a dining room near the work location is used less time is required for the employees to spend in getting there and more time can be devoted to the activities. Attending this meeting must be perceived by the employees as a desirable thing to do; therefore avoid any hardships in getting to the breakfast and from there to the office. The session should open with an informal and good breakfast and no business is discussed during this period of about one-half hour. After this period of social and friendly interaction business should be the agenda for the last half-hour. Only a few major topics should be addressed and the time must be used with great care: no long-winded talks but simple and straightforward discussions of current issues and problems. This is an excellent opportunity for a manager to request suggestions from the attendees. It is an ideal time to give awards and recognition to employees and describe new programs and challenges for the organization. Present these in a way that will appeal to the goals of the employees as well as the organization and encourage participation in helping to make the program a success. The breakfast meeting must end on a positive note with a direction established for the attendees to implement on the job. Everyone should be able to be at their office on time with the sense that it was an hour well spent. Each person should feel now more informed about the programs of the organization and they have been given the opportunity to ask questions of management at this breakfast and have gotten some direct verbal replies. When handled properly this meeting will help employees to understand that management has empathy with their problems and is willing to listen and help. Each attendee must leave this meeting feeling that it was very worthwhile and looking forward to another one in the future. Don't try to save money on the breakfast; make it first class, for the payback in greater dedication, commitment, and loyalty will be well worth every dollar that you spend. The breakfast meeting is an excellent vehicle to improve communication in the organization, and this is often the first step in better motivation.

The Price of Success

The price of success in reaching the goals of an organization is often high, but the price of failure is always much greater. Managers and employees sometimes get little in the way of thrills and excitement from the tasks that must be performed. At times an employee might see little relationship between what he or she is doing and his or her own personal goals. However, the goals of the organization must be accomplished and it is important for each person to realize that the overall program of activities must be carried out in an efficient, effective manner. Everything must be done to produce quality, service, and growth with the lowest costs possible. However, the correct decisions must also be made to assure the shareholders that the company is going in the right direction.

Each person must realize that every task is always done to the best of his or her ability, regardless of how minor the task may seem. If you adopt this attitude, you will have little trouble getting your employees to raise their levels of dedication. Carefully measure the amount of effort required for each task and be prepared to expend it at the necessary price. This might be some extra hours of work on or off the job, but if you aren't prepared to pay the price then give the job to the person who will show the needed commitment. If you can't or won't do the job right, then don't do it. Know in advance the price of the inputs and the rewards from the outputs. Often the price can be reduced by breaking large tasks into smaller ones where the solutions are more apparent, easier to implement, and less risky. Often you can motivate a person to accept the larger challenges when you help them to attack the problem by reducing it to a number of small issues.

You cannot motivate a person to achieve his or her goals if the goals are unknown. Sometimes people need to back off and reset their sights at a lower level if they have set unattainable goals. A pragmatic person tries to keep a sense of balance and sets goals that are with a little extra stretch within his or her reach. What are your managerial goals and what are those of your employees? When goals are identified and put in writing it is easier to motive a person to accomplish them. Even self-motivation is easier when you have defined in writing a program of where you are going.

Managers have a primary responsibility to keep work both interesting and challenging. This is difficult, especially when many of your new employees may be recent college graduates who have mastered such skills as financial analysis and managerial economics. The employee can easily feel an ability to step in and master most of the assigned tasks. What is often lacking is the perspective of the company that has grown with seasoned employees over many years. You must motivate new employees to review the progress and history of the company and to get a better understanding of the needs of the customers and how the company's products and services address these concerns.

See that each employee has the opportunity and experience to work in many different functional areas within the company. Experience is still the best teacher; you must motivate your staff to tackle new assignments that will bring them new insights and improve their abilities to make better decisions.

All problems and issues must be addressed directly; this can be done by fostering a penalty-free environment in which an employee feels safe in try-ing new ideas and taking risks. Reinforce this procedure by offering rewards that compensate for the efforts that have been taken. Many managers feel that spreading a problem over the organization assures a more rapid solu-tion. Involving too many people, without a firm hand in charge, causes the levels of communication and coordination to break down with resultant less-than-satisfactory decisions. You can best motivate people to work hard in solving problems by working hard on them yourself. Keep a good rapport with all interested parties and show an interest in how they are handling the situation.

A manager must also motivate him- or herself to improve personal technical skills and leadership abilities. The half-life of a manager today is only three years. That means that within three years you will find one-half of your skills and abilities are obsolete. Many of the concepts and tech-niques learned in business school in the past are no longer valid, and contin-uing to use them is very risky. Pressures are increasing daily for managers to manage for the short-run and to the bottom line. Most technical problems, manufacturing and marketing issues, and pricing problems cannot be crunched into numbers quickly and decisions made by shooting from the hip. The mission statements of the company should require that all managers focus more on the long-run rather than the short-run solutions to growth and prof-itability. When you evaluate and measure people on a short-run basis you are only encouraging them to view events in a myopic fashion and to look for quick fixes. The most significant sin that higher-level management com-mits today is focusing on the short-run bottom line results rather than the long-term growth and survival of the company.

Conventional Motivation Approaches

Over half a century has been devoted to analyzing how the most precious resource of the company—its people—can be used more effectively. Unfor-tunately, progress has not resulted in any major breakthroughs. Managers today still find it difficult to achieve that higher level of commitment, dedication, and improved performance. There are reasons why conven-tional motivation approaches fail; when given proper consideration these might result in some effective solutions to the problem. First, conventional motivation approaches fail because managers set a price for success too high for employees. In such an environment where a manager has established excessively high levels of performance, it is difficult to achieve wholehearted cooperation and commitment from many employees. The price paid to accomplish the goals is often perceived as too high and not worth the effort. Managers often set the price too high for success because they are implementing short-range rather than long-range plans (five years or more). A manager must look at the policies and practices of the company and identify what behavior and attitudes they develop in employees. For example, is the thrust to develop highly skilled employees for specific technical assignments or is the thrust to develop broad backgrounds of experience so that employees can be more flexible in work assignments and meet the more general needs of the company? The goals set for employees must take the company's policies and practices into consideration; however, they must also take into consideration the objectives of the functional departments. As the manager you must clearly identify the subsets of the organization's goals that you are assigning to employees. Don't set goals too high, but also don't set them too low. Either extreme will cause you to have to exert motivational pressures that are unwise and ineffective. Second, another reason that conventional motivation approaches fail is because many managers do not show that they care about the interests of the employees. The results of the 1924 experiments at the Hawthorne, Illinois plant of the Western Electric Company revealed many insights regarding how to motivate employees. Yet managers still do not apply some of them wisely. You will recall the efforts to study the effects of lighting on productivity. Lighting was increased only for the test group; however, both the test group and control group increased production. Why did the control group increase productivity when they had no increase in lighting? Further studies focused on the assembly of telephone relays where the work environment was also improved and productivity increased. Yet, when all the improvements in working conditions were removed, and the lighting was even reduced, the productivity jumped even higher rather than plunging drastically as was expected.

What accounted for these unexpected findings? It was not the change in the plant and physical working conditions that motivated the women (that is, the changes in illumination and production environment for the "test group" because the productivity of the control group increased also significantly); rather it was the change in the human aspects of the work environment. The lesson to managers then and now was that somebody cared. Employees received recognition by being on either the test group or the control group and all improved productivity. When managers care there is motivation to perform at a higher level. Managers in the Hawthorne experiment expressed a concern in the employees and they developed more self-respect and a feeling of greater value to the company. Also, as employees felt more involved in planning and controlling their own work environment they cooperated more in helping the organization to reach its goals as well as their own. When an employee feels important he or she will be more highly self-motivated.

It is apparent that this well-studied Hawthorne experiment identified the basic needs to be addressed in managing the most complex asset of all: human resources. If the problem has been identified, then why doesn't current management enjoy a payback for this great experiment? Why do managers continue to invest large amounts of monies in employee-opinion surveys, special training programs, and extensive employee benefits?

Interviews conducted after the experiment were of high therapeutic value, and wise managers always realize that the first step in establishing better methods and approaches to motivation is to talk with employees. You realize that employees are critical to the success of your organization, but do you take time to sort through the often-contradictory messages that you get from your employees? Employees are not getting harder to motivate and you know how to motivate them, but you can't if you don't take the time to find out what their needs are and how they can be attained. Do your employees perceive that you and the company feel they are important? When the women at Hawthorne did, there was a wholesale change in their attitude. This is a conventional approach to good motivation but when it fails today it does so because managers do not really convince employees that they are really concerned in their advancement and that they appreciate their efforts.

Hawthorne experiments also found that one of the most significant factors affecting the productivity of the organization was the interpersonal relationships that developed among employees and between employees and managers. People are motivated to higher levels of productivity when they feel that management has put the controls for performing the tasks in their hands. However, some managers today do not practice this approach. Some managers even schedule the work of their people rather than letting them schedule their own activities. Is the manager communicating through his or her actions that he or she doesn't trust the employees to do the job right? If employees perceive this, it will be more difficult to motivate them. The Hawthorne experiment showed that managers need to involve workers in planning, organizing, and controlling their own work if they are to work together cooperatively and raise the levels of productivity. When known conventional approaches for motivating are not used, it is often because a manager sees employee cohesiveness as a threat to his or her control over the activities of the group.

Within each organization there are three elements (see figure 1-2) that must be present to effectively motivate the group. These elements unify employees and managers as they strive to accomplish the goals of the organization. Employees must be given challenging assignments if the organization and its people are to grow. However, managers must also be given assignments that cause them to reach for more-demanding goals and accomplishments. Middle managers must look at the plans that a manager

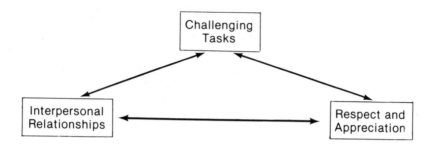

Figure 1-2. Mutual Dependent Elements in Effective Motivation

has in place for him- and herself as well as the plans for his or her employees. Some managers schedule many new demanding assignments for their staffs but continue to do nothing new themselves. Every person must be shown respect in the organization for skills and talents. Appreciation must be extended when demanding tasks are performed in a professional manner. Managers must build in the organization a mutual feeling of respect and appreciation; this results from favorable interpersonal relationships. A manager who fears strong informal work groups has not learned the lesson of the Hawthorne experiments. Such work groups are not detrimental to the organization; rather, they give it strength and a greater dedication to excellence in all that is done. A manager must recognize that a change in any one of the three elements will produce some change in the other two; therefore each change must be carefully orchestrated and carefully implemented.

Third, conventional motivation approaches fail because managers use a mix of techniques that, rather than being complementary, often work against each other. Each technique performs well; however, few managers are skilled in combining them into a cohesive program. One is to establish industrial-engineering work standards for each task. Employees are then measured against them and motivated by rewards or punishments. Unfortunately, once the standards are set they are seldom changed, even when the job and the work environment change. Employees are then asked to perform at levels that might be unrealistic; this is particularly true where standards are applied to knowlege-type tasks. These are tasks that require thinking, creativity, and application of mental processes as well as phsyical activity. Fast-moving technological developments cause many changes in the work environment and as required skills change the methods used for measuring performance must adapt.

Another technique used is to lay out detailed procedures on how each task should be performed. Even the smallest steps are documented in detail and manuals are provided as guidelines for the employees. When questions arise and when an employee needs assistance, it is easy for the manager to refer the person to the manuals rather than offering personal help. All that a manager needs in order to obtain predictable behavior in the organization is to consistently enforce the written instructions. Most of these manuals are written with the goals of the organization in mind and employees have difficulty in seeing how they meet his or her own short-term interests and needs. Effective motivation results in a marriage of the goals of the organization and each person in a manner that is not ambiguous in either direction or means of evaluating.

Employees can be motivated into higher levels of productivity by emphasis on group relationships and group-established goals. Given responsibility and authority the group can manage itself; however, conflict arises when an employee's needs are not satisfied by the group's actions. The unified behavior of the group is necessary for its success and when only partial commitment is present the ability of the group to make and implement effective decisions is affected in ways that are not readily apparent.

Policies and Practices

As any organization grows in size it often becomes more difficult to raise levels of commitment, dedication, and loyalty. Policies and practices that originate with the officers when interpreted and implemented at the functional division levels either lack a clear direction or drown in bureaucracy. Employees see greater distance developing between themselves and their managers and channels of communication begin to break down. The informal meetings that once were the vehicles for better understanding and planning are held less frequently. Information about the company is now learned primarily through bulletin-board announcements and newspaper articles. Often the first news that an employee gets about a new program by the company is through a statement released to the public.

Corporate policies when implemented at divisional levels without adequate direction and authority often cause confusion as to the growth of the company. The use of salary programs for motivation can result in a tug of war between departments for people who possess the needed critical skills unless adequate guidelines have been established. Transfers of employees must meet organizational as well as individual goals. Even with effectively implemented policies it takes a long time for an organization to build a cadre of committed and dedicated employees. Human behavior changes slowly and building positive attitudes toward improved personal and organization values is arduous. New plants can be constructed and new products introduced in short order, but growing a more loyal group of employees takes major investments of a manager's time.

Motivation and Stress

Excessive motivation can raise the level of stress in a person. Millions of employees have their daily lives thrown into disarray because of stressful situations both on and off the job. It has been estimated that stress alone costs American business over $100 billion annually. Managers must be able to recognize stress in their own lives as well as the lives of the employees. To observe stress, study behavior. Identifying stress is only the first step for the reasons for the stress must be understood and programs formulated for coping with issues. Each demand that you make on an employee will be determined by his or her past experiences and how the current situation is perceived. If the demands are not new, then the response will be automatic and simple. However, if the demands are new experiences containing a high level of perceived risk an employee will often subject him- or herself to periods of anxiety. The possibility of failure causes an employee to take protective measures to maintain both a psychological and physiological balance. This adaptive posture can cause the blood pressure to rise, the heart beat to accelerate, and nervousness to increase. It is the demands placed on a person to carry out the adaptive activities that lie at the heart of stress.

Whether the demands that confront a person are pleasant or unpleasant, it is the intensity of the need for the adaptive activities that is stress-producing. The nature and/or degree of either external or self-imposed motivation affects the adaptation or adjustment that a person must make in order to cope with stress. Can stress be avoided? No! In fact, at the right level stress is the force that helps a person to become a higher, more successful achiever. However, problems arise when excessive stressful demands cause a person to be less effective and more inefficient. Tasks are not completed on time and the quality of work suffers. Emotional concerns become reflected in unusual behavior and absenteeism might increase accompanied by psychosomatic illness. These stress-induced illnesses can be manifested in headache, backache, colitis, diabetes, arthritis, chest pains, allergies, peptic ulcers, high blood pressure, and perhaps heart attacks and strokes.

Stress-induced illnesses increase your company's costs. However, there are additional costs that are hard to quantify. When excessive motivational pressures lead to stress both alcoholism and divorces can result. Being married to a job and neglecting yourself and your family carries a high price. Much of the $100 billion annual cost to the nation caused by the effects of stress comes from the person on the job who because of stress-induced alcoholism or marital problems are working at lower performance levels than they are capable of sustaining. It is difficult for a person to maintain a good balance in home and family life if they must work long hours and carry the burdens of the office home with them. Also, be careful of intimidating an employee with a veiled threat to his or her job security in an effort to achieve a higher level of performance. Insecurity often produces tension and anxiety and has negative long-run affects. Perhaps more and better output can be achieved through better planning, scheduling, control, and additional training.

Managers can identify and help control many of the sources of stress encountered on the job by employees. What are some of these sources of stress? The first is excessive amounts of work to be accomplished in far too short a period of time. A fast pace is possible if the intervals of work are accompanied by other tasks that permit a person to pause, catch a breath, and experience new pleasures. An overambitious work schedule might result in less being accomplished as the result of burnout. The decision-making process might suffer, and the wrong steps taken only require additional efforts to correct. A manager has an obligation to see that each employee has a full yet realistic work schedule.

Second, an employee or manager might not have the required authority to handle the levels of responsibility assigned to them. When a person feels that he or she lacks the necessary power to get a job done, the resulting frustration and feeling of helplessness can induce stress. Efforts to motivate a person under these circumstances are ineffective. When you pass an assignment, you must also give them the authority to carry it out or you cannot motivate the person to perform it well. Provide complete and accurate information and data so that alternative solutions to problems can be explored and evaluated. Stress can be relieved when a person feels that he or she has the option to take familiar or comfortable steps. Motivation is improved when an employee feels that you trust his or her judgment and abilities.

Third, you create stress and weaken motivation if every assignment becomes a rush job. Urgent requests always raise stress levels and often the need is less urgent than is expressed. Cry wolf too often and when the need arises to get some work out fast the worker will not be motivated. Most tasks can be planned so that they don't have to be done yesterday. Schedule activities so that large blocks of time are provided as needed rather than jumping from task to task. Set reasonable schedules and motivate people to work smarter and not just harder.

The wise manager encourages employees to do their own planning and scheduling. Controls are built into the work so that each employee can measure and evaluate his or her efforts. Self-motivation then becomes self-fulfilling and the worker controls the work. It is often very difficult to do all of the needed work in the time available; hence, priorities must be established. This can be an effective motivator as it identifies those tasks that require early attention and relieves the pressures that develop when a person tries to do everything in a short time frame.

The relationship of motivation and stress requires you to examine what actually happens to a person and how they react to the event. You can manage many of the events confronting an employee while at work in an effort to make them less stressful and threatening. However, only through good counseling can you help an employee to react to stressful conditions in a more positive manner. You can better assist your employees in handling stressful conditions in the following ways.

First, counsel each employee in ways to better recognize stress-producing situations. When a person knows what to expect, handling it becomes easier. Review events of the past year to identify some of the sources of stress and look at the current environment in order to identify in advance what might be some new sources of stress. If some of your motivational approaches have been producing stress, then it might be time to consider new ones. An open dialogue with each employee is the most direct way to quantify stress-producing conditions in the organization.

Help each employee to do a self-evaluation in regard to stressful situations. Some people hide their feelings and take less-active roles in the group when they have difficulty in dealing with pressures. However, other people will become aggressive and might even demonstrate a degree of hostility. Only by carefully obseving an employee's behavior can you better understand how he or she manages tension and anxiety. Offer the opportunity for confiding and you might reduce the number of problems that the employee is taking home from work. Outside interests and hobbies can provide diversion for a person and often improve mental health as well as personality. At times a person does not respond to motivation because of poor health. An annual physical examination is an excellent investment for everyone, and if an employee has been negligent in this matter ask your company medical department to provide the much-needed assistance.

Many people have not learned how to leave the problems of the office in the office. Provided you can do it yourself you can offer some suggestions; if not, get some professional advice in the matter. A competent advisor can help with this issue and suggest ways in which you and your employees can start on an exercise program that will produce better physical conditioning and a more relaxed, refreshing mental approach to work. Self-confidence helps a person to worry less off the job. Self-confidence is built from a series of successful experiences and you should provide the opportunity for these for each employee.

A manager must be careful not to run at full speed all of the time. You must have some margin of energy left so that when an unexpected stressful situation arises you can fall back on your reservoir of physical and mental strengths. You keep this reservoir at a high level by knowing at what point pressures get to you, and you back off accordingly. Before getting overly concerned about a situation, determine the importance of it and how it will impact the organization. What seems critically important today doesn't seem so tomorrow or next week. When problems get magnified the solutions are even harder to see and evaluate. Avoid acting impulsively on an issue. The immediate solution is often only emotional reactions and quick decisions are often bad decisions. The real issue might be quality rather than quantity, and many managers have decided to address an issue by doing more of the same steps rather than taking new steps. It is easy to focus on the wrong goals when insufficient time is spent looking at what higher-level management wants. You might build a great record of cost control and cost reduction whereas higher-level management has little interest in this area but a strong desire to generate more revenue through the sales of more products and services. Managers often create stressful situations for themselves by trying to accomplish goals that are not the major concerns of higher-level management.

A manager can best motivate him- or herself by utilizing the strategy that the best defense is a good offense. This requires making things happen within a framework of control. A manager must carefully set personal goals that can be achieved without others in the organization paying an excessive price.

Some Mistaken Premises

Some managers do not effectively motivate employees because of the mistaken idea that high salaries will take care of everything. This is a bad assumption because many employees are very dissatisfied with their jobs despite their high salaries. Today more employees than ever before want to have a hand in planning and controlling their jobs and they expect the manager to provide this opportunity. In addition to planning and controlling their jobs many employees expect the opportunity to make decisions or to participate in the decision-making process. You will become a more effective manager when you give your employees the chance to participate in these activities as well as to help set goals and evaluation standards.

Managers in today's world of scarce resources often underestimate the market demands for highly qualified people. You cannot hire or retain employees on high salary alone. Most employees want challenges and opportunities, and without them you will have high turnover. Look at competitive salary structures and exceed them if you expect to draw the best people into your organization; however, when you hire provide a detailed program of how employees will grow in the company and where they might expect to be in the organization in the next three-to-five-year period. The major emphasis must be on growth potential and opportunities. Outline the educational program that you will implement to help the new employee to increase strengths and improve weaknesses. You can best motivate a new employee and current employees as well by showing how you will help them to grow. A manager's primary goal must always be how he or she will develop his or her employees.

Managers often think that once the problem has been identified and a solution developed all it takes is some high-powered motivation to get it implemented. This might by the case regarding a marketing or production-type problem but it is not true when you are searching for ways to increase commitment and loyalty. Finding the true cause of poor morale and low productivity is not easy. What appears to be the cause of the problem often turns out to be very misleading. It is easy to identify symptomatic expression of superficial causes but to address these only provides a short-term fix to the problems and does little to correct them. The forces that build dedication have deep roots and extend in many directions; a Band-Aid on possibly deep wounds will only cause interpersonal relationships to worsen. There are no quick solutions to tensions, conflict, or hostility. Corrective programs must be measured in years, not months. In order for employees and managers to work together effectively there must be a correlation of values and attitudes with common goals and means of attaining them. Organizations commonly have strategic missions to be accomplished over future years yet lack long-range programs for improving the quality and productivity of their business through sound motivational programs.

Higher-level management can do many things to raise the level of dedication, commitment, loyalty, and productivity in the company. Some of these steps follow. Evaluate present methods of recruiting and hiring people. Far too frequently selection of new employees is based on resume and job-application-form data. Take more time in interviewing the candidates for employment and discuss areas such as values, beliefs, goals, and interests. Numerous managers should talk with the new applicant and career paths, training, and salaries should be discussed in more specific terms than is usual. Have a long-range program in place for developing new employees and discuss it in detail. To effectively implement this program move new employees and newly appointed managers into different parts of the organization where broader experiences and new challenges can be found. Some companies move managers into different functional departments about every two years. This puts new blood into the organization. Also, it helps to build a broader bases of generals within the company rather than specialists who know only a small part of how the company functions.

Provide good supervision. This does not mean leaning over the shoulder of a person every few minutes, but it does mean that a person is in charge to direct and coordinate activities. On my most recent visit to Japan to present executive seminars, I was most impressed with the extensive amount of supervision given to groups of employees. This was not resented but welcomed as a vehicle to improve the quality of service offered to the consumer. Proper supervision means knowing when to step in and help and when to move back and let the employees handle the matter.

Keep channels of upward and downward communication clear and free-flowing. Managers cannot properly motivate employees if they do not know what the needs are; needs become known through open discussions. Also, managers who are insensitive cannot expect instructions to be carried out efficiently. Throwing up trial balloons is not a waste of time and is often a very good way to see if an idea or new approach will work. This trial approach allows employees an opportunity to become involved in the decision-making process and as a result feel a part of the action and thus more willing to support it to completion. Managers need to become better listeners and do less talking if higher levels of commitment are to be attained.

Managers must work at providing the kind of work and working conditions that help to meet the value needs of the individual. You can do this best by sitting down with each employee and constructing a development plan for that person. This plan should address the employee's aspirations and interests. You will identify these in your discussions with the employee. The plan should also outline what is needed to develop the individual. Include here what is needed in the way of special work assignments or educational programs. Also, when steps for personal improvement can be identified they should be listed with action steps that can be taken. Include in this plan how you are going to meet the development needs of the employee and how you and the employee share the responsibility of implementing the program

Training-program benefits are long-run in nature; therefore long-range plans must be made for developing employees who will have the needed skills required by changing missions and business conditions. It takes time to evaluate the contributions of new employees and as a company changes levels and direction of growth programs must be revised and improved. Identify the self-motivators and position them in the organization where their actions and approaches can serve as a catalyst to the slower-starting employee.

Self-Evaluation for Managers

What are you doing to improve your level of performance? You must assess your strengths and weaknesses. The following checklist will help you to identify areas that might require attention. Score each item with a **1** if you do it well; a **2** if you know how to do it and try to do it; a **3** if you know how to do it but don't do it; and a **4** if you don't know how to do it.

Organization

Establish clear lines of authority and responsibility.

Properly staff the organization.

Know and pursue the goals of your functional organization as they relate to the company's missions.

Help each staff member to understand how his or her tasks relate to the organizational goals and at the same time satisfy his or her personal needs.

Planning

Plan an adequate-yet-acceptable schedule of work for the group.

Schedule the best use of human resources and facilities.

Establish priorities and involve employees in setting realistic goals.

Endeavor to meet all scheduled target dates while avoiding overtime and/or additional costs.

Production

Emphasize meeting production quotas while controlling costs.

Resolve production problems quickly.

See that each employee consistently meets the performance plan established for him or her.

Coordinate all production activities and make prompt adjustments when required.

Develop and enforce reasonable quality-assurance activities to produce the best products or services with the least amount of rejections, servicing, or maintenance required.

Performance Evaluation

Let the employee set attainable and reasonable performance goals and review them.

Measure and reward the attainment of these goals.

Take necessary corrective actions when performance is at a level lower than expected.

Improving Organizational Performance

Analyze all tasks performed within the organization and eliminate the nonessential ones.

Develop smarter ways of doing each job.

Solicit employee suggestions to improve working conditions and/or methods.

Esprit de Corps

Assign the proper person to a job.

Build a career ladder for each employee.

Give employees feedback on their growth and progress.

Help employees to handle new and more-challenging assignments.

Measure the long-run success of training programs and compare the costs with the benefits.

Reward and promote people for jobs well done.

Earn the respect, confidence, dedication, and loyalty of your staff.

Resolve conflicts fairly and quickly.

Reward and punish as needed with understanding, wisdom, and empathy for the efforts applied.

Keep Growing

Recognize and accept your weaknesses and activate a program to correct them as soon as possible.

Increase your knowledge about technological developments important to your position and the company.

Develop a better ability to improve communication with your employees, peers, and higher-level management.

Your score on this checklist can range from 31 (doing an excellent job) through 124 (need extensive learning and training experiences). A score in the range of 31-50 indicates that you are an effective manager; 51-75 shows that you are a good manager but that the areas you scored as **3** need attention; 76-124 reveals that you should endeavor immediately to upgrade your managerial skills.

Specific Suggestions

The following are practical and simple steps that you as a manager can take to more effectively motivate your employees. Do not try to do all of them at once; rather, pick out the steps that will best address the behavioral changes you perceive are needed now in your organization. Rank these in order of importance and then schedule their implementation gradually over the next two years. High-priority steps should be taken in the next six months, the lesser level of priority over the next six months to one year, and the lowest priority steps over the next year to two years.

1. You should think about the decisions you have made over the past year. How many of these could your staff have made? Why did you not allow them to do it? Develop a list of the types of decisions you will let your employees make in the coming year. Set up a simple procedure whereby you can track yourself to see that you are delegating these decisions.
2. Encourage employees to improve their skills and abilities by doing some research in their respective disciplines and suggest that they write reports for circulation within the organization. This will give them an opportunity to gain some recognition while cross-educating readers in unfamiliar matters. Encourage employees also to make oral presentations to their peers for this will improve their ability to communicate and build self-confidence. Motivate your people to make public presentations in order to gain visibility for themselves as well as the company. These experiences will help to improve their knowledge about the subject as well as fulfill some of the company's social responsibilities.
3. Carefully develop a personal skill profile for each employee. Note where a person needs further education and establish a program to accomplish this at an early date. Look at every position in the organization and identify where there is an exposure if a person becomes unable

to do assigned work. Identify backup assignments and train people to step into the gaps when the need arises. Test your program to see if it will meet an emergency need by having the replacement person handle the position during a normal period.

4. Have a formal career-development program in place for every member of your department and see that you are training your own replacement. Careers must be thought out rather than result from resolutions of events or conditions. Career planning meets two very important needs. The first is the establishment of a course of action that permits a person to achieve personal goals within a reasonable time frame. The second is that it helps the company to manage the human-resource problem in an efficient manner that assures that as the company grows and moves into new ventures the required skills will be available within the company. Start with the individual's strengths and weaknesses and identify what price he or she is willing to pay to improve. The price required for significant and sustained growth can be high and unless success is clearly defined and desired extensive motivational efforts might be required. What is success? Some see it as higher salary, a prestigious title, or position in the organization or the opportunity to be more creative and influential in the organization. To many employees, success is the opportunity to concentrate personal skills and talents on the tasks that they like to perform and satisfy their needs for recognition. The price required to achieve success might be many hours spent at work along with much travel and family separation. How do other members of the family perceive this investment in the employee's career? Often a geographical move is required. When you help employees in career planning you should be prepared to adequately explain the costs as well as the benefits.

Effectively motivating your employees will be one of your most difficult tasks. If it were easy and managers were good at it, we all would enjoy a much more productive society and a higher quality of life. Some important concepts can be stated very simply as follows: First, managers must provide the penalty-free environment where each employee can motivate him- or herself to attain both the individual's needs and the goals of the organization. Second, the highest degree of motivation is not material rewards; rather, it is what the individual perceives he or she is contributing to the family, the community, and the group. Peer acceptance and recognition are very important. Third, as all behavior is motivated, managers must help to bring about worthwhile behavior rather than costly behavior. Good behavior should be rewarded and unsatisfactory actions disciplined. This is so simple, yet most managers ignore its importance to the organization. Every manager must periodically ask him- or herself "How do I motivate my employees?'' "Am I doing a good job?'' "Am I using the proper motivational approaches for each person?'' "Where behavioral change is necessary to benefit the individual and the organization, have I caused it to occur?'' "How do I know that it happened and how have I measured its success?''

2 Leadership Skills and Strategies

Over 60 percent of contemporary executives have advanced professional degrees yet many fail to understand that the formulation of strategy is a continuous process important to the organization and the effectiveness of their skill as a leader. Effective managers not only are able to formulate a cohesive strategy for leading the organization but they are able to see themselves playing an effective role in its implementation. Identifying and improving your level of leadership skills in today's complex organizational structures is not an easy task. As leadership skills can be learned and are transferable it cannot be said that leaders are born and not made. A manager sets a strategy for the growth of the organization as well as for personal growth. These are implemented and achieved through leadership which is a function of managing.

What Is Leadership?

Leadership is the process whereby you motivate people to work toward some predetermined objective. A manager is a good leader when he or she can motivate employees work toward an established organizational goal. It is through leadership skills that employees' behavioral actions are directed and influenced. How does leadership differ from managing? Many of a manager's tasks such as planning, scheduling, and evaluating work are not behavioral in nature; therefore they are not leadership functions. Leadership is a subset of the many functions involved in managing and it is the vehicle by which you get things done through people. Many managers are not effective leaders as they have difficulty getting things done through people. Often, it is difficult to tell what a manager is doing because he or she is doing every thing him or herself, much to the dismay of the organization.

The Leadership Process

The process of leadership requires three interdependent factors (see figure 2-1). The first factor is the manager; the second, the employees whose behavioral actions are being directed toward the accomplishment of an established goal; and the third, the work situation that has given rise to the need for leadership.

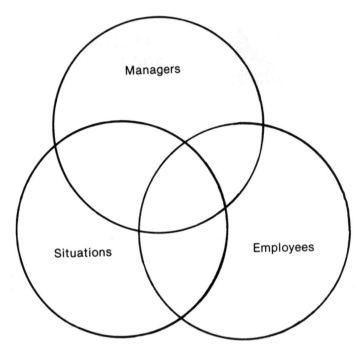

Figure 2-1. Leadership Factors and Relationships

Effective managers demonstrate their leadership abilities by directing the work of employees in an integrated manner to achieve the goals and objectives of the group. The terms *goals* and *objectives* are often used interchangeably but are quite different in practice. When you set a managerial objective for your organization you are establishing for the group a particular aspiration. Goals you set for the organization also are aspirations to be worked for and attained at some future date. However, goals often are subsets of objectives for they are easier to grasp and their accomplishment requires less time. The objective often contains many goals which combine to attain the objective. For example, your objective might be to achieve dominance of the European markets for your products by the end of the decade. In order to attain this objective many goals must be achieved. Some of these goals might be building a stronger marketing force in the areas, establishing overseas production facilities, providing product education to overseas customers, and hiring employees native to the area to manufacture and market your products. You can see from this example that goals require far less time to accomplish than objectives. Also, goals are carefully planned sequences of short-term-action programs, each of which is more specific and of shorter duration than the more-general long-term objectives.

When an objective is set, as in the preceding example, you have in broad and general terms set the course for the organization. A distant target, which will take years to attain, has been set. However, over these years this objective might need to be changed as the mission statements of the company change. Perhaps the objective is attained at some later date or is only partially attained. This is not so with goals for they are specific statements of results to be expected that can be accomplished in a short period of time.

Managers must realize that objectives encompass many forces and factors in an environment external to the organization whereas goals can be managed with the resources of the organization and with a high predictable degree of accomplishment. In the previous example the objective to achieve dominance of the European markets for your products by the end of the decade might be very dependent on international economic conditions, political stability in the areas, and social conditions—all of which you have very little control over. Your ability to exert leadership to managing behavior in these situations is nonexistent. You can exert more leadership in achieving goals than most objectives for you can better manage in the short-run the resources and the interpersonal relationships that are so critical to success. Going back to our example again, one of the goals was providing product education to overseas customers. As manager of this activity, there is something you can do to achieve this goal. You can assign resources to develop product-education brochures, write self-study-education courses, and develop classroom courses and demonstration packages. A goal permits you to make resource commitments and manage them wisely. Your leadership skills are demonstrated by how effectively you plan and schedule the work and how efficiently your people perform the necessary tasks.

There is another element in effective leadership that must be addressed in regard to objectives and goals. Both of these are measurable but the characteristics of how you measure them are different. In our example of an objective, that is, achieve dominance of the European markets for your products by the end of the decade, a quantifiable measurement for this objective might be to capture more than 60 percent of the total European market sales for your product lines. Characteristically, this objective might take many years to accomplish and can depend significantly on forces and conditions well outside of the influences of your organization. On the other hand, typical for goals, they can be expressed in absolute terms and accomplished in short periods of time. A quantifiable measurement in our example of a goal, that is, providing product education to overseas customers can be expressed as produce in the next year six product-education brochures, four self-study-education manuals, three classroom courses and three demonstration packages.

The leadership process requires the establishment of both objectives and goals. Later we shall see how these fit into formulating strategy for the corporation. It also requires that there be dynamic interactions on a planned basis of the three factors we looked at earlier, that is, managers, situations, and employees.

Effective Leadership Traits

Is a manager born a good leader or is he or she developed into being a good leader? For many centuries people believed that great leaders were a result of heredity and kings and queens possessed this special talent through their blood lines. Managerial leadership traits can be inherited. Leaders often tend to be brighter, more socially participative, more self-expressive, more self-confident, and more dominant in group interactions than nonleaders. These characteristics, when not inherited through genes, are nurtured and grown through the environmental forces and factors provided in a home of parents with these traits. Leadership traits, if not already a part of a person's characteristics, can be learned. Intelligence levels can be improved through training as can a higher degree of social interaction and self-confidence. Many of the characteristics that you possess are major contributors to how successful you are as a leader. They contribute much to your posture as an executive and the good news is that these characteristics can be improved through education and training.

Your leadership abilities are measured on how successful you have been in influencing the behavior of your employees in specific situations. Most managers adapt a style of managing employees and situations in either one or a combination of three approaches.

1. One approach is to give detailed directives to employees. It frequently involves telling them what to do, when to do it, how to do it, and, infrequently, why to do it. This approach is often effective given a crisis when firm orders must be given and immediate compliance required. If the building is on fire you exert your leadership abilities in such a manner. Given a noncrisis situation this approach shows little respect on your part as a manager for your employees' intelligence. Such an authoritarian approach can generate hostility, lack of intitiative, and inhibit creativity and cooperation. The manager who gives directions to employees for all situations is often locked into written rules and procedures that are often inflexible. All too often these guidelines are applied automatically to every similar situation even if the conditions are unique and quite different. There is a tendency for managers under this approach to become overly concerned with production and goals and measurements to face in this direction. Only downward communication exists. Managers focus on making assignments. Corrective actions are geared toward punishment rather than improvement. The message is get the job done my way or you must defend your actions.

When jobs are redefined and responsibilities changed they are monitored very closely and complete and immediate compliance is demanded. Managers applying directives set deadlines and track results closely. Often he or she doubts his or her own abilities to direct the work of the group and hopes to transfer the responsibility to the employees through rigid schedules of target dates and enforcement procedures. It can reflect a hidden fear that more power rests with the employees than the manager wants: thus the attempt to control and restrict its informal use. When a manager feels unsure about effective leadership the movement grows to more closely direct the work of the staff and to tighten up on the organization structure. Often an extremely inflexible program is designed and implemented to handle any and all situations. Higher performance levels that are established are more difficult to attain and when the employees do not properly respond to the perceived restrictive conditions stress results and productivity declines.

2. Another approach is to delegate authority to employees while encouraging them to become involved in the goal setting, planning, and measuring process. Leadership ability is measured by how effectively the group achieves the goals of the organization. The manager guides and directs and this is a cooperative and cohesive approach to group interaction. Self-confidence is built in a person when he or she has the opportunity to make some decisions and see them effectively and correctly implemented. This approach builds on the strengths of a person and managers search out these opportunities. The physical characteristics of a person are difficult to changes unless he or she desires to control food intake better and exercise more often. However, managers can help to establish development programs for employees that will improve voice, posture, manners, and appearance. Also, many business schools and management-training programs have helped employees to learn how to make better decisions and to build their self-awareness. Everyone can learn how to communicate better and relate to other employees and each step in this direction raises the levels of self-confidence. Effective managers lead the way by developing themselves.

Managers show the characteristics of being a successful leader by delegating decision-making responsibilities. Delegating does not mean abandonment for unless a person feels comfortable in approaching you for help and guidance, you only elevate his or her stress level and raise the fear of failure and its consequences. The group should be motivated to work as a team with respect for each others' skills and talents. Some managers set conditions of competition between employees to gain higher productivity and soon develop an organization of independent superstars, each fighting for personal opportunities to gain fame, fortune, and success. The wise approach is to encourage team efforts and decision making relevant to abilities of the members. Let the team set their course and measure the progress at established intervals. Managers often stand in the background until help is required or requested. Managers must also have the ability to steer away from offering too-quick criticisms on tasks not yet completed. A good practice under this style of leadership is to avoid excessive instructions for these tend to weaken motivation. The Socratic approach, which raises questions leading to discovery and answers, is a powerful, effective tool for managers. Dedication and efforts must be recognized with adequate rewards because the motivation that this fosters increases the effectiveness of the organization and improves the strengths of the leader.

3. The next approach to a leadership style is for a manager to sell his or her employees on the importance of the job and the need to perform it well. Challenging tasks are presented as opportunities with heavy emphasis on the benefits to be derived from above-average performance. Goals are established in a manner that permits accomplishments to be measured in terms that can be quantified. Much visibility is given to what each person attains and competitive scores soon become important motivators. It is not uncommon to see scoreboards posted indicating the standing of each employee in regard to his or her target and the accomplishment of each person in the group.

To be an effective leader you must be dedicated to your professional responsibilities. You must be committed to the highest level of excellence in all that you do and you expect this from your employees. A very important leadership trait is the ability to communicate at all levels in the organization clearly and with honesty and candor. This must become a part of your posture, whether it be a one-on-one relationship or interfacing with the group. Effective leaders are respected; you gain respect through how you talk and act.

The Situation as a Factor in Leadership

Many great military leaders were not as effective in peacetime roles as they were in wartime duties. Some Presidents have been effective leaders in domestic matters but not in foreign policy. The relationship between a leader and a group changes as situations change. This is particularly true in the growth of a company. New companies are often led by strong and autocratic executives who influence behavior through a dynamic personality and charismatic appearance. The history of the growth of oil companies, airlines, railroad, and shipping companies are but a few businesses where dynamic leaders built profitable companies in a short period of time. Later, as these and also other companies matured the leadership style changed to a more-democratic one reflecting more concern for the needs of the individual. The sheer size of the company often leads to ever-increasing bureaucracy, and close personal relationships and experiences become more impersonal. Often in times of financial stress or rapid technological development the type of leadership changes to one of specialized skills such as the expert in finance or engineering.

A study of most companies will show specific stages of evolution with leadership skills and styles applicable to that environment and the prevailing conditions. Once the environment and conditions change, the leadership skills and styles must change if growth is to continue. In the formative years of a company the leadership skills of creativity, innovation, and promoting, as well as financing, are required. This can be seen in the development of General Motors Corporation for William C. Durant, who created the company, had not only the great leadership skill of promoting sales of a revolutionary new product but the financial skills needed to establish and grow a capital-intensive business. Business history shows that the great founders of companies had certain managerial skills that were difficult to pass on to other executives. These great innovators were highly creative, daring, willing to take risks, and had a venturesome spirit and the ability to make correct decisions on big issues often based on only a gut feel.

As a company grows in size and profitability, a different set of leadership skills are required. The company is now becoming an organization with complex structures and relationships. To build an effective organizational structure that will provide a sound foundation for many years of changing business conditions requires managers with leadership skills quite different from those that formed the company. The company can no longer run on decisions based on intuition for now there must be extensive planning and control of the resources. Failing to use extensive financial controls and important accounting data drove GM close to collapse; Alfred P. Sloan used great leadership skills in planning and managing complex situations. He established effective general policies and then delegated authority to functional operating managers to make and implement decisions.

We can see from the GM experience and many others that management leadership styles reflect personal characteristics and the needs and expectations of the situation. A strong manager seen in the formative early years of many companies can sometimes influence the actions of his or her people in a manner that helps define the needs of the situation in a way that permits it to be managed better. However, effective managers always recognize that the needs of a situation and personal needs can only be satisfied when the needs of the group are met. The group gives the manager the required influence and power to perform the necessary acts of leadership. Regardless of all else, a manager must satisfy the needs of the group.

The Employees as a Factor in Leadership

You must understand that your personality characteristics will play a major role in your effectiveness as a leader. Also, how you attempt to lead the group is influenced by your employees as well as the situation. Highly professional employees require far less direct supervision than others and also require far more in the way of praise and rewards for accomplishments. Highly dedicated professional people live for applause and if they do not get it your status as a leader will decline rapidly. Managers have different styles and if you are a cooperative and helpful manager following in the footsteps of a manager who manages from the book (that is, follow the manual) your employees might find adjusting to the change difficult, if not traumatic. Your support and help is needed and you must allow time for the adjustment to take place. In simulation exercises involving both styles of leadership, the participants often find it difficult to make a quick adjustment. One participant refused to accept the new cooperative and helpful-style manager and insisted that this manager demand the same bureaucratic measures taken by his predecessor. On the other hand, if you step into a very loosely controlled and disciplined environment and begin to enforce some stern measures, your initial acts of leadership might be resisted and you might question your influence over the group. You must hold to your course in a fair and honest manner for behavioral patterns change with time, and you cannot greatly accelerate the process.

A successful leader knows when, where, and how much to move on a given issue and is always sensitive to the employees. Having an interest in each employee and empathy and respect for each person is a cardinal requirement to be a successful leader. Get your people involved in establishing new and better ground rules for running the business and better codes of conduct and behavior. Float a few trial balloons and get some feedback and indications of where the organization and its members are headed. As a new manager in a group, it is difficult to delay the passing of judgment on your ability as a leader. Do not overreact for you may be perceived as one type although you are much different. Set a leadership style that will benefit the group, and it will benefit you. A leader is not always popular, but making decisions is not a popularity contest. You do what is best for the organization and your employees.

Often, a good one-on-one discussion with your employees can help determine what your employees expect of you. You must decide what they expect you to do as well as what they expect you not to do. If your employees expect a major role in planning and making decisions and you fail in giving them this opportunity you might encourage tension, hostility, stress, and conflict. The employees might feel protection and leadership exists in union rules rather than in your abilities as a manager. When employees work in very physically demanding jobs with a high element of risk or danger, they expect leadership from you that addresses their needs and protects them. They will respect you only if you provide firm leadership to them.

Effective leadership begins with trust and confidence, and it ends when this is lost. You have seen in a football game how a replacement quarterback often turns the whole team and the direction of the game around. Often it is not because he is a better quarterback than the man that he replaced, but rather the team feels more confident that he can lead them to a victory. Managers are quarterbacks who must inspire the team to win. Your ability to provide effective leadership in the organization often depends on your ability to understand feelings and recognize needs. The entire organization must work as an effective team and the record books are filled with examples of officers, executives and managers who resigned from companies, not because he or she lacked technical skills but because of problems in the area of interpersonal relationships. Often it is an open clash of personality characteristics, but sometimes it is a failure to meet the norms and standards established by the organization. A banker is generally perceived to be serious and conservative, and to attack these role expectations will reduce your effectiveness if you are a manager in the field of banking. Employees and shareholders often expect a given image and if you present a totally different posture you might raise some concerns. If employees, higher-level management, customers, and shareholders expect you to present a respective businesslike image and you don't measure up to it, you are weakening your chances of being an effective leader. Leadership success is very strongly linked to intelligent role behavior and you must remember that any action or statement that detracts from your creditability or image weakens your effectiveness as a leader in the group.

Leadership Characteristics

One thing that makes a manager successful is his or her ability to see him- or herself realistically rather than to engage in role playing. Employees quickly recognize role playing and your behavior will be seen as artificial. Successful managers have the ability to apply all of their skills, training, and experience to situations in a manner consistent with the goals of the organization, employees, and him- or herself. Growth comes through meeting these goals and adjusting to new ones as the needs arise. A manager's focus must be on the growth of the business and the professional development of the employees. It is necessary to be able to recognize the need for establishing new objectives to meet the changing environment and to help employees adjust to the new demands.

Leaders must not only take great pride in their personal achievements but also in the achievements of his or her staff members. Pride results from quality work and knowing that each person has performed to the best of his or her ability. A good leader has high morale and strong internal motivations that are reflected in how he or she goes about performing the tasks at hand. Success comes from confidence and a successful leader has the confidence—even when things go wrong—to know that he or she can turn it around and pull it all together to get the goals accomplished. To be an effective manager and a successful leader you need to carry a positive attitude, a happy outlook on life, and be reasonably aggressive in setting and meeting goals. You cannot be a successful manager if you sit back and wait for things to happen. You must get out and help make them happen. This requires that you do more for your employees than they expect you to do. Without successful employees there cannot be a successful manager because your growth rests firmly on the growth of your people. How do you help your staff grow? You can do this by giving them every learning opportunity possible. Both you and your people must learn all that is possible about your business and your disciplines. In addition, each person must learn how to work with others in the organization for team efforts are rewarding and productive. This means learning to respect the other person and his or her ideas and positions. It also means a cooperative spirit that puts the goals of the group first and the individual's second.

Effective leaders are effective communicators. Good communication begins with clear thinking and a simple expression of these thoughts. Respect the level of intelligence of your audience and don't discount what they might know about the subject. A good leader has sincere concern for the group and wants to help them in a dynamic and enthusiastic manner to share experiences and learning. A good leader is able to express his or her ideas in writing in such a manner that different people at different times can understand the message and have no doubts as to the intent of the thoughts being communicated. How is this accomplished? Often it comes about only through the constant redrafting of the letter, memorandum, or directive with careful attention to the elimination of all expressions that result in ambiguity or misinterpretation. Often the length of the message causes problems as the excessive wordage increases the opportunities for misunderstanding and incorrect interpretations. Once the size of the message is reduced the interest by the readers increases. How can you be sure that your message is clear? One good approach is to hand it to another person and ask him or her to tell you what it means to them. Good leaders recognize the importance of effective communication and they get other people's opinions on the impact of the message.

Effective leaders are often able to communicate in simple expressions. A brief letter or memo will usually command more attention and action than a long one. One-page documents are read whereas multipage documents are filed in the wastebasket. How effectively do you communicate with your staff? A leader cannot be effective without mastery of the art of communication. Look at some of the recent materials that you have written and see if you can't reduce the verbiage by at least 20 percent. Also, look very carefully at the chord that it strikes with the reader. Have you ever received a letter that rubbed you the wrong way? Did it encourage you to take the actions that the sender wanted? Good leaders never underestimate the abilities of the group and always hold them in high esteem. Be very careful of the connotations associated with words and the combination of words. The tone of your written instructions might appear harsh and demanding unless carefully worded. The tone of a written communication from a good leader always transmits courtesy and respect for the individual. If your writing does not convey this, keep revising until it does.

Successful managers and wise leaders always communicate in a manner that makes it very clear to the recipients what behavioral change you expect of them and why it is in his or her best interest as well as the group's to make it. Look at the last half dozen letters that you have written. If you have not told your employees what to do and why it is in their best interest to do it then why should they do it? If you are to be a good leader and an effective manager, you must improve your business communication skills. How can you improve your leadership abilities through better communication skills? Constant self-review of what you say and write is critical to growth and unless you get some suggestions from your peers you cannot see what needs to be changed. Much of the force of an effective leader is based on his or her ability to communicate verbally. Since we all think deeply about an issue before writing on it, why do we engage in superficial thinking on oral responses? Is it because a quick response is perceived as indicating confidence and professionalism? Well, many professionals have learned that thinking before speaking is not a sign of slow reactions but intelligent pro-acting rather than hasty reacting. Good leaders look at all options and carefully evaluate how each will benefit the organization. Once said, it cannot be retracted and effective managers communicate in a clear and simple manner.

Leadership Behavior

Managers are strong leaders when they inspire their employees to become dedicated and committed to the goals of the organization. Managers know what needs to be done and how it should be done, but often are not effective in communicating it to the employees. Effective leadership begins with your ability to counsel a person in ways that will improve productivity without increasing stress. You must be a good listener and reinforce when possible a person's self-esteem. Be slow to judge a person and slower in discounting his or her abilities. Teach your staff how to develop a business case by evaluating all relevant factors and not to shoot from the hip when making decisions. Quick decisions lead to mistakes and risk the future of the individual as well as the organization. An effective decision can only be reached after an opinion has been formulated and supported or rejected by facts. Unless you can present a case against an action, you cannot truly evaluate the case for a solution. Data must always be collected and presented in meaningful ways to higher-level management. Their concepts of what is important might be very different from yours and you had best understand their needs.

Successful leaders always have the ability to induce higher-level managers to be responsive to the needs of the organization by presenting complete, accurate, and timely oral and/or written reports. Unless you know what higher-level management needs to effectively make decisions, you cannot properly coordinate, schedule, and plan the work of your staff. Only after you know what the officers want, when they want it, and how they want it can you effectively lead your group into providing solutions and answers. Also you must assign sufficient resources to each task as required by the level of response that is anticipated. You cannot motivate your employees to work hard to accomplish unreasonable goals. Most companies fail to continue to grow because they either have inadequate resources or ineffective leadership. Empirical studies indicate that leadership is a dynamic process and that most managers are able to influence the activities of employees to achieve the goals of the organization under even the most-difficult circumstances. You cannot influence your people to attain goals unless you believe in them yourself. Less-than-satisfactory results have accrued from the scientific-management approach which has focused on only the needs of the organization and not the members of the group. Everything cannot be quantified and measured. Unless you are concerned with the individual's needs and feelings you are not going to improve productivity or employees' attitudes and morale.

How do you behave as a leader? Do you fall between the extremes of being an authoritarian manager whose values, feelings, and behavior emphasize the output of the group or the democratic manager whose focus is on the personal relationships and the needs and interest of the individual? Is there one best style of leadership? It depends upon the situations and how you handle them. When the competitive pressures of the marketplace put the premium on driving production up and costs down and the survival of the company is at stake, then leaders are needed who have a high concern for production—even at the expense of some concern for the happiness of the employees. However, it is a high price to pay since companies that demonstrate consistent high growth recognize that its people are its most valuable resources and assest. Your leadership style is based on your feelings and values which have been influenced by your experiences at home and at work. Observe the leadership styles of your peers. Are they effective?

If so, look at why and learn from their actions. However, each person has his or her personal characteristics and what works for others might not work for you. The effective course is to be yourself and improve your effectiveness with training and education. Managers need to balance the needs for production with the concerns for the individual. This can best be done when employees become involved in setting goals so that they are effective in doing the right tasks and efficient in doing them right. Giving employees a reasonable amount of freedom in planning and controlling the work often increases output and improves commitment.

To be accepted by the group a leader must demonstrate that he or she believes the very best about each person who belongs to the organization. Each person must be perceived as being industrious and willing to accept responsibility until he or she indicates otherwise. When you trust people they will trust you and effective leaders make their trust and respect known quickly. Effective managers always look for the positive qualities in each person and build upon them. Many other people will highlight faults and don't recognize or encourage their efforts.

Effective leaders maintain a balance between production and concerns for people. Your style of leadership (figure 2-2) determines how well you handle the short-run demands for output and the long-run benefits from increased employee development. Excessive emphasis on production often leads to burnout and the associated lack of concern for the feelings and well-being the employees reduces commitment. Short-run accomplishments often lead to long-run dissatisfaction if the social-emotional needs of the individuals are not met. Excessive emphasis on the people in the organization at the expense of production has not shown over the years to have produced significantly higher levels of productivity. How then should you a manager determine an effective leadership style? Act in a manner that will strike a balance between the needs of your people and the goals of the organization. Plan the necessary work in a way that permits the maximum amount possible of employee involvement and commitment. When the needs of your

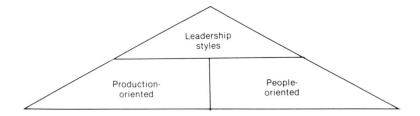

Figure 2-2. Effective Leaders Maintain a Balance

employees are met it is much easier to meet the needs of the organization. You can only know and meet the needs of your employees when you permit them to participate in goal setting and decision making.

Managers must create the kind of work climate that helps each employee to be motivated toward a higher level of performance. When you let employees control the performance of their jobs you will find that they will find new opportunities to grow and produce accomplishments far greater than you had expected. Provide the opportunity to increase salary, responsibilities, status, and visibility and you will be perceived as a good leader. Avoid the highly competitive environment where each person tries to outperform his or her peers, even at the expense of doing things that are not in keeping with his or her character or personality. A manager's primary job is to get things done through people; however, your total efforts must always be greater than theirs.

Managing is much more than being a leader for the former requires much in the way of mental activities that do not involve actions of leadership. Effective managers identify the needs of the group and then provide the leadership necessary to satisfy these needs. Wear the mantle of authority well but earn the respect and loyalty of your people. Offers of rewards induce higher levels of achievement and commitment than threats of punishment and effective managers know and practice this approach. The threats of punishment at best only motivate people to perform at the minimal level expected.

Japanese Style of Management

We have all read much about Japanese management and it has been described in terms ranging from *art* to *science*. Many have been impressed with the success of Japanese firms in both productivity and quality. Japanese management methods and styles have been carefully studied and the question arises if these methods and styles that work so well in that culture can be equally effective in the United States.

Certainly there is a cultural difference between Japan and the United States, but except for historical background the differences today are minor. In Japan many Western styles in dress, food, and life-style are growing in acceptance and here many people have come to like the fine culture of Japan. But how about the Japanese business firms, executives, and employees—can or should their methods be adopted in our business community?

Business in Japan is conducted more tightly than in the United States. This control is done through very close supervision which is not resented by the employees. It is perceived as a way to improve both quality and productivity and this perception is correct. Also it is perceived as necessary for the continued growth of the company and thereby the growth of each employee and this proves to be correct. Many U.S. employees would resent greatly this high level of supervision but it produces profitable results. It is a matter of attitude. Japanese employees look forward to work and do not see it as an evil or hardship. They cannot understand why U.S. employees do not look forward to getting in to work. To them it is an opportunity and a chance to see their friends and work for the good of the company and themselves. Employees in Japan do not see supervision as a negative force, rather as a positive force for it will help them to do a better job and as the company grows they will grow. Supervision is seen as a way to assure that everyone does his or her job and does it correctly. I am much impressed with this attitude. When we discount the role of supervision we weaken quality assurance and reduce productivity.

Japanese workers appreciate the prompt manner in which a manager jumps in to correct a situation and resolve a problem. Japanese managers do this for they realize that their primary measurement is on quality and output. All too often managers in our society avoid the employees and their problems and seek the shelter of their office. This would be a difficult step to take in many offices in Japan as only the extremely high-level offficers have a private office. Managers even as high as the third managerial level in the organization have their desks side by side in the back of the large open-office areas—bull pens as they are often called in our business jargon—and you recognize this person by his or her physical position on the floor and not a name on a private office. Highly paid managers seem quite at ease working in these environments for their central focus is on the performance of the group rather than their personal surroundings and image. Employees work with great dedication and commitment and there is no chit chat even though the desks are close and many people occupy a small area. There is great mutual respect and politeness and at all times the atmosphere is highly professional. I have seen employees reluctant to leave their desks for either coffee or a washroom break.

As managers are in the back of the room they can supervise the office activities very well; however, there is an added advantage in that they can very quickly communicate with each other and make some very effective decisions. Letters and formal meetings are not required. Each manager is a working manager and I believe much of the success of Japanese business to-day results from this leadership style.

Another element adds to the strength of Japanese business today: That is the great dedication and commitment on the part of all employees in doing the best job possible. Great pride is taken in doing even the simplest tasks. Peer pressures are high and each employee knows that they must satisfy their own sense of accomplishment as well as what the group expects of them. This can best be seen in the educational training of professional people. The entrance exams to the prestigious Japanese colleges and universities are very difficult. Students agonize over getting accepted and when they are accepted it appears that much is expected of them in return for the opportunity. Commitment to hard work and long hours begins early. Perhaps then it is not surprising to see that later these professional people are working in the offices well beyond 7 p.m. And also they work a full day every other Saturday. Do the managers do this also? Yes, sitting alongside of a manager's desk in the evening in the office I have looked around and seen the other managers and staff people all at their desks and working, not talking. Most managers in Japan do not get home until 9 p.m. The family has eaten dinner and the children have done their school work. True, many high-level U.S. managers offer the same example of dedication and commitment to the company; however, managers appear to see the work day as lasting from 9 a.m. to 5 p.m.

Another difference in the style of Japanese management is their patience and acceptance of long-run results and solutions to problems. U.S. managers attempt to fine tune every program to gain a quick solution and immediate measurable results. This leads to throwing lots of money and people into a program to wrap it up quickly; this is not always an intelligent approach. If the problem is complicated, much long-range planning is required and implementation must be evolutionary and not revolutionary. Managers cannot build a high degree of loyalty and dedication overnight. Japanese companies are successful because they effectively involve each employee in establishing goals, schedules, quality-assurance programs, planning, and decision making. Quick fixes are rejected and only carefully programmed action programs are implemented.

The very act of involving each employee in the conduct of the business assures the success of Japanese ventures. Participation builds team spirit and loyalty to the organization and permits the opportunity to focus on the needs of each individual as well as the needs of the organization. Employees feel that their dedication and commitment will not go unrecognized and that as the company grows they will grow also. This seems to be proving itself. Job security is important; however, Japanese managers very carefully move employees into more challenging positions with higher salaries. It appears that developing and implementing a career-path program is taken very seriously. Less emphasis is placed on individual merit and accomplishment than we see in U.S. business; however, group accomplishment is given high recognition. This requires the employee to fit well into the group and to advance the cause of the group first and his or her own needs second. The value to this is apparent, for it builds more team players and fewer superstars. Because of the competitive pressures that we have built into our society, we encourage superstars and discourage the team players. Superstars get big salaries and team players hardly even get thanks.

Because high value is placed on the performance of the group, Japanese managers trust them to take an active and intelligent role in the decision-making process. This enables ideas to bubble up to the top. Most worthwhile ideas are created in this manner in contrast to U.S. business where much decision making is made on an individual basis from the top down. The strongly participative style of Japanese managers gives the flavor of an autocratic-form management yet this is not the case since decision making is pushed down in the organization. The concern for the total person and his or her full satisfactions, as well as placing him or her in a responsible position, points more to a democratic form of management than the bureacratic forms of many U.S. companies. In the latter, the individual has but a small role in decision making and feels little responsibility to the group in the implementation of the decision.

In the Japanese style of management the initiative for change often begins at the lowest levels in the organization. Higher-level managers welcome this participative approach and build clear channels for upward communication. Each manager makes him- or herself accessible at the point where the work is being done to facilitate employee involvement and suggestions. When sufficient information is available decisions are made; however, if more data is needed managers ask the employees to gather it in order to support their ideas. These requests are always made in a way that encourages the employee. The employee is always made to feel that his or her efforts are appreciated. Using this style there is less need for managers to issue orders or directives and as the employees are close to each work situation they can recommend the direction that the organization should take. Also, they help to set goals and objectives and establish measurement techniques.

As higher-level management puts the setting of goals and objectives at levels lower than in U.S. companies it requires first- and second-level managers to accept more responsibility for the growth of the business. This is handled well in Japanese firms as managers as well as staff members all have a clear understanding of the business needs and long-range growth strategies. Each employee knows what he or she must do and what attitudes and behaviors are expected. Armed with this knowledge, situations are handled as they arise without the need for directives from higher-level managers. Middle managers, however, have the task of coordinating the development of how the ideas originating in the various departments are presented upward. Also, when other organizations are affected the respective managers must present for adoption by higher-level management an agreed-upon solution to the problem or a resolution of the conflict. Such an approach requires managers to talk often with each other, and this is facilitated by having proximity.

If a problem or issue is complex many meetings are held between employees and managers. Everyone is encouraged to comment and dissenting views are welcomed. In business good decisions cannot be made without considering all opinions and evaluating all alternative solutions. The Japanese style of management produces a high-quality decision and all participants feel a part in the decision-making process. Also, each person feels a sense of responsibility for the final solution and a commitment to its implementation.

Managers in Japan have excellent rapport with all employees. Much is known about the family and outside interests and there is a genuine concern for the person as an individual—not just as an employee. There is also great interest shown in the members of the family. Managers have empathy with a person's needs and a sensitivity to the concerns of the family. Managers join in social functions with the families of employees and are trusted as close friends. Employees are dedicated to the growth of the company as it becomes an extension of the family. Honest mistakes are forgiven for managers know the tasks by having performed them and they help to turn an employee's shortcomings into learning experiences.

Dialogues between employees and managers are always open and straightforward. Close daily contacts encourage this and it is strengthened by feelings of mutual trust. Managers earn respect for they will help to perform some of the employees' tasks when needed and offer guidance. This cooperative spirit between managers and employees increases dedication, loyalty, and commitment to increased productivity and improved quality of products and service.

The leadership style of managers in Japan reflects many of the characteristics required for successful participative management. Foremost is the trust placed in each employee accompanied by open communication. Also, ideas are sought by managers who are readily accessible to all employees and decisions are made through consensus. Managers combine a high concern for the individual and his or her family. Finally, managers create working conditions where the employees recognize and understand the problems and have a vested interest in solving them.

The force that ties Japanese managers and employees together is a common understanding that what is good for the company is also good for the employees: that as the company grows and profits in the long-run, the employees will share in the gains. The goals of the managers and employees are melded together and the company's missions and philosophy are clearly understood. Japanese companies are successful because they integrate everyone into a group and concern for the group has embedded in it concern for the individual. Japanese management puts primary emphasis on the skills of their people and the working relationships. Most U.S. managers give this secondary importance for their primary attention is placed on long-range goals, strategies, and systems to implement them.

Japanese culture requires more than interdependency because of space, population, and heritage than in the United States, therefore people do work more closely together with greater respect for each other and long-term accomplishments. The density of population alone causes a high degree of politeness for each person. Japanese managers still must manage the superstars in a way that teamwork is advanced although individual motivation remains at a high level. My observations are that managers meet this challenge by rewarding the very talented people and high achievers with special privileges. An opportunity to travel or attend a special function is often an effective award.

How the Japanese Style Differs
from Ours

Japanese management style differs from the style of U.S. managers in that less emphasis is placed on corporate strategy. Most U.S. managers develop a corporate strategy that is broad and bold. This is followed by careful long-range planning and a functional decomposition of the corporate strategy results in rather rigid goals to be achieved by each functional department in the organization. The philosophy is that the many smaller strategic programs with established targets will synergistically result in the firm achieving its long-range missions. This often is not the case. The short-run results fall short or are achieved late and at very high cost. Japanese managers take less quickly to designing and implementing strategic formulas and programs. This is because they see a danger in grasping a concept and charging full speed ahead in blind allegiance. There is always the danger that conditions and the markets will change and that even if the initial strategy was correct—and it also could be wrong—the changes might not be observed and/or properly handled.

Many U.S. managers regard strategic formulas as the means to an end and get so dedicated to their implementation that they ignore new technological developments and changing consumer and economic conditions. Japanese managers—rather than relying on their own master strategies—begin a venture based on inputs from all possible sources (for example, employees, customers, salesmen, bankers, consultants, et cetera). As the venture progresses all of these insights are blended together into strategic action plans. It is the ability to continuously assemble even the smallest of these inputs and insights into action plans that are flexible to changing conditions that result in constructive sense of direction. This direction is based on information and decisions generated at the bottom of the organization and is managed upward for approval by higher-level managers. Many of the Japanese success stories can be traced to Japanese executives who, rather than dictating strategy, were flexible enough to mold and modify previously established strategic programs to meet the changing times and conditions.

Although much of the success of Japanese companies can be credited to the described characteristics of Japanese management style, much credit must also be attributed to the conditions of the past three decades. Many Japanese plants were rebuilt with higher levels of technology and automated processes which helped to reduce production costs and improve quality. It is often easier to improve product quality when modernized factories are equipped with the latest in labor-saving and robotic-type machinery. The suggestions of the quality circles can be implemented effectively and efficiently on a large scale. The culture promotes a penalty-free environment where a young employee set speaks up and contributes ideas for the group to consider. Superimpose on this a very high sense of nationalism and the high level of work ethic becomes a way of life. There are other factors that help to make a manager's job a little easier. Japanese people are very polite and sensitive. A situation rarely reaches a stage where conflict arises or resentment develops. Sincere mutual respect for each other results in win/win arrangements rather than win/lose.

It is inherent in the culture of Japan to be honest and trustworthy and to perform your duties well. Those in management positions are respected, honored, and obeyed. Given such traits, the ties within a group are strong and these groups are the cement that binds the company into a cohesive organization that can stand firm against changing markets. To help even more the policies of the government have been supportive of business and the firms, universities, and governmental agencies work for common goals. It appears to be much more productive for the government to spend large sums of monies in support of business rather than in preparing antitrust cases that divert many resources into nongrowth activities. It is encouraging today to see our government helping U.S. business rather than being burdensome or impassive. Foreign governments for many years around the world have supported their own national firms and have given them many competitive advantages in the international markets.

Choosing the Right Leadership Strategy

A strategy is a careful plan or well-thought-out method for achieving a certain goal or objective. In many of your daily tasks you use a strategy as a framework to guide you in making decisions and determining directions and choices. When it comes to the survival and growth of the firm it is the strategic thinking by the officers that determine success or failure. Why is it that some firms have good strategies but somehow fail to achieve great results? Often it is because a clear strategy was not executed properly. The strategy tells the business organization what it should do but not always how it should do it. Strategy and its implementation must be carefully orchestrated for success. This is most important today when growth by acquisition is very important to growing firms. A firm cannot survive if the long-range growth strategies are not in harmony with the business-conduct practices and policies employed. Given a poor strategy and ineffective implementation, the script reads failure.

What are the strategies that guide your organization? Who is setting the goals and directions of the firm? Are they only reactions to competitors and market conditions or are they being set with growth targets in mind? Are outside forces driving you in directions that are not in your best interests, and what can you do about these? Many businesses today are being faced with great changes due to deregulation, yet high-level management has in some cases developed no long-range strategic plans to cope with the new environment. This is in some companies causing confusion all through the functional departments. They are looking for a course to follow and have none. Effective leaders get things done through people and you cannot do this when the path to follow is not even known in the organization. At the root of most of the difficulties with the less-than-successful companies today is the lack of sound strategic planning and wise leadership to enforce it.

Good management strategies are reflected in the amount and quality of long-range planning implemented in the firm. Are these long-range plans merely an extension of what you are doing now, or have you decided where the company should be ten years from now and what it takes to get it there? Drifting with current organizational structures, product lines, marketing programs, and servicing policies will in most cases lead to failure in the future. What business should you be in ten years from now and what kind of leadership style is needed? Build a sound blueprint for the future and concern yourself less with writing exciting stories for the shareholders to read. They will care less if you can't continue the growth in earnings they have come to expect; changes in management happen suddenly and without warning.

How cohesive is the strategy of your organization and are the leadership styles complementing it and moving it in the right direction? How do you know? You ask questions of the members on the management team. Where do they see the organization going and how is it going to get there? What are they doing and what do they need to do differently? Are the markets of the future identified and what new products and services are needed? How is the state of technological development affecting the business and how will it impact the firm's resources? Resources are more than monies and skilled employees hold the key to any strategy developed and its successful implementation.

Strategic leaders are constantly looking for clues and reactions to decisions. They do not follow rules, procedures, and regulations to the limit but encourage creativity and adaptability on the part of each employee. Also, a strategic leader constantly looks at his or her own experiences and the history of the organization and then evaluates its relevance to the situation at hand and either uses it or comes up with a better approach. If you are to be a good strategic leader you must not expect perfection and you must not be disappointed if all of your plans do not work out as you expect. Your leadership abilities will come into focus only after you have strategically planned the goals and direction for the organization. Included in this are your plans and methods to control, measure, and monitor the results. Primary emphasis is placed on what needs to be done to assure the long-term survival of the firm and that is followed by what strategic steps must be implemented in order to improve profits, produce better products, provide better customer service, and develop the employees.

Higher-level management is responsible for the establishment of the business missions that will affect the long-run survival of the firm, the establishment of company policy and practices, and the delegation of authority to make decisions within the middle-management levels. However, middle management also has a responsibility and an obligation to perform both long-range planning and short-run objectives. It is at the first-level-management positions where the control over the performance of the operations takes place and the most difficult task here is the motivation of the nonmanagement employees who have technical expertise and yet feel that far too often the rewards do not match the accomplishments.

Effective managers include in their strategies the analysis of the profitability of each unit and clearly will take necessary actions if the unit cannot improve its profit picture in a short time. One large company built this into their managerial strategies and passed on a 65 percent increase in dividends to the shareholders after the program had been in effect only one year. Effective leaders learn quickly that if a unit is not producing adequate profits it must be reorganized and restructured more in respect to what the market requires. If your strategy is aimed at maximizing the generation of cash and you have operations that require and lose large amounts of cash, then you must take some strong measures. One of the largest automobile manufacturers in the world recently sold off its appliance business in which it had made a great name and good reputation. Why would leadership strategy dictate such a move? It is the primary responsibility of management to manage the assets of the business in such a manner as to maximize the profits profits for the shareholders. It is important not to keep carrying on the old business if it is no longer profitable. Managers must conduct the business in a way that utilizes all of the assets to generate maximum returns to the stockholders.

Even if your business is very profitable it takes massive transfusions of capital today to grow the business. The number of acquisitions and the number of business units divested are increasing at an annual rate of 10 percent. This indicates that as part of leadership strategy there is an increasing emphasis on eliminating the less-profitable operations. It also indicates that more managers are looking further out and asking him- or herself what business the firm should be in ten years from today. What was profitable in the past decade will, I assure you, not be profitable in the next decade.

Are there any problems that you should consider in implementing a strategy that emphasizes the divesting of the less-profitable operations? Yes, there is always the chance that competition will decrease between firms in that product line and this could mean a reduction in production costs and selling expenses, and hence, perhaps good profits for you if you had not sold off the business. It is not always a wise leadership strategy to sell off the less-profitable units if they are carrying a large portion of your overheads. Additional capital investments with some automation might improve productivity, quality, and profits. If you cannot go this route, perhaps you can parcel parts of the operations out to some of your contractors or vendors at an acceptable profit.

Some managers apply a strategy for growth that results in diversifying into both related and unrelated businesses. When the diversification is into a related business the skills and experience that the firm has can be put to good use, and the newly acquired company can play a large role in generating better profits and increased technological developments. Often this permits greater operating efficiencies, lower production costs, and increased revenue. Often it can help to build cash flow and this can help a capital-intensive company. How about when the diversification is into an unrelated business? Is it wise? Yes! Sometimes it is very beneficial because it permits a more-efficient management team to come in and untract a stalled organization. Often it provides an opportunity to put the firm's capital into ventures with a higher return on the investment. Sometimes the acquired firm has a highly leveraged debt position and this might lead to some tax benefits.

A contemporary manager in today's rapidly changing world uses strategy and tactics to manage diversification in a way that will improve the firm.

Effective leaders compare the pretax profits of the firm against the industry averages. Your growth might have been good and acceptable to the stockholders, but did it match or exceed the growth of the other firms in your business? This is what you should be measured against. As a higher-level manager you might put in place a strategy that requires first-level managers to take strategic responsibility over the product line and to grow the share of the market. If competition is not aggressive this might be an effective strategy; however, given a different picture do you want to give up profits for the sake of building the market share at the risk of declining profitability? What will be your answer to the stockholders who look at the bottom line (that is, the earnings)?

Some leaders adopt a strategy that gives the highest priority to the culture ethnic in the community, encourages great team loyalty, and promotes hard work with creativity and cooperation the first step to success in the firm. Is all of this of much value if the consumers are not buying the products? What happens if profits decline? Do you cut costs and reduce the quality level of the product and services that you are offering? You had best not. Profits can vary in the short-run but once you reduce the respect that your product has in the eyes of the consumer you have suffered a long-term loss. To sell an inexpensive, low-quality product is the fast road to failure. Good growth and stability of earnings come only from offering high-quality products and services. Suffer on the profits if needed but don't lose your image for it might take a decade or more to regain it. People buy quality; don't forget it!

Leadership strategies must also focus on the problems of the international markets as well as the domestic. The opportunities on a global basis represent a marketplace for the future far greater than most managers comprehend. However, this requires special skills in leadership as the customs, regulations, and needs of the employees are a challenge since they differ from those in America. As over 75 percent of a manager's time is spent working with and through people it is important to understand their needs and attitudes. A manager is a leader when he or she gives directions to employees, responds to the actions of his or her employees, and represents the employees in their dealings with other people in the organization. Effective managers are leaders who help to build pride in employees for what he or she has accomplished. Pride in the performance of work leads to higher quality products and increased productivity.

One strategy that some leaders are considering is the reverse of growth through acquisition; it is growth by breaking up the firm into separate companies wherein the stockholders have a proportionate ownership. One element that needs to be closely examined in this action is the impact of the capital-gains tax on the company and the income taxes on the stockholders. If the separation can be done under the law without incurring some tax liability for the company and the stockholders, then some companies are giving this strategy more attention. This process of breaking up a company is sometimes referred to as demerging, it is the opposite of merging with other companies to become a larger firm. Why would you want to consider such an action? Most firms want to become larger, hence why would you consider getting smaller? There are some merits to this strategy. One is that it gives a lot more incentive to top management if they can be the head of a smaller company rather than a lower-level officer in a large company. This is often because the degree of recognition is much greater as the head of a small firm and also there is greater opportunity to use your skills and talents where they can be more meaningful and visible. If it is a problem in your firm to motivate people because the pyramid is getting narrow, then this is a way to give them new incentives and challenges. Would you rather be a divisional vice-president of a large company or a president of a smaller company? Many officers today are leaving the large companies to find the excitement of being the president or chief executive officer of a small firm.

How does demerging affect the employees? This can be a positive step, for many employees are able to identify much more closely with a smaller firm and feel that they are a part of the decision-making process and are responsible for the growth of the business. This might not be true of all employees as some put a high value on the prestige of the big firm and the connotation of a greater success on their part which might or might not be correct.

How do stockholders react to this strategy of demerging? It is often with mixed emotions; however, most feel that the market value of the individual firms would add up to much more than the sum of all of them combined into a single company. Often stockholders gain as the price of the stock of the smaller companies add up to more than the price of the stock of the larger company. It is often possible for three or four young and aggressive tigers to accomplish more than one larger, yet more-experienced tiger. Often the smaller firms can move more quickly and this is important in international markets. Also, there is not the cloud of antitrust trials hanging over the growth of the smaller firms. However, are there any words from the devils's advocates on this matter? Yes, there is a great strength in the financial resources, managerial talents, and research-and-development efforts of large companies. From the manufacturing and marketing aspects, there are the economies of scale that benefit the large companies. Nevertheless, there are many executives today who are looking at the benefits of demerging. Effective leaders employ good strategies and this always requires you to look at issues from both sides with an open mind. The approach in the past decade was to buy and merge with as many firms as possible for this brought profitability and growth. Many managers now realize that bigness does not always assure higher profits and that in fact larger profits might come from owning numerous small-but-dynamic firms.

3 Attitudes Toward Risk

A manager's life is filled with opportunities and risk. The replacement of the manager is often the first step taken when things do not progress as well as higher-level management had expected. It is surprising how many managers do not realize how quickly they can be replaced, often for some rather superficial reasons. You can be doing a good job yet higher-level management may want new blood in the organization and may make changes. A manager does not have the same relationship with the organization as his or her staff. Managers sometimes get credit when things go well, but they most always get blamed when things go wrong and often it is a noncontrolled event. Employees, particularly if they are unionized, have some rights and you must prove their performance was poor and that they made some very wrong decisions. Managers often are quickly judged by their managers and the outcome can be a fast termination. As organizations change managers must also change since the talents that made you a manager are often not the managerial skills needed for your new position. You were perhaps quick to take risks before but now you react more slowly. New higher levels of management might be very conservative and your open criticism and risk-taking approaches might cause concern.

You might be doing a great job as manager; however, if your manager who was your mentor and sponsor is replaced by someone less friendly, you might be in an exposed position unless you perceive his or her attitudes toward risk. An unnecessary risk taken by you might provide little in the way of rewards yet the price of failure can be very high. It is easy for managers to develop feelings of insecurity and to begin to discount what they have to offer to the company. Sometimes it is true the abilities that a manager has to offer the company are no longer needed or wanted; however, the good news is that the current shortage of managers is so great you do not have to be overly concerned with the opportunities for success. The skills that you have learned in one company in managing people are applicable to many companies; hence you must not avoid risk for the sake of job security. You should always shoulder risk and understand that managers are paid to take risks. If you cannot avoid risks, then you must be aware of what information is required in order to manage risk, have the proper attitudes toward risk, and know how to assess risk.

Assessing Risk

How do you assess risk? Is it the same way that your manager and his or her manager assesses it? Does your staff assess risk the same way that you do? Decision makers must take a position and often they will try to pick a point between the extremes of being too conservative and gambling. One condition that has a bearing on your attitude toward risk is the amount of monies at your disposal. This applies right up front regarding the risk that you take in managing your position. If you are financially independent you can afford to take greater risks that if you are not. In making a business decision this is also true: With adequate funds you can step in and prevent the risk situation from getting away from you and turn a failure into success. Many bad decisions are salvaged with great transfusions of capital, a circumstance that at a later date tends to make the existing risk seem much lighter. With sufficient funds you can deal with a posture of strength and this gives you greater self-confidence. With higher self-esteem you appear more forceful and can often influence people enough to make a poor venture succeed. Also you might feel that you are in a position to suffer less personal loss if the gamble goes against you, so you take the plunge. With little amounts of funds to put at risk, the gains can appear to be insignificant; thus you tend to become more conservative.

Another condition that can affect your attitudes toward risk is who owns the monies involved in the venture. If the funds are yours, you might be able to take greater risks than if the funds are supplied by a banker who might monitor you very closely with ratio analysis which causes you to become more defensive and cautious. Managers take the degree of risk that he or she perceives the organization expects to be taken and poor communication here causes problems. Do you correctly understand higher-level managements attitudes toward risk? If you don't, find out where they stand. There is always the tendency to be more conservative than the officers of the firm expect. The fault is not yours, but rather that of higher-level management. The cause is the enforcement by management of unwritten, potent punishment and reward systems. If you take a risky action and the results are not good, you often get little encouragement because of your willingness to step up to an issue. You might even get accused of using poor judgment in not properly evaluating the conditions and the options. Mistakes are not forgiven very quickly; hence there is risk in trying. However, what if you take the risk and the results are quite successful? Unfortunately you are seldom rewarded and you are told that it was part of your job. With no praise forthcoming you soon decide that taking unnecessary risks is a no-win-high-loss game. Once you perceive this you become more conservative and cautious in risk taking.

A turtle can go no place without sticking its neck out. How then can a firm grow if it hides within its shell by discouraging managers from taking risks? Successful managers encourage people to try new things and provide a penalty-free environment for these actions. Give reward to the venturesome and offer encouragement and assistance to those who are trying and need help. If you foster an environment where everyone plays it safe, the organization will not grow, profits will decline, and innovation will be only a dream.

Attitudes on risk must be fully communicated upward and downward in the organization. Unless there are some guidelines, each decision maker in the firm will apply personal judgment to the issues. The communication should take the form of written instructions illustrated with examples. These should be reinforced with in-house seminars that give practice in making decisions under risk. Do you need this kind of program? One way that you can find out is to construct an in-basket set of business-decision-making cases or problems. Simulate the real world by asking everyone in the organization to make a decision on each and to support their actions. You should not be surprised at the vast range of risk postures you will find displayed.

The element that makes risk difficult is that it requires you to make allowance for many things that you cannot forecast or understand. You handle this by assessing the probability of the given event's occurring and you assign a value to it. Generally this is best done by expressing the percentage possibility of it occurring. Establish ranges for each option under review and apply the probability. This results in a quantitative numerical measurement that is a weighted average for each course of action. These can be compared; however, mathematical-decisions analysis does not always point you in the right direction. Many variables have been reflected in the weighted quantified number and often in the long-run these forecasts are questionable. By giving a value judgment to the elements of uncertainty you have tried to quantify them, but when you assess the venture in its entirety, intuitive reactions might lead to different conclusions. When in doubt, give serious consideration to your intuitive feelings and when emotions have subsided and you can find no significant reason for discounting them, get the opinions of others and move ahead if they are in agreement. Often building a best case and a worse case for each issue helps to crystalize thinking and puts risk in perspective.

The risk and uncertainty of future activities that affect decision making can be reduced if you estimate carefully the costs and benefits associated with the venture. Do a good forecast of sales, revenues, and investment requirements and then relate these to how it will help you to increase the profitability of the organization. In addition, identify and evaluate all of the elements of risk associated with the venture and then begin to eliminate each by anticipating what actions can be taken to minimize the risks. For example, if you want sales to reach an anticipated level you must be sure that more advertising or better sales training will produce these results.

Sound decision making and risk avoidance that can result in greater profits for the firm might put more emphasis on the long-run than the short-run. If you assess the risk correctly for small decisions you improve your abilities to make better decisions on large projects. Also recognize that the avoidance of a higher level of risk in the short-run might be a wise decision but it might not be a wise decision in the long-run. The U.S. auto industry gambled for the short-run by staying with the big cars but lost in the long-run when the small foreign imports produced better mileage and less servicing, higher quality, and took away 27 percent of the market.

One way you can maintain a consistency in respect to your attitudes toward risk is to build a history file of your decisions. When unexpected new decision-making situations arise, you can reference this for guidance. You should have in that history how you quantified some of the uncertainties and how you evaluated some of the opinions that you received. Also contained should be some statements regarding the attitudes of management at that time regarding risk. Effective managers must take intelligent risks in order to continue the smooth line of growth of the company. Behind each of these risk decisions you must know the size of the potential losses and the magnitude of the potential gains. You will find that most marketing managers in the organization will be very optimistic and they will tend to downplay the risks associated with new products and the entry into new markets. You might have to be the counter-balance or check to keep these decisions from going too far afield. You can get a measurement on the possible losses that could result from marketing decisions through the use of good market surveys. Do some very realistic forecasting and do some product testing in the marketplace to better assess the degrees of success or failure. Select only the most profitable opportunities and build aggressive marketing plans around them.

Marketing managers must particularly recognize the presence of risks and the forms that they take. All risks should be assessed in the light of its worst, most-likely, and best-possible result. Each risk must then be evaluated in regard to how it financially impacts the organization. When historical data is available this process is made much simpler and you have reduced the risk of the unknown. The benefit of objective historical data is that it provides a relatively sound way to measure risk and makes decision making more successful. However, even with large amounts of historical data you will still be making some subjective judgments based on your experiences and how your current higher-level management feels about risk.

When historical data is not available, you must size up the maximum loss of the venture, determine ways to prevent the negative conditions from hurting the operations, and implement a program that will reduce or eliminate the losses. For example, many times market studies or research reports can be used to identify ways to advertise, distribute, and sell products to help obtain greater profits with less risk. Managers live with risk and must take intelligent and reasonable risks if they are to grow and the organization is to move forward.

You can use computers to help you to better evaluate the risk involved in alternative courses of action. You can test the consequences of many proposals or options by using what-if type questions. Using a simple model, you can evaluate the amount of risk by feeding in various ranges for the conditions and probabilities that you see. Through simulation procedures the computer can compare costs and sales data and produce charts that will help you to understand better the elements of risk and the potential for profits. As the computer performs rapid calculations you can quantify the elements of risk and weight the results using different options. You can use the information that is stored in the data base for the modeling of the risk factors or simply enter new assumptions. Simulation permits you to test ideas in a quick and inexpensive manner and improves the quality of the decision-making process.

Risk and uncertainty in decision making can be reduced by doing better forecasting, and this can be achieved by keeping history on past decisions. For example, if you realize that in the past on similar investments you overran the estimated costs by 15 percent then you can build this into the cost figures for the current decision. You also can manage risk and uncertainty in making capital-investment decisions by adding an adjustment factor on to the return on investment (ROI). The investment in a given situation might be exposed to greater risk because of political, social, or economic instability; therefore projects are accepted only when they meet the normal ROI plus a given percentage to compensate for the risk. These adjustments might be only a few percentage points but in high risk situations you might increase the ROI by 10 or more percent to qualify it as an acceptable opportunity.

You can approach capital-investment proposals by using three levels in estimating costs and benefits. Determine the worst, the most-likely, and the best set of figures. Then match these against the level of confidence that you have that they can be attained. This confidence level or probability-of-achieving level should also consist of three positions: that is, a low, medium, and high degree of success. Attitudes toward risk are often different in smaller firms as the adjustments to changing conditions can be implemented rapidly. As there are fewer levels of management, a greater amount of decision-making power rests in the hands of only a few managers and a course can be set or changed quickly. Also, as the manager has closer relationships with the employees than in a large company, greater cooperation can be secured for programs that directly reduce risk. Whereas a large company must follow the slower procedures for assessing and managing risk, a less bureaucratic small company can often capitalize on the opportunities missed by other firms because they can take early actions in the marketplace. Because the small firm does not have such extensive commitments to product lines, manufacturing facilities, and has more flexible distribution channels and marketing organizations than larger firms, they can attempt something new at far less risk.

How you as a manager look at risks can sometimes be influenced by economic conditions. Some managers have raised their levels of risk taking in periods of high inflation in the belief that the higher costs of doing business can be passed on to the consumer and that the risk of not acting now will only increase as prices rise and the capital investment amounts required increase. Also if continuing increases in interest rates are perceived many managers will show a higher-risk profile and be more willing to take on debt before the cost gets higher and also to pay that debt off over the years with cheaper dollars. When inflation rates exceed the interest rates, managers often hesitate less in borrowing for the company. It also is easier as the value of the firm's assets have been driven up by inflation and this provides a greater base for borrowing. Another factor that affects management posture on risk is that inflation sometimes serves as an umbrella for marginal or less-well-managed companies to secure price increases and protect profits. This provides a form of protection against inefficiencies in operations, unwise decision making, and accepting high risk courses of action. Even taking a greater amount of risk in building inventories might prove not to be of considerable concern because with rising prices on low-cost inventories the sale of these items improve the profits. Even the risk taken by buying the equipment needed to build the inventories is reduced because the interest payments on the debt work as a tax shield and give added incentive to expand the business. Managers in periods of deflation must recognize that the retention of risk-taker posture can prove damaging to the company if cash flow and liquidity is declining. When you move from inflationary economies to deflationary economies, you must consider adjusting your attitudes toward risk and take a more conservative stance.

Technological developments require large investments in research and development and often larger investments in turning the results into commercially profitable products. This entire process is fraught with risk but the rewards are great. Some managers shy away from being the innovators and risk takers; instead, they prefer to wait and copy success as soon as possible. Meanwhile, the resources of the organization are employed on other activities. Although there is a risk that producing a quite-similar product might be a patent infringement, this does not generally dissuade managers from using this marketing strategy. How is the patent infringement risk reduced? The answer is often by doing some novel packaging accompanied by a change in the style or characteristics of the product. The color or ingredients, shape or size, and application or uses can be modified just enough to present a different image. Management's attitude toward risk is as vital to manufacturing as marketing decisions. The investment in manufacturing operations in foreign countries is rarely an easy decision to make. The Japanese auto manufacturers found that major changes were required in operations and organizations when building cars in the United States. In Japan many of the component parts of the auto are built by numerous subcontractors. This gives the auto manufacturer a great competitive advantage over U.S. manufacturers by permitting a tight control over inventory and rapid adjustments in production to cyclical changes in the industry. In order to maintain a competitive posture, the Japanese auto manufacturers in the United States must get in place equally attractive subcontracting arrangements. Also, risk is increased for the higher labor and material costs in the United States affects the profit margins. Also, with stronger unions in the United States the risk of costly labor-management disputes is an added burden. Much of the risk in hiring employees is handled in Japan through the screening provided by difficult hiring tests. In addition, new employees must have a high scholastic standing and pass demanding physical and mental examinations. Many times, extensive personal inquiries are made on the character of the person and the manager has great control over the training and relocation of the employee. As a Japanese manager, you can appreciate the risk of establishing a business in the United States and hiring employees in a market where you have less control over the organization and manager-employee relationships. How you perceive risk determines how aggressive you are in entering foreign markets. What are normal and standard operating procedures in one environment can be much different in another.

Many managers see foreign markets as ripe for picking; many times in recent years this has proven to produce a small harvest. Often it is the sudden and unexpected political changes that sour the investment. What is your attitude and higher-level management's attitude toward the consequences that result from changes in the direction or structure of a foreign government? Multinational firms are always looking to find better ways to forecast and handle overseas risks. There are service firms that you can subscribe to that use sophisticated models to help predict political, social, and economic change in countries. However, there are different opinions as to the value of the information received because it implies a mathematical precision when it often rests on subjective inputs. Because much of the information is judgmental, it should not be used to quantify the decision-making process. It is another good source for assessing risk only when it is carefully evaluated by specialists with insight into the respective countries and situations.

Managers must be somewhat skeptical on long-range forecasts of political risks in foreign countries because conditions can change drastically and quickly. Because of this, you cannot rely solely on recent personal and business associations that you have had or current pronouncements of the governments. Some firms try to hedge the risk by purchasing political-risk insurance from private underwriters; however, the premiums are high and the policies rarely protect you from large losses. When you have your own staff of international specialists and keep them separate from the day-to-day operations of the company, they can issue reports to executives that will help the latter to avoid making unwise decisions. The objectivity of this group is very worthwhile because there is a high degree of risk in the decision-making process when the inputs are provided by a few close associates. There is risk in acting improperly and entering a market or country at the wrong time, but the risk is just as great if you do not enter at all.

Effective managers use past experiences and history to judge the degree of risk in a venture. If the conditions and resources at hand parallel a past situation, then evaluate the elements that made that decision an effective one and repeat the process. Managers must take risks if the organization is to grow and if market share is to be increased for the product line. If developing a product or service internally presents much risk then consider the use of outside vendors. To reduce the risk that quality and costs are not as expected, you must clearly identify what is to be done. This requires detailed specifications and adequate controls to minimize changes once the contract has been assigned. All changes must be justified from a cost-benefit point of view. Get references from other people who have used the contractor and get at least three different bids to assure that the price is reflective of the real-market conditions. Also, reduce the risk of a less-than-satisfactory performance by periodically sampling the nature and quality of the contractor's work during the life of the contract. Identify in advance of starting a project all of the major areas of risk and how they will be managed. A high-risk proposal requires you to invest your resources on a gradual basis until more is learned about what is needed to contain the risk.

All programs that involve risk require that you have in place a contingency program. The greater the financial risk to the firm, the more checks and balances must be in place to reduce the scope or halt the activities if the return on the investment is in doubt or the successful implementation is not assured. If ways cannot be found to avoid risk, then you must hedge them in a manner that will protect the organization.

Risk of Multinational Corporations (MNCs)

Throughout the last decade, enormous progress has been made in building a closely knit international economy and the markets have adapted to the task of recycling an unprecedented flow of funds from surplus to deficit countries. Some of the Third World countries and some of the countries in the southern tier of Europe have experienced rapid growth in income and standards of living. Managers in multinational companies must realize that many countries have more room now to steer their economies in new directions. However, the adventurous spirit that once characterized much industrial activity and was very vital to rapid growth has been temporarily restrained by the uncertainties in international money markets. The current decade can be seen as a growth opportunity for many countries engaging in long-term strategic planning. For the first time in many years, growth abroad is likely to exceed growth in the United States and the greater risk is to be out of these markets rather than in them. How can you assess the risks that are faced by multi-national corporations? First, by having a better understanding of international economics and its changing profile. Inflation rates shown less divergence between countries and the Concerted Action Program recently adopted at Bonn has resulted in countries recognizing the overriding importance of not allowing sluggish growth, sectoral difficulties, or trade imbalances to serve as pretexts for actions that would undermine the framework of free trade among nations. Difficult challenges will be faced by executives of multinational corporations, and to understand how to implement an effective overseas marketing program it is important to understand the changing international interests and pressures. Some countries will find it hard to generate enough jobs to reduce unemployment, and they might welcome the activities of your organization in proposing new business facilities. However, GNP will remain low in some of these countries and many of them will have weak economies because of excess capacity in many basic industries. The risk involved in running your plants at a high rate of capacity increases when you are located in an area with existing excessive plant capacity. Also with low rates of investment in plant and equipment, the creation of new jobs and improved consumer spending might not be promising. If you are marketing consumer products or services there might not be much demand for what you produce.

The risk of attaining new venture capital at reasonable costs is increasing as the large current-account surplus of the countries making up OPEC (Organization of Petroleum Exporting Countries) are decreasing. Meanwhile, the combined deficit of the so-called non-oil developing countries is expanding and this could cause added risk for the multi-national corporations doing business in these areas. There are significant problems and risk that arise in doing business in foreign countries. You must be able to identify the problems and relate them to the long-range strategies that you are implementing. You must be aware of the ethical conflicts and practices that exist in various countries. How do you compete in a market where your competitors engage in possible deceit or bribery? To manage risk, you must examine the regulations in various countries where you plan to conduct business and understand the proper division and extent of power between the government and the multi-national firms. In some European countries, there is now "co-determination" whereby the board of directors must have a high proportion of representation of employees and even outside union members on the board. Are you prepared for this in doing business in these countries? Executives today are faced with changing political structures and hard-to-forecast economic movements both at home and overseas. There are increased government regulations, growing demands from outside groups, and changing attitudes of employees toward their jobs. All of these elements make risk more difficult to manage.

You should give your attention to the following five major elements of change that are making risk assessing and management increasingly more difficult to handle.

First is the role and impact of nationalism. The trend of protectionism will continue and this will foster more inflation as it increases the spreads between the economies of the developed countries and the nondeveloped countries. Follow carefully all new decisions on international-trade agreements for they will effect how many companies can compete in European Common Market member countries. Look at the practice of various countries that are giving preference to local manufacturers and relate this to how your firm, if it is multi-national, can retain a high visibility in the country that is practicing protectionism. In some countries big is good; yet in the United States there are people who think that big is bad. Multi-national firms want to be good citizens in a foreign country; however, in many countries sales often hinge on political decisions rather than on building a business case. The level of risk in the decision-making process increases unless you understand how people in government think and will act on an issue that will directly affect your operations.

Second is the identification and nature of the customers. In many foreign countries the young people want to buy and wear American-style clothes. Marketing these products in these markets would not be a high-risk-level decision; however, introduce them incorrectly and failure could result. The question of "what business are we in?" requires very careful study in foreign markets as well as domestic markets. You should look at such things as whether or not the country is developing into an industrialized nation, whether the business is susceptible to nationalization, how you create customer needs and meet their measures of value, how you manage your public relations, and how you go about raising the capital needed to establish and conduct the business. Pricing the products always carries elements of risk because what a person will pay for quality varies significantly from one country to another. Technological developments within a country are often closely related to economic growth and there can be high risk by introducing a product or service that is beyond the needs of the consumers.

Third, technological developments can result in profound changes that make the assessing and managing of risk a difficult task. Technological changes today are more revolution than evolution; some business executives plan for products with expected lives of not much over three years. Investments are made in products only when the payback—the return of the initial investment—is less than three years. Improved technology is one of the solutions to the problem of inflation and increasing business costs and it must be encouraged by government, business, and consumers. The climate for research and development has deteriorated in the United States but this is not the case in many other countries and the technological leadership of many U.S. industries is endangered. Unless the challenge is met, it will become increasingly difficult to sell some products in the domestic market against foreign competition. Exporting these products into the foreign markets is fraught with even a higher level of risk. Robotics will sweep manufacturing operations over the next decade like a great tidal wave and computers that operate at high levels of sophistication are analogous to the automobile industry at the Model-T level.

Fourth, social changes makes managing risk a new ball game. Co-determination and other practices in foreign countries puts management in a position where their ability and opportunity to manage change is greatly reduced. Some of the practices consist of increasing resistance by employees and unions to merit pay systems and the increasing steps to sell ownership in the business to the local people. Multi-national firms must endeavor to perceive the direction that the social structure has elected and proact with effective strategies rather than to react with emotional and impulsive decisions.

Fifth, the attitudes of employees are different in many ways from one country to another. In some countries, where mealtime wine is commonplace, employees expect it to be served in the company cafeteria. As the firm must draw near and address the needs of the employees, the employees must also recognize the goals of the organization and its problems. There is mutual responsibility to prevent any disharmony that puts added risk in the path of successful growth for the company. Europeans, for example, assign more authority to governments than do Americans and they care far less about competition. Americans put great emphasis on individual rights and the growing communitarism ideology assigns a high value to membership in a group. How you manage effectively depends on how you are able to understand people, perceive changes, and assess risk.

Risk Spreading

Inflationary pressures and increasing debt burdens can often seriously inhibit the ability of a capital-intensive company to build new plants and facilities. When additional capital is required it often becomes necessary to spread the risks of the business. Many multinational companies today are building major plant, laboratory, and office facilities in countries where costs are difficult to forecast because of inflation and are even harder to control. Some of the expansion takes place in remote areas of the world where labor is scarce, materials very expensive, taxes rising in quantum leaps, and political pressures as well as the risk of confiscation of some of the firm's assets rising. As the risks can be enormous and difficult to predict and manage, many executives look for ways in which they can be spread among other companies as well as among the governments of the countries where the investments are being made. In addition to spreading the risks among governments, other parties can be used such as suppliers, customers, and investment banks. It is the profitability of the investment that leads other parties into accepting a share of the risk burden, and as each of them has different goals and objectives putting a good financial package together is not an easy task.

Using the computer-simulation model can help in evaluating the many elements of risk and constructing an appealing package to reduce the firm's exposure. It must begin with a very careful assessment of all of the start-up costs and all of the related operating/maintenance costs during the life of the venture. Benefits and costs must be related and the inflow and outflow streams of each must be compared. Profitability is determined and the investment decision made with the help of the net present value, internal rate of return, or payback financial-justification techniques. Investment alternatives are ranked and risk is assessed. Some countries have a posture regarding investments from overseas sources that requires careful evaluation. Possible obstacles might be a direct expropriation of the facilities or the ownership of more than 50 percent of the business. Other elements that raise the level of risk are constant increases in taxes and foreign-currency restrictions. When evaluating the social and political stability, try to assess some weight that you can add to raise the level of the ROI to compensate for the conditions. Some large international banks help to spread the risks for your foreign investments when they are a sponsoring member in the venture. As much as possible, risks should be reduced through insurance programs or sponsoring agencies. Often sponsoring agencies have positions of strength with the involved foreign government and can help by restraining the government from acting in adverse ways toward your projects.

Effective managers realize that committing the company to excessive amounts of debt might impact cash flows and restrict profits and growth. Bankers often ask for agreement forms to be signed, which assures them that the parent company is giving some form of guarantee to the lenders so that these funds can be shown as direct liabilities. Spreading risks often produces costs that are significantly higher than would be expected were the parties handling the risk to require additional insurance-premium payments. Private lenders will often assume risks, and commercial banks are helpful in assuming some of the risks in foreign countries. However, it is always worthwhile to investigate getting funding or risk insurance from government agencies for the rates might be lower. You can often acquire funding or risk insurance from overseas customers; however, unless conditions are favorable the terms might be high.

Better Planning, Less Risk

Managers can often reduce risk by giving more attention to gathering the data and evaluating the opinions that improves decision making in the planning process. You should begin by identifying the elements of risk and endeavoring to quantify them based on history and experience. Do you have adequate resources? Many firms have spread resources so thin that what was a safe and sound venture now suffers and the program to plan for risk, which over 70 percent of major U.S. firms have in place, begins to crumble. Planning for risk is a program that will not always improve your forecasting but it will help you to manage future events. Its major contribution is that it makes today's decisions more mindful of the demands that the future will place on the organization and its resources.

A sound plan for managing risk begins with identifying the company's missions and the functional departments' goals and objectives. The policies that are established provide guidelines for making decisions given situations that can be outlined in advance of their occurring. The policies provide enough flexibility for managers to quickly implement action programs yet help to identify the questions that should be asked in order to make an effective decision. It is often assumed that managers are risk takers; however, this often turns out to be correct only when the rewards for taking the risks are large. Managers are paid to take risks and the better he or she plans for the handling of potential problems the less traumatic it will be when unexpected problems are added. The degree of satisfaction that you attain in achieving an objective has a value, or utility, to you. Once you have established this level of value, you can better assess the amount of risk that you are willing to handle. As you will have a unique utility value to the goals that you plan and achieve, the degree of risk that you will endeavor to manage will be very personal. Other managers will not set the same values for those goals and will assess and accept risk quite differently than you. The result is that there often exists different levels of risk taking and attitudes toward risk within the organization. Attitudes toward risk become very personal and subjective, and each manager plans to handle risk individually.

When you properly plan, you reduce risk because you make decisions in a manner that is more structured and disciplined. You will follow a more consistent and predictable pattern in selecting options and alternatives. Unfortunately, many managers are not consistent in their handling of risk because they have not laid any groundwork for handling complex problems and for preventing minor situations from becoming complicated. Often the amount of data that must be gathered and evaluated is so large that without a preplanned program to attack it the extraneous and worthless information often gets treated with the same importance as the essential data, and confusion leads to an impulsive and usually incorrect decision. Effective managers plan for innovative growth of the organization and new products and services are always born in climates of risk. What you market and manufacture now is your bread and butter, but it will not be in the next decade. You need to plan for risk and encourage the taking of risk if the company is to grow. If you want innovation within the organization you must build it; you do this by creating a penalty-free environment when everyone will propose new ideas and plan for their implementation by considering the nature of the risks that might appear. Growth means accepting risk and managing it through careful planning. Successful managers often mix long-term projects with high-risk and short-term low-risk projects and measure the gains and losses of the composite of these on a long- and not short-run bais. Research and development is an area where risk is at a high level, particularly in pure research. Later, in applied research when the idea becomes a potential commercial product the risk declines. One major company has stayed with pure research on a given subject for more than ten years because the risk was perceived as being worth the investments and efforts. As long as the firm continues to see some practical application to the pure research efforts, they continue the activities. Executives in many companies plan for the continuous growth of revenue from new products and create the environment where managers must take risks at levels that are perhaps higher than they would like. Managers must believe in what they are doing, accept the risks involved, and go out and fight for the dollars needed to fund the project.

Many new products and services spring from outside of the company and you must talk with customers and vendors to get their ideas and their assessment of the risk involved. New products or services must meet the future needs of your customers if you want to leap-frog competition and gain increasing share of the market. The productivity growth in the United States has for many years lagged behind that of Europe and Japan. This is due to U.S. managers having an aversion to risk taking accompanied by a low rate of saving and capital investment. Managers often avoid the risks of the long-term projects and invest capital primarily in short-term opportunities. Show a three-year payback on an investment and you get a green light to move into it; however, if many years are needed to pay back the investment required to build new plants and automate production facilities, the venture is perceived as being high risk. Only careful planning and the development of a good business case turns these situations into go decisions. It is not a risk to invest monies into improving the productivity of the employees; rather it is a risk not to invest the funds. The avoidance of what has been perceived as risk for more than two decades is responsible for the low productivity in business today. This being the case, it is management's attitudes toward risk that has harmed the economy more than the lack of venture capital. In order to meet the competitive advantages of foreign firms, you do not take a safe posture by being content to gain small profits by licensing and acquiring small innovative firms to expand your product lines.

One reason to take only the short-term approach to managing risk and improving profits is due to the decentralized approach in decision making. Often the officers in the functional divisions of the company are both physically and organizationally far removed from the source of the company's mission statements. Without good communication it is difficult to understand the nature of the risks and how they should be handled. Many of the executives therefore exercise great caution and conservatism in allocating resources to new areas of technological development and growth. The risk of failure is perceived as being greater than playing it cautiously: hence fewer rewards but less-devastating penalties. Successful managers know that the big-money winners of today will not be the profit makers tomorrow, so don't sacrifice future new markets and customers with excessive attention to today's business. You must take the risks required to introduce new products, new services, and structural reorganization. Growth never comes from following the market and letting the other fellow be first. You can't copy the market and grow; you must be an innovator. You also can't import your technological expertise by buying foreign-made products for you don't lessen risk—you increase it. As you become more dependent, you have less control and fewer options on your decisions. Those who avoid risk soon become followers rather than leaders. There is no question that the managing of risk and assessing new capital investments are difficult tasks to balance; however, the key lies in how complete your planning strategies and alternative options are.

Managers spend much time in planning the efficient use of capital and human resources but insufficient time in assessing risk. Just a simple assessment of the probability of success is helpful. Use the history of past decisions as a guide and apply it to the new situation. For example, if last year you reduced the price of a product by 12 percent and estimated a 50 percent increase in sales, then what were the final figures? If sales increased only 30 percent, can you relate this to the current price reduction's being considered to arrive at a more-accurate estimate of increased sales? You can and should estimate the affects of a decision prior to implementing it or even proposing it to higher-level management.

Decisions Involving Risk

Even very simple decisions carry with them elements of risk for you are looking at many causal variables and hard-to-quantify unknowns. Each alternative could have many different outcomes and each of these must be evaluated. In order to manage this process effectively, you should break each situation or problem up into clearly defined parts where definitive results can be forecasted and evaluated. Often, simulation models can be used to manage this process and to help to assign quantified values to many of the elements that make up the complex decisions. The mathematical models, when used to define the variables, can also assign the probability of risk that has been assumed for each of the parts in the hypothetical solution.

As many decisions involve much uncertainty, managers must identify the course of action that will result in the most satisfactory resolution of the situation in keeping with the corporate mission statements and the goals of the organization. You reduce the risk of unsatisfactory decisions by applying probability to the possible solutions. Probability means that you assess the percentage of time that a specific outcome occurs when the action is repeated a large number of times. The probability of getting a tail on flipping a coin is 50 percent, but you cannot predict with certainty the outcome of any single flip. You deduced this probability from your facts about the condition of the coin (one side head, one side tail). When you have sufficient knowledge about the conditions involved in a situation, you also can deduce the probability of the outcome. However, you should use history and the data that you have collected on past experiences and relate this to the new problems to help arrive at better probability figures.

Making decisions under conditions of risk requires a manager to take a series of orderly steps as follows:

First, identify all alternative courses of action that you can apply to the resolution of the situation. Each of these must be in harmony with the mission statements of the company and the goals of your organization. If you have doubts about a course of action, consider it but don't take a "no, it won't work" attitude too quickly. Managing risk requires a very careful application of building a business case for or against a position. Unless you build a case against a position you cannot build a case for a position. Good lawyers know exactly what the other lawyer will present in order to reduce the risk of a surprise move and to build a sound case for their cause.

Second, examine the forces, factors, and elements that affect each alternative course of action and quantify how, when, and where they can impact the outcome. Next, estimate the probability of each outcome from the alternative courses of action. These estimates are from the history at hand or the best forecasts from those with experience in these matters.

Third, determine an expected dollar value of each outcome. The use of decision-tree techniques is worthwhile here. The expected value of an action that results from a decision that you have made is the average result that would be expected if the action or decision were carried out many times under the same condition. The decision-tree analysis rakes each possible alternative course of action and relates it to the estimated probability of producing a given payoff.

People with a high need for achivement are not gamblers. They do not take excessive risks for they carefully determine what must be done in order to succeed, and they are careful not to underestimate or overestimate the required resources. Success is often perceived as being on top of the problem and controlling the final results. It is important to control the surrounding actions and events as much as possible. High achievers want to be in a position to influence the outcome by working on the problem rather than leaving it to chance.

Many people often go to extremes in their attitudes toward risk. They are often either wild speculators who seldom learn from their losses or they are ultraconservative and avoid all exposure to risk. The attitude is often determined by how willing the individual is to accept responsibility for losses. Both the gambler and ultraconservative type of person wants to be free of all responsibility. The gambler blames the loss on things beyond his or her control. The ultraconservative will not take a chance because if something can go wrong he or she might be blamed for the outcome. If you are managing either of these types, it is important through counseling to try to move them nearer to the middle of the road for this is the ground of achievement-motivated people. Why? Because it is perceived by them that a moderate amount of risk is required if they are able to use their skills and abilities to influence the outcome of their tasks. Both managers and employees respond to risk best when the goals given to them are moderately difficult but potentially achieveable. Achievement-motivated managers also prefer a moderate degree of risk for it gives challenge and visibility to their skills, efforts, and abilities.

The Risk of Not Imitating the Japanese

For many years managers have seen in U.S. firms an increasing cost disadvantage in competing with foreign manufacturers. This has been very apparent in the competition with the Japanese production of automobiles, electronic equipment, and textile products. The weakness in American industry has risen from falling productivity and increasing labor costs. The risk is that if our industries do not follow the Japanese approaches for increasing efficiency by raising productivity and lowering costs, then what little trade advantages we have will disappear in the next decade. Perhaps it has been a complacency with market share that has led U.S. business to ignore for over a decade what foreign manufacturers, particularly the Japanese, were doing to increase their profit margins on goods and services.

Some of the problem has been caused by the attitudes toward risk taken by U.S. managers. An aversion to risk taken by many managers has steered firms into programs that did not improve productivity and slow the rise in labor costs. U.S. Bureau of Labor statistics show that Japanese auto manufacturers have a cost advantage of over $8 per hour in comparison to labor costs in the U.S. auto industry. Why have U.S. labor costs gotten so high and given the Japanese an enormous advantage in manufacturing costs? The risk of plant shutdowns due to strikes have made U.S. managers fearful of taking strong positions against rapidly climbing labor costs. Management has quickly expanded fringe benefits and approved automatic wage gains that were not linked to improved productivity. Production costs steadily climbed, but management blamed it on inflation and passed the higher costs on to the consumer in small-but-frequent price-rise increments. The consumer didn't resist because in inflationary times if you don't buy now the price will only go higher. Disinflation might bring a much-different consumer attitude. Managers had best be aware of this change.

Further adding to the costs of products has been the cost of ever-expanding ranks of managers. Who would take the risk of not having a sufficient number of managers when the forecasts for business growth have been highly positive? To make matters worse, many people had estimated that there would be a greatly reduced supply of managers in the next decade. The risk of coming up short of professional people and managers was too great; hence, many firms have gone to great lengths to retain employees who should perhaps have not been retained. Professional people perform knowledge work, and this is difficult to measure. In addition, management has forgotten the adage that you should earn more only when you produce more.

Managers in U.S. industries have also shown another aversion to risk that we do not see in Japan. This has been the fear of jumping in with total commitment to technological developments that can reduce manufacturing costs. First, there is the risk that the payback on the capital investment will not substantially improve the bottom line profits in the short-run. This tendency to measure success in the short-run rather than the long-run is to blame for most of our problems. Second, managers perceive that there is a risk that there would not be any displaced costs for union-contract gains and that organized pressures would result in little reductions in operating costs. Cost avoidance also seems of little value as managers like to assess benefits in short-run terms. Managers with less aversion to risk taking have already automated many of their company's procedures and are gaining the rewards of improved efficiency and higher productivity. Those managers who risk not adopting the technological changes—as have the Japanese— will continue to experience increasing cost disadvantages in competing with foreign manufacturers.

However, U.S. managers show an aversion to a risk of listening. They often do not want to hear from the employees. It seems strange that managers who were once not in managerial positions forget that people other than managers often have geat ideas. It is as if once they are given the title of manager only their ideas have merit. The Japanese worker often does have more-advanced tools to do the job, but more importantly they have more opportunity to speak up regarding how the job should be done. Why do many U.S. managers feel it is risky to let employees engage in planning production, scheduling work, controlling quality, and participating in decision making? A popular business saying was "Work smarter, not harder." Why have we turned our backs on this when it has worked so well for the Japanese?

Many U.S. assembly lines have large numbers of parts on hand, which take up much room and increases the size of the plant. The Japanese have few parts at the work station because they schedule them to arrive as needed; hence, their production facilities can be smaller, thus resulting in considerably lower production costs. Tight quality control on the part of everyone further drives down production costs as there are fewer rejects and less material waste.

Japanese managers believe that there is risk in not letting employees participate with management in running the business. These attitudes have proven correct many times. Risk is less dangerous when it is shared between management and employees. When employees participate with management many small improvements result, which in turn lead to higher-quality products, improved productivity, and lower costs. These benefits generally cannot be achieved with large-scale programs directed from the higher levels of management downward. Japanese workers identify with the goals of the organization and want to see the company grow. They are also willing to take risks. William Ouchi has labeled the Japanese approach to implant a disciplined social hierarchy in the business environment as the Theory Z approach. A Japanese employee does what he or she is asked to do because of discipline but even more, I feel, because he or she wants to see the firm grow. There are some in U.S. management circles who say that we cannot follow this approach with success because the American worker will not accept the discipline. I must differ: American workers will not only accept the discipline, but they are asking for it in a loud voice. Everyone respects a tightly run ship for they know that this will get them where they want to go. Also, American workers want very much to see their companies get back into the world markets with a posture of strength.

Yes, there is job security in the Japanese labor market and perhaps American workers perceive the risk of being fired; however, given reward and recognition for a job well done, you will find the American worker will work with even-greater dedication than his or her overseas competitors. It is true that Japanese employees give outstanding service to customers, but it is not from a fear of losing his or her job. There is no perceived risk of loss of job because of poor performance, but there is the risk of the loss of self-esteem and this is a risk that most employees will not take under any condition. It has been said that the Japanese employees work hard and long hours not because of the interest in the growth of the firm but because of the fear of displeasing their managers and also that this is why they work so hard to improve quality and improve productivity. I must take exception to this thinking. Continuing levels of high performance are not gained and maintained by fear or the risk of punishment. Japanese managers and employees are risk takers and the decision-making-by-consensus process is not a submission to discipline as has been suggested but a method to increase involvement and assure that the views and opinions of everyone in the organization have been heard. It is a testimony to respect for the individual. Some have suggested that to learn from the Japanese methods for handling risk and building strong organizational structures is a waste of time. They also say that to give this added respect to the individual will reduce our competitive advantages around the world. This is not ture, for unless we learn some lessons from the higher level of the employee involvement in the growth of the company we will have less, not more, of a competitive edge. The Japanese process has been described as a method of cajoling employees into doing what management wants them to do. This is not correct: The Japanese worker perceives that the risk of failure to the firm is the risk of failure to his or her own personal life. There is no pressuring; rather there is a sense of all being involved and working for the well-being of everyone. The Japanese managers recognize risk, they accept it, and they manage it because they know that growth comes only with taking intelligent risks.

Profits and Risk

The word *profits* has different meanings to many people; therefore they tend to exaggerate the size of the corporate profits and minimize the risks taken in order to achieve it. Most people feel that profits make up over one-third of the total gross national product, but we know that prior to taxes it is less than 10 percent. Much of what is termed *profit* is only a return to owners of what they have supplied to the business. Some of this is interest on the owner's capital or wages paid by the owner to him- or herself.

The business owner must get some reward for the efforts and risks involved in establishing and running the business. If you receive no more than wages that you could get by working for another person, then why should you risk your capital in a venture that might fail or produce a minimal gain. The entrepreneur or innovator is deserving of a profit for the risk that he or she has taken. The greater the risk, the greater the rewards. Those executives or managers that only run the established business receive wages that are commensurate with the risk that they take. Profits are the returns that go to the innovators or entrepreneurs who provide the venture capital or, in some cases, the shareholders who continue to infuse capital into the company. Why should the innovator receive profits? It is he or she who provided the idea, process, or capital and was willing to take the risks of the new venture. The innovator rarely has any aversion to risk and with a high commitment of their talents, time, and monies are deservant of the rewards of the profitable successes. Innovational profits are linked with uncertainty and risk and must always be encouraged.

Uncertainty and risk can be managed in a manner that reduces the element of gamble but it does so at the expense of some of the profits. This is done by pooling and spreading the risks over a large number of risk takers, thus helping to cancel some of the impact on some of the parties. An insurance company will use mortality tables and spread the uncertainty of the risk over a large number of policyholders. Each policyholder then reduces his or her relative riskiness as does the insurance company through the mathematical laws of probability. The insurance firm might even go further in pooling and spreading the risk by off-loading some of it—with a reduction in profits—to another insurance firm.

Many managers who have an aversion to risk expect to get a profit from taking the risk. Companies then that go forth with risky ventures must be able to recover profit margins that adequately reward them for taking the risks while providing adequate rewards to those that made the risk-taking decisions. Any business activity that involves a great deal of uncertainty and risk taking will engage people who are risk takers. Risk takers should be rewarded for managing risk and not letting risk manage them.

Risk Analysis

Proposed capital investments should be classified as a high-level risk when the resources to be committed are large and incomplete or inaccurate cost-

and-benefit data forms the basis for the decision. Managers often focus only on the capital to be committed; this incomplete analysis for the human resources is expensive for any venture that requires professional talents. A wise approach is to invest capital and human resources in a stage-by-stage approach. The gradual commitment of resources permits management the time needed to gather more data and to carefully evaluate it. Also, many ventures change in scope and importance as business needs change to match changing environmental conditions. Further, time is required to match performance against the planned schedule of activities, analyze the measurements, evaluate the accomplishments, and perhaps modify the plans if required. Time is also required if you are to exercise quality control prior to committing more resources.

It is possible to gauge exposure to risk in a proposed capital investment by observing how wide the range is between the low and the high estimate of costs and also benefits. The wider the range, the greater the risk. In the initial stage of a proposed capital investment, these ranges should be at their widest width. Hence, the risk is greatest and commitment of resources should be the least possible to successfully do the job. At later stages in the development of the capital investment, more and better cost and benefit data is collected and the ranges should narrow. This indicates a lower exposure to risk and larger amounts of resources should be committed. At every stage in a proposed capital investment the more accurate the cost and benefit data the lower the risk in later expenditures. Forms should be used to standardize the procedure for collecting cost-and-benefit data and assessing risk. These forms must be designed to meet the specific needs of your business; hence, they cannot be included in this book. Managers in many companies will give you the opportunity to look at the forms that they use; with minor modifications you can adapt them to your organization.

When you are assessing the risk of a proposed capital investment, you are looking at the possibility of recovering your initial capital investment in a short period of time and with an acceptable risk. Often the outcome of the investment is in doubt since you might only partially realize the full value of the benefits. Also, you might not realize the benefits in the time period that you have expected. Another risk is that the actual costs might exceed your estimates and perhaps even your benefits. How do you handle these unknown future outcomes? Assign some probability to each of them based on your experience, history, and the judgment of others in the organization. Identify the potential adverse factors, estimate their chance of occurrence, and determine how they will impact either the costs or the benefits. The greater the adverse factors, the greater the risk associated with the venture. The more knowledge that you have about past similar situations, the better you will be able to gauge the magnitude of the risks. What makes assessing risk difficult is that most firms do not have good historical data and it is hard to quantify unknown situations. A proposed capital investment might appear to be low risk in that the costs can be controlled and the production schedules met, yet if the quality of the product is poor the venture is high risk.

Risk comes in many forms: that is, exceeding costs, underrealizing benefits, lateness, and unsatisfactory quality. However, there is another risk that most firms face that can have serious consequences. This is the right solution to the wrong problem. Many managers do not know what the problems are that require their resources and pour wasteful resources into doing the wrong thing. Risk jumps to a bet-your-job level when you either do not identify the problems or cannot give them a proper priority ranking. For example, growers spent millions of dollars on developing new machines to harvest tomatoes with less damage to the fruit, yet the problem was not in the machine but in the thin skin of the tomato. The solution was the development of a tomato with a firmer skin.

Risk is great in today's high-technology industries. Technological developments move at such a rapid pace that products are obsolete within a few years. Some manufacturers of semi-conductors rank their investment proposals only by using a two-year-payback period. The reason is that if they cannot recover all of their initial capital investment within two years, the risk is too high and monies should be invested elsewhere. Risks are great in manufacturing new products. Sales of some products soar when they become fads, but consumer demand can be short-lived. Sometimes the forecasted demands for new products and services are overly optimistic and the actual demand falls far short of expectations. Another risk is that often regulatory laws are passed, reinterpreted, or aggressively enforced, which results in the need to modify or discontinue a product or a service. The probability of any of these events and their impact is not easy to identify or quantify and a statistical approach to assessing risk is difficult. Perhaps the best that you can do is to judge the situation as one of low, medium, or high risk.

Measurement of Risk

Risk analysis, which includes cost/benefit analysis, requires a large volume of data. The collection and evaluation of this does not come cheap. A small data base only leads to inconclusive if not very misleading results. The best approach is to make assumptions and forecast within these constraints. All ventures should be followed with a post-hoc study to improve the data base for future risk-assessment use. Was risk improperly assessed? If so, by how much, and why? Risk deals with the probability of an adverse event's occurring and if it did not occur, then do we attribute that to luck or to misjudgment of the risk? You might not be so lucky the next time, so you can't count on luck. On the other hand, if you misjudged the risk, more insight and/or guidelines for assessing risk are needed. Only a careful study of what happened will permit you to rule out the events that happened by chance and to identify those events subject to probability. Take the time to do this.

Perhaps you identify a proposed capital investment as a high-risk venture. You might have instituted more extensive controls than usual to control the risk. The venture is successfully concluded. Were you wrong in identifying it as high risk? Perhaps you were wrong and it was a low or medium risk. Perhaps you were right: It was high risk and your extensive controls did the job. Only a careful analysis after the venture is completed will help you in the future when you are assessing and handling risks under similar circumstances. Risk measurement and assessment is done not only to attempt to identify early any adverse events that will affect the project but to help to reduce risk by planning for these adverse events in order to avoid them or reduce their impact. It is not possible in this book to give you a blueprint for controlling and assessing risk. The forms in which risk appears varies with the nature of the business, managements' attitude toward risk, and the changing markets. However, some suggested steps for helping to manage risk are as follows:

1. The risk that arises because activities are omitted in the normal conduct of the business can be reduced through the use of policy and procedure manuals, handbooks, guidelines, and statements of practice. Reference sources that contain checklists and sample forms reduces the possibility that necessary activities will be overlooked or not handled correctly.

2. The risk of poor quality can be reduced through the establishment and publication of procedure-and-standards manuals. Work can be broken down into tasks with built-in quality-control checkpoints to measure the product against the specifications. Producing a quality product or service becomes the responsibility of each employee and is a significant factor in employee performance appraisal and evaluation.

3. The risk of missing target dates can be reduced by doing more short-range scheduling with your staff. Each person is responsible for a deliverable product at a given date and must manage his or her time accordingly. When target dates are set on a realistic basis and the employee has been involved in setting them, they become self-fulfilling.

4. The risk of unexpected adverse events increasing the costs or delaying completion of the project can best be handled by immediately informing higher-level management and suggesting alternative courses of action. Additional controls to monitor subsequent events might be implemented. Also additional commitment of resources might be in order. Review the original plan and make needed changes. Risk only increases when you try to implement the wrong plan at the wrong time.

5. The risk of coming in over the budget, under the benefits, or over the time allowed can be reduced by better estimating and tracking actual results against these numbers. At each stage in the life of a project, you will get better numbers regarding costs and benefits. Alert management to expect this and pass upward the new numbers. Tell management when your original assumptions are no longer valid and forecast the affects of the new situation. Managers do not like surprises; therefore address the risks, quantify them, and propose a program of action to handle them.

The responsibility for finding new ways to avoid or manage risks is an integral part of a manager's job. Identify risk quickly, look at the potential costs, and immediately develop an action plan to manage it. The first approach of committing large amounts of resources is not always the best solution. A better step is to get some experts involved in discussing the problem and developing solutions.

4 Managing Change

The manager's world is a world of change and seldom is one week like another. Many variables require your attention and you often do not know what the next problem will be until the telehone rings. Many people within the organization want change. Some perceive it as an improvement to the current situation whereas others want change for reasons you might find difficult to know and understand. You manage today in organizations that are complex and where change is a way of life that cannot be avoided; however, change can be very costly and must be controlled. You must manage the great number of variables that confront you wisely because change creates unknowns and most people fear the unknown.

Focus on Change

Effective managers apply a structure to managing change by taking the following steps:

First, as change often involves many unknowns you must focus on getting the right amount and right kind of information needed for making the correct decision. You will perhaps never know all that you would like to know about the people involved in the change. You will, however, have a sense of how successful your past decisions were through feedback from people within the organization.

Second, as change is implemented over a period of time—often shorter than required—it should consist of a series of orderly steps. Each step addresses specific needs which can be scheduled. As decisions are made in small incremental stages, when possible, the quality improves because you have the time needed to collect and analyze the information.

Third, as change is often met with resistance, you must improve your ability to diagnose resistance and develop better skills in overcoming it. Resistance can arise from small groups within the organization in the form of political pressure.

Fourth, as change requires understanding and awareness by everyone in the organization, it must be implemented through education and involvement. This requires good communication and a high degree of in-

103

teraction and commitment. Those with the responsibility for managing change must be sure that a long-range plan is in place with goals and strategies outlined.

How can you manage the change process in order to achieve the established goals within the time and monies available? Begin by getting quality information on which you can make some good decisions. Change rarely occurs overnight; therefore keep an ear alert for comments about why and how things might be done differently in the organization. Collect the kind of data that is necessary to evaluate these comments. Executives do not like surprises and implementing changes should not come without careful planning and endorsement. You must encourage everyone in the organization to openly discuss the need for change in a penalty-free environment. You often must probe deeply into the interpersonal relationships within the organization in order to avoid the ambiguity that can lead you to make poor decisions. Talk directly with your first-level managers about the need for change. He or she will appreciate your attention and will help you to get complete and correct data.

All alternative solutions to a situation must be carefully examined before you implement a change. In order to properly evaluate the alternatives, you must collect all of the data necessary to weigh the facts. It is important to assess the risk of each alternative and choose the most creative solution with a high probability of success. Quick decisions should not be made if at all possible and get a high degree of participation and involvement in the formulation and design of the change. It will take time to plan a change, but it will take longer to build awareness, interest, concern, and cooperation at all levels in the organization. Even the most carefully planned change can fail if it lacks needed high-level-management support and endorsement. Often it is necessary for key people to get involved in the design and implementation of the change in order to give it high visibility and acceptance in the organization.

Evolutionary Changes

Often the most effective changes are evolutionary in nature. They begin with a few ideas and expand to embrace many people and functions. This approach to change is good because resistance is slower in developing than with a quickly implemented new way of doing things. As technological developments take time to form—as do market changes and regulatory procedures—you must plan your changes to meet their time schedules. You cannot control their pace but you can the speed with which you implement the required changes. Provide ample resources and open good channels of communication with higher-level management so that they are supportive of your actions.

Whenever possible, changes should be tested with a sample group to provide data about the effectiveness of the change and the acceptance among the people involved. As you have not yet announced a specific solution to the problem, you can get reactions from the group and examine other options. The next step in the change process is that as each new way of doing things becomes defined and accepted it becomes imbedded in the ongoing activities of the organization. There is less risk in implementing change this way than if you were to announce a change in such an emotionally upsetting manner. Because you are indicating flexibility in the design and implementation of the change, you do not place your personal credibility on the line. Implementing the change with a small group does not affect the entire production of the organization. It gives you time to modify the change as needed and it helps to sell the change once the rest of the organization sees that it is working well. Also, it permits those that are involved in the change to participate, this will help to overcome any possible resistance or, at worst, keep it on a small scale. Look for the strong supportive people in the group for they can help to endorse and recommend the change to other people. You should have a consensus of support for a change from those people in important positions before you implement it on a large scale. Each of these people, like the others, have individual and organization needs that they expect the change to satisfy. Unless their confidence level is high, you will not get strong support. Get support for a small part of the change, implement it, and then move on to gain support for the next piece of the decision. Once the change has settled in and is working well, you can announce new policy statements and goals.

In complex organizations it can take many years for a change to be accomplished and accepted. Many of the related decisions are made in incremental stages as more and better data becomes available. Those who helped to make the decisions in the early life of the change move on to other jobs and responsibilities and new people become involved in the design and implementation of the change. In some organizations the time span and number of participants precludes you from identifying just who was responsible for the change. As other people become involved in the change they add new insights, talents, and creative ideas; as a result, better changes result when adequate time is taken to mold them. Even though change is evolutionary, it is done cohesively. You must have a proper sense of direction and establish goals if you are to use your resources wisely. Each step in planning for change requires careful cost-benefit analysis and risk assessment. Your plan should be written like a script with assumptions and forecasts documented. When the environmental conditions change and the script is no longer valid you go back to the initial goals, reconfirm their correctness or announce new ones, and change your plan accordingly. Before each step is taken in implementing change a new consensus is reached regarding its relevancy to what business the firm will be in tomorrow, not today. Consensus for the change must come from the higher levels of management because they have the background and experience to examine it from many sides. It takes time and monies to design and implement change, but once it is underway it gains momentum; that is why it must be the right change at the start.

The Change Model

Managers often describe the problems that accompany the implementation of change as a resistance to change. Production might decline, morale fall, and absenteeism or lateness increase. The change may or may not be the cause, for many small changes occur daily in the organization without producing problems. People often need to alter their attitudes and behavior when change is introduced into the organization, but this is an adjustment and will not become resistance if the change is understood and perceived as being good for the individual as well as the organization. The following illustration (figure 4-1) will help us to see more clearly how people adjust to change and how you can facilitate the process.

Productivity in the organization is at level AB as indicated in figure 4-1. You implement change and productivity falls as indicated by the line BC. The magnitude of this decline will depend a lot on how much acceptance and consensus you have developed for the change. When the people involved in the change see that it is in their interest as well as the organization, line BC is short and the dip in productivity is shallow. Managers who manage change effectively are aware of this and sell the merits of the change well in advance of its implementation. Until people get comfortable with the change, productivity is at a plateau shown by CD. How effectively you manage change determines how far the CD level will be below the AB level and the duration of time (length of CD) it remains there. The implementation of a good change eventually results in improved productivity as shown by line DE, and it reaches some point E which is much higher than the level AB. The implementation of a bad change drives productivity even lower as shown by line DF, and it reaches some point F which is far lower than the original level AB and interim level CD. How do you manage change so you arrive at E and not F? You do it through the three elements shown in figure 4-1—that is, attitudes, behavior, and productivity.

The first step is through attitude. If you properly sell the benefits of your well-designed change, the people involved will realize that it helps rather than harms them. Also, when you help them to understand that high-level management supports and endorses the change they will see it as a good solution and worthy of implementation. Once you have established

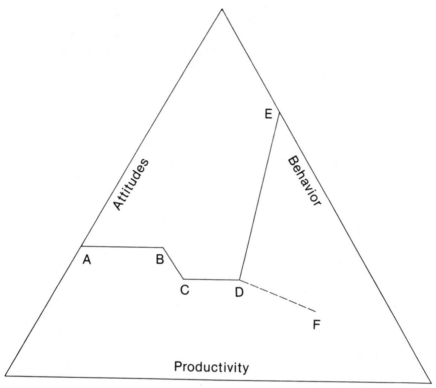

Figure 4-1. Adjusting to Change

constructive and positive attitudes, you are ready for step two. The second step is the modification of behavior. The motivation for this must come from within the people involved in the change; therefore it is important that they see that the change benefits them as well as the organization. When possible, offer some rewards for implementing the change; these rewards might come in the form of promotions, salary increases, or even better working conditions. Once the desired behavior is in place, the third step becomes a self-fulfilling prophecy. Productivity will improve and production will increase as the change takes hold in the organization.

Some managers prefer to handle the adjustment to change in a reverse manner. Using a Machiavellian approach, their first concern is with productivity. The thinking is to drive hard to get productivity up and after you have made the numbers (proved the change works), the behavior will adjust and people will develop the proper attitudes. If you use this approach you must realize that a forced behavior is not as effective and durable as a change that comes from within the person. Also, attitudes might eventually be formed that accommodate the change but it might take a long time to form and they might only be superficial. When you force people to accept change you increase the risk that resistance will develop and the change will not be successful.

Why Change Is Resisted

Managers need to know how to recognize resistance to change; if you know why people resist change you improve your abilities to handle resistance. Organizations must change, as well as you and your people, to meet the new demands of business. Rigid organizations are short-lived. When organizations change, many employees feel threatened. They see changes in their jobs and work relationships as a source of problems that they are not sure they can handle. They are afraid of change primarily because of their insecurity. If they only feel insecure you can help to alleviate some of their concerns. However, if they are insecure you have a much more difficult task in helping them to adjust to change. Every change is accompanied by some emotional concerns, which take time to resolve. Almost all changes take longer and cost more to implement than planned; therefore many managers are afraid to make changes even when they are necessary.

People at all levels in the organization often resist change because they look only at how it affects their interests and values rather than the interests of the organization. Many people overlook the benefits to the organization and some people can't even see the benefits to themselves that will arise from the change. Most people seem to be concerned primarily with what they perceive the change will cost them personally. The question is less what can I gain than what can I lose. A perceived loss in responsibility, authority, status, or opportunity to grow is identified as a loss of something of value. Actually there may be no loss due to the change, but if the person believes that there might be then resistance can develop. You must communicate the details of a planned change very carefully so that people do not perceive that they will lose when they really will gain. Should a number of people in the organization decide that the change is not in their best combined interests, they will join together to block the change or, if it has already been implemented, work at sabotaging it.

Change is also resisted when people do not trust or understand the reason for the change or the implications of the change. An organizational change represents a solution to a problem or situation. Management gains the trust of employees when they clearly describe the problem, explain why it must be addressed, and propose a change that is in the best interest of the organization and the people involved in the change. Poor communication leads to misunderstanding and this in turn to lack of trust in management's actions. You must continuously search for misunderstandings, and this is best done by asking employees to verbally give you their interpretation of the change and what they perceive are the implications. A change that is very much in the best interest of a person might be resisted by him or her simply because he or she does not understand. You do not know if this condition exists if you do not discuss the change, prior to its implementation, with the employees.

Another reason people resist change arises from how risk is assessed. People at all levels in the organization assess risk differently; some are risk takers whereas others are risk avoiders. Most people do a mental comparison of the benefits of the change versus the costs of the change, and if it does not appear that they have a high probability of being a winner they want no part of the program. Don't assume that because you have and understand all of the relevant data supporting the change that other people either have it or understand it as well. You must build a good business case for making a change, and if you cannot you had best wait and see if the change is needed. Many times no change is the best course of action to follow. The role of the devil's advocate is an important one if you are to manage change successfully. You must encourage people to play this role and respect their comments when they resist your proposals. When everyone says a fast "yes" to a proposed change, then you had best not go ahead with it until you think it out more clearly. It is easy to highlight only the issues that support a case and sweep under the rug the matters that people do not want to discuss.

A person might also resist change because he or she cannot cope with new experiences. The change might require working at a different location, with new people, and using different skills. The current job environment might be secure and comfortable, and even though the change is seen as good by that person, he or she might resist it for any number of reasons which both he or she and you might find hard to identify. The need for changes are often intellectually accepted by a person but resisted or rejected because of perceived stress-producing and emotional forces that he or she feels incapable of handling. A person who has lived all of his or her life in a small country town might turn down a great opportunity to grow in the company because it requires a move to a large city and the person fears that they cannot handle the new environment. This might never be admitted, but it could be the true reason for the resistance rather than the superficial statements that are voiced. Adapting to change means a restructuring of attitudes and behavior and a person must want to do it or it will not get done. Your job is to help the person realize why he or she should do it and how they can handle the change and be further ahead in life.

If a change is to be successful it must start with the right attitudes among those involved in the change. You can help to develop these through encouraging early participation by many people in the planning of the change. Get involvement up front and don't wait until implementation time to cultivate it. There is a fear of the unknown that accompanies change and it is not so much the fear of the tasks changing as it is the personal relationships changing. When employees participate in making the change they have the opportunity to address these issues and to more clearly recognize what they need to do in order to adjust. Promote the positive results to be derived from the change and concensus can be reached at all levels. Should the employee see him- or herself not gaining from the change but in fact losing, he or she has the early opportunity to discuss it; before you implement it you can look at other options. The change most likely to fail is the one that comes to everyone as a surprise.

Frequently, people make adjusting to change more difficult than it has to be because they become overly concerned with the technical aspects or physical routines of the change. People must have confidence that the technicians have done their job well and focus more on the interpersonal relationships and how they will change. You must help to guide the thinking in this direction so that the change is better received in the organization. Adapting to new work procedures is not nearly as difficult as adapting to new social arrangements and interactions within the organization. It is easier to make the adjustment when a person has participated in structuring the new arrangements. Participation doesn't mean just being present at meetings; rather, it is offering opinions and suggestions that are considered with due respect. The nature and the magnitude of the change are rarely responsible for the degree of resistance to change because major changes can be made effectively as long as the interpersonal relationships are handled well. People who work closely with each other usually have little difficulty in making even major changes because they respect each other. However, when change is introduced from outside of the group, it might be perceived by them as a threat to their well-defined personal relationships. You must take great pains to see that changes not initiated in the group are introduced by people who are respected by the group. Also, those outside the group who are introducing the change must have close contact with the people in order to understand the group's complex social arrangements and how they might be affected by the change.

It takes time for a change to work successfully, even when there has been no resistance. You cannot hurry the process for if you do the people involved in the change will feel that they are being pressured into accepting and might offer unnecessary resistance. This pressure to implement the change quickly puts some elements of friction into the interpersonal relationships. Quality and production might both decline, which adds additional pressure to accepting the change. What can really make this a dangerous situation is if the people implementing the change accuse the group of resisting the change. Resistance will then develop with even greater intensity. You must have patience and give the change a chance to settle in and be accepted in its original or modified form. You must also see that those people implementing the change have a great deal of patience. This is difficult for these implementors because their job is to introduce the change and quickly show that they have done a good job as it works well. Time will work with you in implementing changes, but push too fast and it will halt implementation in its tracks. The bottom line should always be "was the change accepted and does it work well?" and not "how quickly was the change implemented?"

When you introduce change, keep it simple and be straightforward in all forms of communication. Confusion only impedes consensus. Also, change must be introduced by people with positive attitudes and a desire to be of assistance to those involved in the change. Go in looking for resistance and if it is not there you will create it before you leave. Be a good listener and sensitive to the comments that you hear.

Overcoming Resistance

Figure 4-2 shows the four major situations in organizational change that can produce resistance. Each situation requires a different approach if you are to overcome resistance.

The most common factor that gives rise to resistance is insufficient information. This is missing or inaccurate data, and either or both of these prevent people from forming a consensus to implement the change. Once you provide people with all of the correct information needed to understand and evaluate the merits of the change, they can more easily be persuaded to support it. When the details have been explained and there is nothing to fear, resistance has a difficult time getting started or growing. As early as possible, educate the people involved in the change why there is a need for it, how the change will be implemented, when and where it will be done, what is required of them, and how each person and the organization will benefit from the new way of doing things. Such an educational effort is not small, but it is critical for getting support, acceptance, and endorsement of your proposed change. You can communicate the information in written form; however, oral presentations to small groups provides people with an opportunity to ask questions and to surface their concerns. This benefits you also for it gives you the chance to evaluate your program to be sure that you have all of the accurate data needed to make a wise decision. These educational sessions are also great opportunities to encourage involvement and participation.

The very lack of participation by people involved in the change can produce resistance. If they do not have a part in the designing of the change,

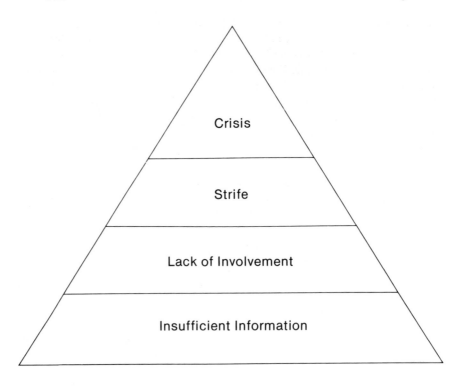

Figure 4-2.. Resistance-Producing Situations

they often feel that it is not a good change and might be reluctant to support it. Some people find it difficult to become committed to a course of action unless they have had a hand in planning it or at least their inputs were requested and their opinions heard. Participation and involvement helps to get acceptance of a change, but it also does something else for you. It helps you to get more and better information should what you have be incomplete or inaccurate. A word of caution is in order here for this method of preventing or reducing resistance—unless properly managed—might result in changes that satisfy many people but are not good approaches to solving the problem or in the best interest of the organization.

Situations involving strife are difficult to handle for resistance to change takes many forms. You must address two different conditions. The first is the internal strife of your employee because he or she must adjust to the change. The change might be acepted as good for the organization but he or she fears that it will not be in their best interest. You must help the person to see that the change will be beneficial and that it will not be as emotionally unsettling as anticipated. Often this is accompanied by the fear that they will not be able to do the work the new way; therefore it is safe to stay with the old methods. Provide training in the new procedure and offer whatever emotional support is required. People who find it difficult to adjust to change need guidance, not criticism. Have patience and help the employee to build his or her self-confidence by offering some praise and compliments when the new tasks are done well.

The second condition of strife is that between people or groups of people. It arises when a person or group perceives that the change is not in their best interest and that they might end up losers rather than winners. If that person or group has power to offer significant resistance to the change, the implementation of it will be difficult. It is important that they do become a winner if you want cooperation; therefore you must offer them something of value for their support. It becomes a case of trade-offs where each side negotiates an acceptable position. The win/lose condition is resolved and a win/win result is achieved. When you are faced with strong resistance you might use this approach; however, you must keep in mind that once you open the door and negotiate a change the demands might escalate and where do you stop?

A crisis situation can produce large measures of resistance to change because of the pressures of the many factors involved. A quick solution must be found and implemented; therefore managers do not have time to develop educational programs. Often there is not enough time to get a lot of people involved in formulating the change and implementing it. One method to handle group resistance is to select a person in the group (or outside the group) that the people involved in the change respect and give him or her a highly visible role in formulating and implementing the change. The purpose of this act is to gain the support of the group and you are not concerned with getting detailed involvement and advice from that person in designing the change. You have picked the person to represent an endorsement with minimal involvement. The problem often is that the person becomes highly involved in the design of the change and this might not be in the best interest of the organization. You might reduce this risk some by selecting a person who is so busy that he or she will limit their involvement but still give the change support and endorsement.

Another way to overcome resistance in the crisis situation is to present selective information about the matter in such a way that the problems appear alarming and people will then want to quickly implement the change to protect their interests and the interests of the organization. You must be careful using this approach for overmagnifying and dramatizing events too frequently will weaken the respect and trust that your people have in you as their manager. However, when you do not have time to use other methods for dealing with resistance or the other methods fail, you can use this approach successfully. As a final approach in a crisis situation where it is critically important that the change be implemented quickly, you can force people to accept it. You do this by threatening them with a loss of promotional opportunities or even the loss of their jobs. Employees do not like forced changes; therefore it is an approach that is high risk and should be used only when all other options have failed. You must also be very sure that you have sufficient authority to force the people in the organization to accept the change before you use this method.

We have looked at four resistance-producing situations and approaches applicable to each for dealing with resistance to change. How successful you are in overcoming resistance depends on how well you diagnose the situation and apply the proper approaches. Most managers make the mistake of using one approach regardless of the situation. This lack of flexibility comes from his or her management style. If he or she is very authoritarian the approach is of a coercive nature, and if very democratic the approach is of a participative nature. We have seen that the different resistance-producing situations require quite-different approaches. To successfully manage change you must be flexible. Use the approach that will best handle the situation and not just the approach that you feel comfortable with. Also, resistance-producing situations are often blends of conditions and more than one of the four situations we looked at may be present at the same time; hence, a combination of the approaches used for each might be in order.

Common Mistakes

A mistake frequently made by managers is to quickly implement a change when it could be implemented slowly. A hasty decision can be a wrong decision and once implemented it is hard to back it out of the organization. If the situation is not one of crisis or strife, then take whatever time is needed to get sufficient information and adequate participation in designing and implementing the change. Plan the change carefully and construct realistic implementation schedules. Should you not properly plan the change and try to implement it quickly, you reduce your chances for success. Small details overlooked in the planning process add to the length of time required for the change, and many small unexpected problems can slow the momentum and resistance can build. The greater the scope of the change and the more people involved, the more likely it will fail if implemented too quickly.

In addition to carefully planning the change you must anticipate the type and amount of resistance that might arise and where in the organization it might come from. Unless you are prepared in advance, when the time comes you might apply the wrong approaches for dealing with resistance. If it appears that you will need high-level-management support and endorsement of the change, then lay the groundwork for it as early as you can. Make some presentations to the officers so that they understand what the change is all about and why it is needed. Should you need more authority to deal with resistance than you have, make your case known and request the authority. Have the right amount of power to act when the need arises for in dealing from strength you improve your posture should you need to negotiate with resistors. Collecting data and getting involvement takes time so don't hurry the process—particularly if the stakes are high or there is no crisis situation.

Another common mistake is to not get enough involvement in the design and implementation of the change. Too many people involved might be as harmful as too few; however, most managers get lots of facts but only a small number of opinions—and these usually from too few people. Often, much time is spent in getting supporting data yet little effort goes forth in searching for those people who have dissenting views. Even when their views are presented, they are often really not heard and they are rationalized away as being not applicable and of little value. If you want to make a change work, carefully analyze all of the reasons why it won't work; once you resolve these you are on safer ground.

Forces of Change

Where will your employees work tomorrow—in the office or at home? It has been predicted that prior to the end of this century over 15 million employees will be working at home. Many decades ago, this was commonplace and in many foreign countries today work is done at home. Adjusting to these changes will not be easy for you, the company, or the social structure. Many companies today have programs in place where computers are used at home and the employee avoids some of the commute into the office. This is known as telecommuting, and it will grow at a rapid pace during the decade. It will help many people who have conditions preventing them from daily commuting—that is, small children at home, disabilities, and so forth. It will raise new problems to you as a manager for you will now be managing people on a remote basis and communication and mutual trust will be very important. Will you find it difficult to adjust to this changing business environment? You should not, unless you fear that you are losing some control over your people. Should you lose control? There are no reasons why you should lose control if you have in place good performance plans and a respected honor system. Certainly, if your employees are working at home with computers the moment that he or she logs on or off you have a record of activities. You do not need to risk the problems that go with oversuper-vision by telephoning frequently to determine the status of the job. Weekly progress reviews in the office will give you an excellent picture of what is be-ing done and where help is needed. There might be, however, a problem with infrequent organizational interactions, and managers will need to ad-dress this by providing opportunities for meetings or seminars that are in-formative, educational, and motivational.

Contemporary managers must continue to learn new skills for growth and survival. With the current pace of technological developments one-half of your managerial abilities will be of little value in three years. The job that you were hired to do will change and the tools and techniques used today will be obsolete tomorrow. You cannot isolate yourself from the flood of technological innovations now sweeping the world of business for you need them to be an effective manager. The computer puts vast amounts of data at your fingertips and helps you to make more rapid and better decisions. It improves your ability to develop and implement extensive networks for handling information. At the press of a key, data can be transmitted around the world and managers in multinational companies can review and evaluate facts or discuss opinions. Now interactive terminals and space-station linkage permits managers to communicate in seconds with people throughout the world. The scope of decision making has expanded and with it come greater responsibilities. The nature and practices of management change at an ever-increasing pace to match the momentum generated by the vast exchange of knowledge between varied disciplines. Correct decisions must be made quickly; the wrong decision is costly. Have you lost your edge because new developments or theories have evolved in your field and you have ignored them?

It is through change that an organization and a person grows. The nature of your work changes and the employees that you manage change and new techniques will require new production methods and new products for tomorrow. When you are comfortable and feel that you are on top of your field, then watch out: Complacency is dangerous. This is the time to get back to reading and attending some seminars or university programs. Evaluate some of the new theories and pick at least one new approach to try in the organization. Have you spent an excessive amount of your time on the social relationships in the office with your employees? This has its value, but if you have given it more importance than upgrading your technical skills, you might make some wrong decisions regarding the direction of your business.

A flood of technological innovations is not the only factor today that requires you to manage change well. Foreign governments and the competi-tive overseas companies bring about extensive pressures on profits and growth and this often requires new strategies and marketing practices. There are changes in the labor force brought about by early retirements and changes in labor negotiations to accommodate the white-collar unions. A manager is faced with putting in place increasingly more expensive in-house training programs or paying higher salaries and competing in the market-place for those with experience or advanced degrees. Recruiting is a big and costly job, but retaining these bright young employees gets harder each year. Those with the skills and talents each year set higher goals and expand their willingness to move from company to company for better opportunities.

As new employees with higher levels of formal education and greater mobility enter your company, you are challenged to match what they have to offer. You must be flexible and able to anticipate their needs and demands quickly. Many new employees today have a strong sense of indi-vidualism and a low tolerance level for bureaucracy and hierarchical au-thority. New employees not only want to be part of the decision-making process but they expect to participate; if you screen them out you turn them off.

If you sit back with a passive attitude toward change, it will control you. Evaluate what is happening in the organization from many different points of view. Look at how situations affect the organization from the perspective of the shareholders, customers, employees, and higher-level management. What will happen if you make no changes? Are most of the problems minor and do they have little affect on the strength and growth of the company? Perhaps change is not required; if so, then the adjustments might be minor. Change is not made just for the sake of making change. Many managers new to an area feel that the first thing that he or she must do is to make some changes. The most successful managers and executives that I have known have stepped into new jobs and made no changes for at least a few months until he or she found out what was going on, identified the problems, and come up with good reasons for well-designed changes. The managing of change begins with the identification of the problem. If there are no prob-lems, change might not be in order. There might be some minor conflicts between people in the organization and in the interest of better harmony it might be good to resolve them; however, if these conflicts are not harming the interests of the organization or the individuals the price of change might not be worth the benefits. In fact, some disagreement and minor conflict might be beneficial in helping to raise issues that need attention and in maintaining checks and balances. When disharmony results in a loss of pro-ductivity or the lowering of quality, change is needed.

Every manager should do a yearly self-appraisal of his or her skills and attitudes toward change. You must not be the last to go to school and im-prove your abilities, and you must not be afraid of change. Managers are hired not because of what they did yesterday but because of what they will do tomorrow. You might have the highest degree of competency in your field, but if you will not take risks and manage change wisely you are not going to grow. Can you handle a terminal and get the kind of information needed to make the right decision? The time is at hand when the manager who cannot interface with a terminal, pull data from a data base, and simulate decision-making exercises is obsolete. If you are not comfortable with the grasp that you currently have on the tools of your profession, then do something quick.

You must manage another change and that is the changes taking place in the labor markets. Over the next decade there will be a reduction of young people entering the work force by about 25 percent. This resulting shortage of new employees coupled with higher-salary and benefit cost will require managers to plan and monitor their human resources very closely. Perhaps we need an insight from Japanese managerial practices; we might develop closer company loyalties among employees to reduce labor turnover. If it is true that many young employees today are less influenced by high salaries and accompanying high levels of responsibilities than over past decades, then you must devote more time to learning what motivates people. The need to handle technological change will be surpassed by the importance of handling human resources effectively.

If you are a manager in a multinational firm, the pressures for you to manage change successfully will be growing at an unbelievable pace. The nature of overseas markets constantly present new dynamic problems in respect to demand for your goods and services, consumer tastes, government regulations, pricing and currency fluctuations. Many times you must live right in the markets themselves in order to get the true flavor of conditions and understand the problems. Reading reports and correspondence—even making telephone calls—will often prove to be a less-than-satisfactory substitute. Business environments in many foreign countries are vastly different than the United States, and they change dramatically from year to year. Marketing and manufacturing in America often takes a much simpler approach and is far more flexible to environmental changes. To grow you need experience in international marketing for even if your firm does not plan to do business overseas, foreign firms are doing business here and you must know how they think and act. One of the most significant changes to be faced by managers in U.S. firms will be the increased competition they will face in domestic markets from foreign firms. It is one thing to say that you will ignore the foreign markets, but when the foreign firms take away your local markets you had best be prepared to implement some strategic changes.

How Japanese Managers Handle Change

You must manage change intelligently if you are faced with the challenge of Japanese firms. The business climate in Japan is such that there is a high degree of cooperation between business, the universities, and the government. Markets there are very difficult for outsiders to enter and you must sell high-quality products that have been produced at low cost. In order to do this many U.S. firms must invest large amounts of capital to build more-efficient plants and the amount of venture capital today is in short supply in America. This is due to increased taxes, reductions in savings due to taxes and higher living costs, and the pressures of inflation. It takes great capital resources to implement technological changes. However, in Japan there is an abundance of capital for investment purposes since the personal-saving rate averages three times what it does in America. A great deal of capital is put into basic research and development and as the results get translated into marketable products and services, the competitive posture of the Japanese firms will rise. Monies are invested in basic research and development as long as there is a potential for commercial development of the product. It is not uncommon for basic research and development to continue as long as ten years on promising products or services. Applied-research-and-development projects often are funded for five or more years and generally prove profitable. With a highly disciplined labor force that is very loyal to the company, there are few strikes in Japan; this permits development programs to continue without interruption. Also, as the employees are well educated and highly motivated, they take productivity and quality very seriously and become truly concerned and dedicated to levels of high performance.

Japanese managers manage change well because they are very well informed on international markets and technological developments in their respective fields. A new product is not funded until a detailed study has been performed on the market potentials and the needs of the consumers. All of this is done with the full support of the government, which coordinates the activities of the universities and the business firms in that matter. The policies of the Japanese government supplement quite well the marketing strategies of the country's business firms; this is an intelligent approach. If other nations are to become competitive, they must adapt the same close harmony of the government, universities, and business.

Managers in the United States need always be aware of the antitrust enforcement programs. However, a manager in Japan finds him- or herself sheltered by the government and a host of associations and professional organizations that will protect business. Japanese business leaders and governmental officials cooperate in establishing national goals that are in the interest of everyone interested in growth. Managers cannot become the slaves of government reports, controls, and bureaucracy if American business expects to get competitive and regain their rightful share of foreign markets. Change keeps accelerating in importance and magnitude, yet less and less time is available to devote to it. Managers have handled change very well in Japan by increasing the degree of participation by employees in the decision-making process. This has resulted in higher productivity and improved quality of goods and services at lower costs. Employees have become even more dedicated and perceive their success as being directly linked to the successful implementation of changes. Capital investments are made to automate assembly lines with robotic equipment. These automated assembly lines improve quality and reduce costs. These changes are profitable for the company and they also benefit the employees through job security and salary increases. Because of a large supply of capital, Japanese managers can make changes and invest in automation and technological innovations with an eye on the long-term profits rather than the short-term gains.

What are the sources of funds for Japanese managers to implement change? The major source of capital funds has been the banks. Therefore as debt is used and less equity there is a lesser amount of shareholder pressure than in the United States to generate quick profits and pay big dividends. Profits can be held in retained earnings and used to expand the company.

The rapid and diversified growth of many firms makes it difficult for a single executive to make every decision with full insight into the problems and with a clear understanding of the data. Japanese firms attempt to solve this problem by making decisions regarding change a consensus act among higher-level managers. These managers are knowledgeable for in most cases they have had many years of service in the firm and know the business very well. The program of action for handling change then in this setting is the result of a group decision based on extensive experiences, shared goals, and mutual interests. You will find that taking steps to increase automation is not perceived as a psychological threat to employees when they understand that their job security is not at stake. When a change results in staff reductions, Japanese managers handle it by using early retirements on a voluntary basis.

One change that is apparent in Japan is that executives in many of the electronic companies are chosen from the ranks of engineers rather than from the disciplines of marketing, finance, and law. This is to prepare the firm for the changes that are seen coming because of rapid technological innovations. It is felt that an engineering background will help an officer to develop strategies to assure the survival and growth of the business. Doubtless a knowledge of the latest technology is a valuable asset for an executive; however, it is important to realize that the executive decision-making process requires a great understanding of human resources and the ability to persuade and negotiate new approaches to work are important. The process of moving technical people into higher-level-management positions is done with care and slowly in order for the person to gain the necessary managerial skills.

Forces for Change in Foreign Countries

Managers handling change in multinational corporations where they are responsible for overseas operations must know the cultural values, language, customs, and laws of the country. Also they must know the production capacities of their competitors and the type of research-and-development activities that they are conducting. Important, too, is a knowledge about the labor markets and the attitudes of the unions in the country. The business pressures are sometimes difficult to handle because in some countries the unions have a major voice on how the company is run. They frequently push hard for social programs to be sponsored by the firm as a commitment to social responsibility and obligation to the community. Unions often have a very strong voice in how a manager uses his or her resources. They often get involved in the decisions about staffing the organization and offer strong job protection and support to their members. At a moment's notice a union—often just to demonstrate its power—will magnify an issue and close down a plant. Firing an employee can be a very difficult task; it puts the burden of proof back on you. You need to hire people very carefully; this begins with a sound screening of job applicants. In Japan new employees are screened very carefully for the hiring process is looked on as a lifetime association with the firm.

Working hours and schedules are often quite different in foreign countries and if you are to be successful as a manager in these climates you need to accept the established patterns. Don't try to change them to fit your way of life. In some European countries, the work day starts very early and ends early, whereas in many South American countries the employees arrive later in the morning but work later in the evening when it is cooler. In many European countries it is the custom to close at midday for a few hours while the family enjoys dinner at home. The business stays open later in the evenings and the evening meal is light. Also, in many European countries the firms close in July or August for weeks or the whole month while employees take a holiday.

Executives and managers understand that in some foreign countries titles and degrees are very important. They all have been acquired with much hard work and they are held in high esteem and with much respect. A manager often learns many skills and disciplines in the universities and colleges rather than on the job as is often the case in America. Formal studies take many years and great expense; competition is keen to get into the universities. A technical person rarely becomes a manager without first completing a great deal of formal managerial training. As these managers are developed through structured educational programs, the practices taught are quite fixed in direction and content and seldom encourage creative or innovative thinking. The philosophy is that the ways of managing are the products of years of experience and these ways are not quickly changed. In American business you find quite the opposite; the approach is to be creative and flexible and try new techniques and ways of doing the job. Within a short period of time a traditional organization structure might be changed to a pool, team, or functional arrangement and even a matrix structure. Management by objectives or a zero-based-budgeting approach might be quickly implemented and almost as quickly abandoned. Managers of foreign firms would never go through so many changes in such a short period of time. It takes many years before new techniques are implemented. In many countries organizational structures and operating procedures and policies are in place becuase they have worked well for years and changes are not made unless very serious problems arise.

Many foreign firms realize the profit potentials, safety and growth of the U.S. markets and in ever-increasing numbers are investing monies into the ownership of American firms. When the foreign firms are not buying into established companies they are setting up their own or producing at home and exporting to the U.S. markets. Many firms in the United States are finding today that the marketing of their products both in the United States and overseas is impacted by the low-priced and high-quality goods produced overseas. If you take industry leadership for granted today, you are making a big mistake. The ranks of the fallen can be seen in the airlines, autos, television manufacturers, watch and camera producers, and many others. Competition is intense—particularly from Japanese firms who start small in the marketplace with the specialty areas which are highly profitable. They then move aggressively into the other markets where profits can be achieved through economy-of-scale manufacturing. The strategy of some Japanese firms is to penetrate the low-price end of a product line and then when they have learned how to handle the marketplace and distribute the product to move into the higher-priced products with greater volumes and higher profit margins. Handling change in the markets that you are responsible for requires that you have in place programs that will monitor very closely the amount and intensity of competition across the entire spectrum of the marketplace.

In order to increase their marketing effectiveness, foreign firms often form international syndicates where licensing-and-distribution agreements are assigned in overseas markets. Sometimes the royalty arrangements with the licensees are sufficient to create a market; however, at a later date when the foreign firm uses different marketing strategies this new market penetration with increased competition to the licensees impacts their profits and forces them out of the business or into price wars. What might this new strategy look like? One approach is that the foreign firm will use a network of dealers to distribute their products in the U.S. markets. This strategy can be very effective if the U.S. competitor employs an internal sales force which is expensive to hire and to train. Often this force takes six months to a year to become effective. This is especially true in marketing high-technology products where just learning the products requires much time by the salesperson. As the dealers in the network often get high markups, the selling incentives are great and profits are helped by other operations picking up much of the overhead of running the business. Managing change in this climate calls for much hard, fast, and intelligent work for survival. You might have to meet price cuts with price cuts, quality challenges with new and better products, and dealer networks with marketing through the same channels. If your firm is to remain healthy and grow, then how you handle change in the foreign markets is very important.

Proact to Change: Don't React

Most difficulties that managers have in dealing with change results from the lack of having in place a program for handling situations when they arise. A spontaneous reaction is usually the wrong one. Changes must be implemented only after careful planning. If you have in place a program that will gather the data required to make a good decision regarding changes, then the emotional upheaval in the organization will be less serious and changes can be taken in stride. Experienced managers know that the first step when confronted by change is to take no action at all. Many times, the haste to act in a situation is dangerous because it is an emotional reaction. A sound approach for managing change is always to ask "What are the costs if no changes are made?" Will sales opportunities be lost? Will expenses rise? Might revenues decline? Making changes when they are not necessary not only increases stress but it increases the opportunity for resistance to change to grow. Unless all of the opinions have been heard, all of the facts evaluated, and all of the for and against arguments studied, any quick decision or implementation of change is likely to fail. When a plan is in place for handling change you have available to you and all other managers a program for gathering, analyzing, and evaluating the costs and benefits of alternative ways of solving the problem. I have seen very few problems that did not have more than one very good solution. In addition, a program that permits you to proact with a plan rather than react with emotion assures a consistency with which decisions are reached in keeping with the facts, opinions, conditions, climate, and management's attitude toward risk. Having procedures established reduces the pressures of the moment and allows you to think of innovative ways to handle the change.

Approach changes with a quiet mind and a relaxed manner. Good decisions are not made when emotions and feelings are high; a successful manager knows the value of having a calm temperament in implementing change. A wise manager looks beyond the problems of change and sees it as an opportunity and challenge for him- or herself, the organization and its people, and the firm. Change often provides the opportunity to see yourself and others in a different light and to gain fresh insights as to relationships, strengths, and weaknesses. It is often the chance to gain new skills and learn new disciplines. Change often challenges you to search the full spectrum of your experiences and abilities so that you become a more meaningful and valuable person. Change can alter relationships and make you a happier and more satisfied person both at work and at home. Managing change can be a synergistic force for you because it can take your strong characteristics and your self-confidence and, through perhaps stressful experiences, mold you into a more-effective manager.

You can prepare for change by getting opinions as to where change is needed and how it can be installed with minimal emotional stress. You must also gather opinions on the role of new technology in your firm. The first step is to identify the opportunities for the new technologies. The second step is to identify the specific applications where change is required and where the new technology can be employed. The third step is to propose the equipment and methods required to implement the change.

Identifying opportunities for change begins with a study of the organization and its objectives. Data can best be gathered through interviews that generally last about one hour; the comments then are carefully recorded. Each manager should be asked to describe what major improvements they would like to see and what gains they perceive might arise from the changes. Once the change opportunities have been identified, it is good to rank them in order of most critical to least critical to the successful growth of the organization. Look at both the value to the organization and the degree of risk for each change. One class would be the changes that have only modest benefits to a small part of the organization yet present very little risk. They are safe moves but of minor value. A second class would be those changes that impact much of the organization, have high benefits, but a fairly high degree of risk. These you would consider as worthwhile while carefully managing their implementation. The third class is an extension of the second class for these changes would affect most of the organization and have excellent long-term benefits, but they are risky. Managers are paid to take risks so you must look for ways to handle these opportunities and not walk away from them.

If new technologies are being introduced to your organization along with new equipment and procedures you should try to implement them on a small-scale pilot approach. This reduces the magnitude of the risk and allows you time to correct the implementation methods, techniques, procedures, and practices in order to overcome any resistance that might develop. Any resistance that develops is on a small scale and the communication and education to correct it is easier than were the change to cover a large part of the organization. Once a change is working well on a small scale it is easy to expand for now other people appreciate its benefits and will ask that it be implemented in their area. Many changes result from computer-related technological developments, and most of these offer dramatic increases in productivity and better managerial controls. As with any other change, the approach is to introduce these with a minimal amount of resistance and emotional upset. This is difficult for many people when offices are automated and information is stored in distributed data-base systems. If you are involved in these matters, you must learn how to manage the system prior to the change and you must talk with other managers within or outside the organization who have had experiences with these new methods. The implementation must go smoothly and the employees must accept it as being in their best interest. Often the users of the new technologies do not understand it, do not appreciate its benefits, and often feel insecure or threatened.

Introducing a change, specifically if it is technological in nature, requires that in the planning stage you prepare for some element of dissatisfaction and resistance. First, you must have in your program a strategy for handling it; this requires that you understand the amount of hostility or resistance that can be expected from the change. A high level of resistance means that you must implement slowly in order for the people to realize that the benefits of the change far exceed the losses. Second, you must consider the positions of power held by the employees resisting the change. If they have more power than those who are implementing the change, then higher-level-management support is required and this must be visible and vocal. Third, if you are implementing change you must search out those people who have the skills and interests needed to make the change a success. They must become involved in the change, and they must stand up and voice their support. Fourth, if the change must be implemented quickly, all time-consuming approaches to minimizing resistance are worthless. Action must be taken, but always with sensitivity, empathy, and respect for the rights of the individual. Remember that the individuals facing the changes need to know what the new technological changes are about. At least give them the time to fully understand what the changes are and how they will make a better career for them.

People that are affected by change always want to know how it will affect them. This is understandable for unless they perceive that the change will help them, they usually do not want it implemented. In fact, once employees decide that the change will not be beneficial, they will usually decide to resist it and once this is done you will have trouble turning their attitudes around. You always need to sell them early as to why they should want the change. You must get your employees interested in the change in order to get them involved in the design and implementation of it. Don't expect quick acceptance. People must try it and find that it benefits them and this takes time. However, if the change is not working you must be prepared to back off and look at some new approaches. Get your employees involved in this situation for they might have some good ideas to accomplish the objectives but through different methods. Many managers make the mistake of trying to force a change that is not compatible to the environment and conditions and it generates much hostility. If the change is accepted, give it time to settle. Nothing creates more emotional upheaval than to follow one change quickly with another.

The Quick Fix

You must be careful to avoid any possible fast solution to a complex problem because often this leads only to changes that go in the wrong direction. How do you prevent this? First, don't overreact and think that you must solve the problem the same day. Talk with your people and get their insights, experiences, and opinions and come up with a workable, and acceptable solution. When you bring them into the decision-making process you open the door for greater commitment and a responsibility to implement necessary changes. You should establish a network that provides inputs from your staff, higher-level management, customers, and external professional advisors. When a change proposal is presented to you, go further than just reading the report. A letter, report, or memorandum cannot give you all of the data that you need to make an intelligent decision. You must get some first-hand information by doing some one-on-one interviewing with the people involved. If you are to be an effective manager, you will talk informally with all levels of people in the organization that will be affected by the change. You do this before the change is announced and implemented. Often the information that you get from a direct interview is worth far more than the data presented to you in some task-force report or the recommendation of a committee.

Employees who are not in a staff position like to talk with the manager when a sincere interest is shown in their ideas and opinions. They can provide you with some good options and you should listen and not be too quick to implement the first workable solution to a situation. Consider all of the alternatives and select the best one that is in the interest of your employees and the organization. Get your staff involved in looking at each alternative solution and let them know that no final decision has been made. Your staff should be developing more data as you discuss the issues with higher-level management. Use higher-level management to give you some new insights and, if possible, some commitment and support. Change takes time; don't try to push it.

You will find it hard to implement a major change unless you have the full support and commitment of higher-level management. Once you get this support, let the organization know it. Changes are rarely accepted at face value. The forces that appear to the employee as threatening often lie deep; time and much empathy are needed to make the change work. Most changes that fail are a result of managers' trying to implement them too fast. Don't present a change as an ultimate solution to a problem because nothing in the business world is this simple. Rather, present it as a step in the correct direction with more innovations to follow. This leaves the door open to new ideas and changes in the current program should they be required.

Less opposition to change is encountered if you move slowly and introduce the new way of doing the work in small incremental steps if possible. If you do not make the change appear as a critical issue, there is less pressure on the employees and the adjustment doesn't appear to be forced on them. Most major changes require a high degree of executive commitment and political support. The endorsement of an officer is valuable, but it is even more valuable if the officer is in the functional department where the change will be made. Often a major change needs the backing of a task force to reflect the divergent needs that were considered in the design of the change. The task force must do an honest and complete job and not just issue a white paper supporting management's long-range plan. The members of the task force can present either short-run or long-run solutions to problems as called for by their mission statement; however, all members of the group must be carefully selected for their abilities and held in high esteem in the organization or their reports and recommendations will not receive the recognition, support, and acceptance of the employees. Never discount the contribution of an efficient task force in bringing about change for functional groups in a firm often have parochial views. These are handled well when the people designing the change on the task force are from different parts of the organization.

You should move slowly when introducing change that requires work to be done in a significantly different way. The people in the organization need to support it in order for it to be successful; this will take time along with some good experiences with the new procedures. Seek out the dissenting opinions before and during the change and truly welcome these opinions as a way to make the change more effective. To promote the opportunity for dissenting opinions you might leak out some elements of the change as it is being planned. This floating of a trial balloon has the advantage of getting the employees to think about the possible changes rather than being hit by surprise. During this period, they have the opportunity to voice their feelings and perhaps even suggest better ways of designing or implementing the change. Also during this time, those factors that could result in hostility and resistance have a chance to surface and can be managed with a more-relaxed manner. Provide a stimulating and challenging environment for then participation in change is easier. Make the need for the change highly visible, but hold off committing yourself to a specific course of action until you are able to gain adequate support from the employees and higher-level management. Should the support not develop, then you do not have to publicly reverse a position and you do not lose credibility with your people. By not imposing a change quickly, you allow people in the organization the time to support your views.

Managing Computer-Project Changes

Change is any event, action, or edict that may affect the resources, time, or scope of a computer project (figure 4-3). If you are to manage a project

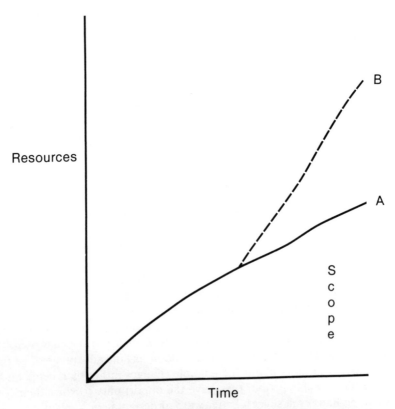

Figure 4-3. Computer Projects

well, you must successfully manage the changes that might affect the elements of resources, time, and scope as shown in figure 4-3.

The starting point in the process is with the scope of the project. The scope of a project is carefully determined by studying the needs of the people requesting the project. This requirement study identifies the transactions (or tasks) to be performed, the reports that are required, and the information screens that will appear on the cathode-ray-tube terminal. These screens can be used for inquiring about data and displaying calculations performed on the data. The data gathered in the requirement study is collected by interviewing the people who will use the computer (the users). The interviewing is conducted by staff members of the data-processing group and representatives from the users' own functional departments. The requirements for the computer project are then put in written form and the interviewers and interviewees sign these requirement statements as being complete and accurate.

These agreed-upon requirement statements of clearly identified tasks and functions (called specifications) to be handled by the computer form the scope of the project. Just as a surveyor establishes two points and connects them with a straightline (called a baseline) from which all future measurements are made, the scope of the project serves as a baseline for managing the changes requested. Now that you have a defined scope for the project you are able to estimate the resources that will be required. The resources are the monies and people needed to make operational the computer equipment (hardware) and the programs (software). As resources are made available, you assign them to your scheduled activities and over a period of time, which you have estimated, your people design, program, test, and install the project. The scope of the project is defined by the specifications as point A in figure 4-3.

However, changes are requested that can result in different specifications and the scope of the project can expand to B. These requests for changes, called change proposals, come from many sources both within and outside of the organization. A change proposal might be generated internally due to some problems in a computer program. Change proposals also can be generated externally by new demands of the users or vendors. A new problem might arise and the solution requires a change, or perhaps new legislative requirements by the federal or state governments results in a change proposal. You must have a formal procedure to handle proposed changes. If you do not, the scope of the project can change from A to B as shown in figure 4-3 and if you have not been given additional resources and more time to handle the expanded scope, your project will not be done on time nor within the amount of money budgeted.

The formal procedure for managing computer-project changes begins with a change-request form. The purpose of this form is to give you the information needed to evaluate the impact and quality of the proposed change, to determine if everyone affected by the change has been consulted, to obtain the necessary approvals to make the change, and to plan and schedule the change. To provide you with the needed data the change-request form should contain the name and location of the submitter, a description of the change being requested, the reasons for the change, and who and what will be affected. The change-request form should be signed and dated by the person who has the budget responsibility for the project. In many companies, a change-coordinator position is established and he or she gets the change request and is responsible to see that it is properly evaluated, changes are properly coordinated, and quality and installation guidelines are followed. Plans are then made to make the change and to install the change should the proposed change be approved. These plans included the procedures for designing and testing the change, how resources will be allocated, what documentation is required, and what educational efforts are needed.

The change-control procedure helps you to manage changes to computer projects not only to secure the additional resources and time needed for the expanded scope of the project but also to schedule and control the changes in a manner that reduces the number and severity of problems that might be caused by the change. The change-request form is an important record; however, it is supported by a change log. This log is a summary form showing the date and who requested the change, the nature of the proposed change, and the dates when the change was approved, scheduled, and made.

All proposed changes must be carefully examined to assure that the quality of the project that it applies to is not going to be harmed and that the quality of the change itself meets all standards. In addition, the change must be assessed as creating no problems when it is implemented, and the change must be justified in terms of costs and benefits. Also, all important changes should have written approval and if the change affects a large or complex system there should be a sign-off by all interested parties. Use the change log to track the changes; record the date when the change was implemented and its success. If there were any deviations from the scheduled change plans or if the results did not meet expectations note these as remarks. Also note in the log if a change is rescheduled or cancelled.

Effective managers of computer project changes know the importance of maintaining a high level of user satisfaction. This is accomplished by keeping control of the problems and resulting changes. You must know what the users' needs are and prioritize and plan your projects so that reliable systems are available when they are needed. Open good channels of communication with the users so that they are kept up to date on your activities. Maintain clear lines of communication with everyone involved in making changes to a computer system. Also you must communicate upward to higher-level management. Give them reports on the problems that arise, the solutions, the proposed changes, and the status of the changes. Report on the number and nature of the problems and if you discern any trends. Describe the solutions to major problems and inform management as to what resources were required and how they were used. Discuss with management the nature of current-computer-project changes and the changes you expect will be required in the near future. Should it appear that adequate resources will not be available in the time frame allowed by management, you can see if there is a business case for going outside of the organization to use vendors or to buy software packages.

There are some questions that you can ask yourself that will help to achieve better control over computer-project changes. First, have you established a position that is responsible for coordinating and tracking all changes, and are log entries and schedules maintained for all changes? Second, is it mandatory that all hardware and software changes be proposed through a formal-change-request procedure? Third, are change-request forms, change logs, schedule sheets, and problem-reporting forms available and are the procedures for their use written and distributed? Fourth, is a formal-risk assessment and cost-benefit analysis performed for all changes? Fifth, are all changes tested and all written approvals obtained prior to implementation? Sixth, do you prepare reports to higher-level management indicating the number and nature of successful and unsuccessful changes and their impact on the organization?

Managing change in data processing is a challenge. To manage change successfully you must develop and implement a change system that is applicable to your business and is responsive to the environment. A change system is required in order to formalize the change process, provide documentation, improve communication, and make higher-level management more aware of problems, solutions, and changes. The primary concern in developing and implementing a methodology for handling computer-project changes is to provide better service to all users of the data-processing facilities.

The Corporation Must Adapt to Change

Corporations, like individuals, must adapt to change if they are to grow. If you are to effectively manage change you must begin by understanding how your company has handled change in the past. Study the history of your firm and see what the problems were and how they were resolved. How did the changing markets affect the product lines? Did technological developments change the importance or direction of research and development?

Were creative approaches used that changed production methods, distribution channels, or methods for financing the company's growth? From the history of the company, it is possible to learn many valuable lessons that will help you to better plan for the future. New problems are often old ones in different form. A study of yesterday's decisions will provide you with a sense of the company's attitudes toward risk.

Where can the company's history be found? The firm's archives are very worthwhile and you should start there. Often you will find reports, books, and films on how the company has grown. Much of the material will provide you with insights about earlier problems and how they were resolved. Unfortunately, these materials do not often focus enough on the details of the decision-making process behind the change. You will find that every minute spent in studying the history of your company to be a valuable use of your time. You should analyze how the past problems arose, the alternative solutions that were proposed, and how the changes were designed and implemented. Look for answers to the following questions: What policies formed the basis of the decision and how were the management practices modified? Did the organization require a restructuring? Did change meet with resistance and how was it handled? How were people motivated to change their attitudes and behavior? Did productivity improve as a result of the change? How was performance measured and what were the levels of quality before and after the change?

The following areas are important to study for they indicate the nature of previous changes and how they were handled. First, analyze the management structure of your company. Has it been centralized or decentralized and if it changed, why? What conditions gave rise to the change and was the change effective? You should ask, "Were the structural changes made to better adapt to the environment and business conditions or were they made just for the sake of doing things differently?" Some managers feel that they must make changes to show that they are doing something creative. If there are good reasons to change the structure then change it, but if not leave it alone. However, management relationships and organizational structures are rarely permanent and effective managers know when these have outlived their usefulness to the company. Organizational structures must be fluid for what has worked in the past, or is working today, seldom meets the needs of the future. Tomorrow's problems are different and the organization must be able to quickly adapt to change and implement solutions. Some companies have centralized operations only to find that at a later date the changes in the labor market or community required decentralization. A slowness to recognize, accept, and adapt to a change always slows growth.

Second, study marketing strategy and look for the trends as well as the steps taken to broaden or diversify the product lines. Were the steps the

right ones and were they necessary? Did it result in a greater market penetration and increased market share? Were the moves profitable in the long-
run? Have the product lines been too narrow or too broad? Many companies become very profitable by going for a small-but-specialized market
where competition is light and profit margins are good. Going head to head
against a large, established competitor with many products and an efficient
and effective marketing force can be very risky.

Third, look at how your company has handled capital budgeting needs.
Was the reliance in the past on debt or equity and why? Was there a strategy
for the use of either or a mix of the two? What other means were available
to raise investment capital and why were they not used? For example, had
convertible debentures been considered and rejected? Many firms that
historically have relied on debt with its leverage have found themselves
strapped with large interest and principal payments that can be handled if the
business is profitable and growing but can cause severe cash-flow problems
in bad times. A study of your company's history will reveal some interesting
insights on how financial policies were established and how they were implemented into good or bad practices. When you find that incorrect or
poorly timed financial decisions were made, try to uncover why and how the
situation might have been better handled. It might have resulted from financial procedures that were too flexible or not documented and managers ex-
ercised judgment that focused only on the short-run results.

When you spend time in studying the history of how your company has
lived with change you can benefit from the mistakes and wisdom of those
who managed before you. You will gain a greater awareness of how the
company grew and a more meaningful perspective of how to manage change.
The study of your company's history is a valuable diagnostic tool for
understanding the nature and importance of change in your business. In
order to fully understand the organizational structures, management relationships, and technological developments that give meaning and success to
your long-term strategic plans, you must know where and why the company
made changes and how it affects the business today.

As a business grows it often develops bureaucracy and different management structures and styles. You will learn from what the company has
done in previous periods of growth that it is now the wrong thing to do.
What once worked effectively in one environment cannot be transplanted
successfully in a different environment. By being conservative and pater-
nalistic, a company might have protected its employees in the past. However, today if competition is fierce and profits are under pressure, such
traditions and management attitudes might destroy the aggressiveness of the
organization and even more markets will be lost. Instead of the employees
being protected by the practices their jobs are being lost if the company fails
to grow.

New legislation, technological developments, and changing markets can force a company to examine its policies and practices and to hire and develop managers that are more aggressive and better understanding of the marketplace. Sometimes organizational structures need to be radically changed and functional relationships must give way to market-oriented structures if the company is to continue to grow. Companies in markets that have become deregulated must reexamine their mission statements and long-run strategies. If new opportunities are profitable, you must seize them quickly and everyone in the organization must be willing to change the way he or she works. You manage change effectively by retaining when possible the sense of direction and values that have been established and accepted in the past. Unless new policies and practices are required, don't be too quick to throw out the old methods. However, when structural and strategic changes are required move quickly in order to establish the proper foundation for the decision-making process. Carefully record these events, decisions, and changes so that they become a part of the written history of the corporation. This collection of information is a store of knowledge that others can study and analyze in the future. Provide the ability for new managers to see the events that gave rise to the changes and help them to grasp the problems in their true business, political, social, economic, and emotional contexts. Also they can then see why the decisions were needed, how they were made, and when they were implemented. People over the years come and go in a company and information kept only in the minds of the managers is soon lost or when passed on to others gets distorted. When changes are not fully recorded in writing, managers work at a disadvantage for it is more difficult to make good decisions. You will find that over a period of time people forget why a decision was made and how it was implemented. The ability to reconstruct events is lost and gone also is the data that gives you a long-term perspective on the company's missions and its identity. The recording of any change that involves the corporate strategies, research-and-development activities, capital budgeting and investment decisions, and personnel decisions and practices. Corporations, like people, might find they are unable to adapt to change and new ways of doing things simply because they have no written experiences from the past to look at. How a corporation adapted to changes yesterday provides insights into how to adapt today and tomorrow.

Change and Conflict

Conflict between people arises because of differences in values and how a person perceives the values of the other individual. When you implement change, care must be taken not to threaten a person's values for these are not changed as easily as are job descriptions. When a person's values come under attack, an intense need to protect and preserve them arises; this can result in hostility to the change. You might find that your authority is being challenged and this can lead you into a conflict situation where you must rule either in favor of the organization or the individual. Often both cannot be the winners. To make the correct decision and implement the change successfully, you must understand the employee's as well as your own values for working. For example, pressure might come from higher-level management to fill a position or promote a person and you feel the individual proposed is not the best choice. How do you handle this matter? Do you quietly go along and avoid conflict with your manager and risk conflict with the deserving employee that is passed over? Will you be able to implement change successfully in the organization if the group sees you as a manager who does not have their best interests at heart? Do you present a case to higher-level management that raises mild objections yet only a token effort of fighting for what you believe? You have minimized the potential conflict between you and your manager but have you gained much support from your people for the change? Would you stand by your value judgment and resist the pressures from higher-level management? You now risk potential conflict with management, but your stand is in the best interest of the group whose support is also needed to implement changes.

Managers often get put in positions where it becomes a win/lose situation as a result of changes or requests for changes. With the exception of a crisis, almost every situation allows some degree of bargaining and negotiating. You must not do this too quickly; however, many managers are far too slow to even entertain the approach. Turn the win/lose situations into win/win and all parties will endorse change and work hard to implement it.

Just as conflicts arise because of organizational changes they can also arise from the activities of people off the job. What if one of your employees participates in a civic cause or program that your company feels uncomfortable with? Is there a value conflict which must be addressed? There might be a difference in what the employee sees as his or her interests and what you perceive to be in the best interest of the organization. Is the performance of the employee at work being harmed by the outside activities and interests? You might have a conflict when you attempt to suggest forms of conduct for the employee off the job, but it might well be in the long-run to the best interests and well-being of the individual, his or her family, and the organization. If the activities are of significant concern to management, then professional counseling might be called for in order to bring about different attitudes and behavior. These types of changes are never easy to make. However, you might have a responsibility to become involved for today many communities expect an ever-increasing concern by managers of their role and the role of their employees in local activities that are held in high regard. You and all of your employees must represent the company at all times and in all environments in the most respectable manner possible. You must always establish high standards and you must practice what you preach.

Values for working develop early in a person's life and they are strongly affected by the individual's environment, experiences, and family relationships. Trust and respect for the individual must be a major ingredient in all changes if conflicts are to be avoided. Bureaucracy can give rise to resistance to change and can result in some measures of conflict if rigid organizational structures and reporting systems are not flexible. This does not mean, however, that there should be an absence or lack of continuity of policies and programs for their stable support prevents confusion and the indecisive actions that often follow. A change can result in a conflict between functional departments if not properly handled. Just as an employee might perceive a change to not be in his or her best interests, a department might feel threatened with a loss of status, authority, growth potential, funding, or staffing. A company will stop growing very quickly when tension, friction, or ill feelings develop between groups.

Many people are ambivalent about conflict and change. It is through the conflict present in many sports that a person extends him- or herself, changes attitudes, behavior, and performance and becomes a winner. Most people like to be a part of a winning team; hence, conflict is often welcomed as the opportunity to gain reward and recognition. Sometimes a person engages in conflict within him- or herself in order to perform a sport better. For example, you change your game to get a better bowling or golf score. Often the organization puts a person in conflict with him- or herself by giving them a higher quota or standard than their previous one. Sometimes a person or groups of people are put purposely into conflict with others to see which solves the problem first or in the most creative manner. Departments compete against departments and divisions against divisions for awards and recognition. Sometimes the competition is so great that conflicts flare up and the company is hurt rather than helped. This can result in contention for resources, shortcutting of procedures, bending the rules, or a lowering of the quality standards.

Growing organizations are always faced with changes and you must manage them by anticipating how and where they might arise and through greater employee involvement in implementing the change reduce the risk of conflict. You can often avoid much conflict just by asking employees for their opinions and suggestions. Then you must listen very carefully to their comments. The more that departments, staffs, divisions, headquarter groups, and field units focus on their own needs and goals and not those of the company the more dysfunctional will be the interactions and the more each group will go in their own direction. Your challenge is to blend the intense internal loyalty into dedication and commitment to the needs of the firm. People must see others in the organization not as competitors for resources but as team members who are willing to pool their strengths for the good of the organization. What is the nature of the climate in your organization? Is it too competitive? If so, then resolving differences will be difficult and changes will be hard to implement. It is always good to reward people for their special efforts and to give positive strokes when needed; however, be careful that you don't develop a group of superstars who will not and cannot work with other people. The strengths of the organization must be directed against the competition in the marketplace and not in internal battles for more resources and rewards. In order to give managers insight into other departments and to encourage the need for cooperation, some firms rotate managers between departments every few years. In addition to these benefits, the organization gains through the changes the new managers introduce to the groups. Also after a period of time the managers develop a broad base of experience. This helps them to make better decisions when they arrive in positions of higher-level management.

5

Forecasting
Techniques

In almost every decision you make there is a need to make some kind of forecast and you should know the different forecasting techniques (see figure 5-1) and be able to choose the right one. Forecasting techniques have evolved from being a luxury item that was considered an art and done often out of curiosity into a science as increasing insight has been applied. A manager must be able to forecast market demand, estimate the affect of pricing changes, and be able to cope with economic changes.

Many forecasting techniques have developed over the years and some of these are very scientific in their approach, yet forecasting still retains many elements of being an art. Some people with background and experience in the subject being forecasted have an uncanny ability to make sound estimates on intuition and not very much data. They will often find it difficult to explain how they made the forecast as they have put together in their mind many small pieces of relevant information and reached a good conclusion. People with these abilities should not be excluded when you are developing a forecast and we will look at some techniques that use these skills.

Technique Selection

You will make better forecasts, and hence better decisions, if you understand the many methods of forecasting and use care in selecting the correct techniques for the situation at hand. The factors you must consider in selecting the right forecasting technique are as follow: First, do you have accurate and sufficient historical data? The Delphi technique is a valuable forecasting technique in the absence of historical data. Second, how accurate must your forecast be and how will it be used? Models are an excellent forecasting technique when properly constructed and when the inputs are accurate elements of data. Third, how far into the future are you forecasting? Developing scenarios about the future can blend both insights and judgment in a nonscientific yet effective way. Fourth, how much time do you have to make the forecast? With sufficient time you can negotiate with people; if you are estimating the length of time required to perform a job, their involvement can become self-fulling commitments to the results being forecasted. These and many other techniques will be discussed in this chapter.

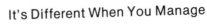

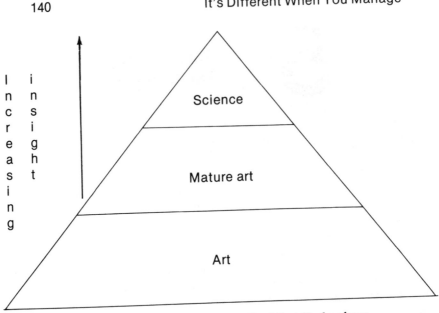

Figure 5-1. Forecasting: An Evolving Technology

For forecasting purposes your organization will never have too much historical data. Keep history files on every forecasting problem and situation. In these files identify the elements and nature of the data collected, their relationships, what the original forecasts were, the forecasts during the life of the problem or project, and the actual outcome or results. Also include an analysis of the effectiveness of the forecasting technique used. With all of this as a starting point you have a better understanding when a forecasting situation arises as to which techniques will best handle the problem. In order to use the best forecasting technique you need to understand the purpose of the forecast. Forecasting the price of a new product must be done with great accuracy if the size of the market and the selling price is of a nature where it has a significant impact on the company's revenues and profits. On the other hand, only a general estimate based on past experiences might be sufficient for forecasting how much additional inventory should be added to the shelves if the item can be quickly manufactured and sales are predictable and slow. In the case of forecasting the selling price of an expensive new product, you might consider the use of sophisticated models (discussed later under the heading Causal Models); however, for the building of inventory the use of a simple moving average (discussed later under Time Series Analysis) would give you a good forecast.

Methods of Forecasting

The three basic methods of forecasting are qualitative techniques, time-series analysis, and causal models. The qualitative method is used where there is little or no historical data. You are looking for the opinions of experts and their judgment based on their past experiences. Time-series analysis seeks out causes for movements in the data. It looks at relationships and patterns and makes projections based on past history. Causal models express mathematically the causes and the changing relationships between the factor to be forecasted and other relevant factors. These models often use the results that are obtained from the time-series analysis. We will look now in detail at these three basic methods of forecasting so that you can use good judgment and know what forecasting technique best fits a specific situation. Good judgment comes from experience and experience comes from poor judgment. The following might help you to avoid some of the costs associated with poor judgment.

Qualitative Techniques

These forecasting techniques are effective when you have experts available but not historical data. The expert's judgments and experiences are systematically pooled in a manner that turns the qualitative information into a representative quantitative forecast. This is an easy approach that requires little preparation and quickly produces a forecast. However, this method of forecasting is primarily a group guessing exercise and if the participants are not experts the quality of the forecast might not be high. Let's look at some of the methods used in the qualitative techniques.

The Delphi Method. The Delphi method uses a panel of experts in a systematic manner to obtain from them a forecast. You endeavor to arrive at a forecast that represents the consensus of their views. There are a series of rounds of requests for a forecast from each panel expert and as the responses are always anonymous each person feels free to change his or her forecast. The results of each round of forecasting is summarized and the results are given to the experts. They now can weigh the data and offer a new and better forecast. It is important that each expert on the panel perceive that all other members are experts or they will not value the inputs highly and will be reluctant to change their forecast on the next round. As in any method of forecasting, the subject of the forecast must be clearly identified and understood.

The Delphi method gives accurate forecasts whether they be short- or long-term. It produces a forecast at a very low cost. Also the panel of experts do not have to be at the same location for the requests for the forecasts and the feedback of the responses can also be handled by mail. The method consists of four rounds of questionnaires as each round refines the forecast. A consensus of opinion is reached by the end of the fourth round and additional rounds make very little significant improvement in the forecast. In each round (after the first) the panel of experts are given the following information about the previous round: the mode (greatest number of responses), the median (the mid-point of the number of responses), the mean (a weighted calculation of the forecasts and number of responses), and the interquartile range (IQR—the interval of the distribution containing the middle 50 percent of the responses). All of this data with the full distribution of all of the responses is fed back to the panel of experts at the end of each round. One other set of important information accompanies this: the comments provided by each expert as to why his or her forecast of the current round falls outside of the interquartile range of the previous round. These inputs should help the panel of experts to make better forecasts on the next round.

Let's simulate a Delphi forecast. For our example the panel of twenty-eight experts are asked to forecast the first year sales of new product "X." The responses for the first round are collected and when summarized it appears as follows in table 5-1.

In the first round the median is $72,000, the mode $73,000, and the mean $72,900. The interquartile range is $70,000 to $77,000 and the range of distribution of all of the responses is $63,000 to $81,000. The panel of ex-

Table 5-1
Product X: First Round

Forecasted Sales (in thousand $)	Number of Experts Making This Forecast	Analysis of Responses
63	1	
68	3	
69	3	
70	2	
71	2	
72	3	. . . . Median
73	5	. . . . Mode
75	1	
77	1	
78	3	
79	2	
80	1	
81	1	
	28	Mean = 72.9

perts is given all of the preceding first-round data and each is asked to make a new forecast. Also if their second-round forecast falls outside of the first-round IQR the expert is asked to comment on why he or she has made this new forecast. The second round when summarized appears as in table 5-2.

Table 5-2
Product X: Second Round

Forecasted Sales (in thousand $)	Number of Experts Making This Forecast	Analysis of Responses
70	3	
71	2	
72	2	
73	3	
74	4 IQR	. . . . Median
75	5	. . . . Mode
76	2	
78	3	
79	2	
80	2	
	28	Mean = 74.6

Comments of experts whose second-round forecast falls outside the first-round IQR:

78: Product "X" is similar to product "Y" which pulled $78,000 in its first year; I estimate the East-coast market at $20,000, the Mid-west market at $35,000, and the West-coast market at $23,000 for a total of $78,000; a gut feel based on experience.

79: Based on several years of history with other products; results of questionnaires to distributors on earlier new products that are like product "X."

80: Forecast East-coast market at $28,000, the Mid-west market at $37,000 and the West-coast market at $15,000 = $80,000; previous new-product experiences when I worked for other companies.

The second-round median is $74,000, the mode $75,000, and the mean $74,600. The interquartile range is $73,000 to $76,000 and the range of distribution of all of the responses is $70,000 to $80,000.

The panel of experts are given all of the preceding second-round data and asked to make a new forecast and explain their forecast if it falls outside of the second-round IQR. The third round when summarized appears as follows in table 5-3.

Table 5-3
Product X: Third Round

Forecasted Sales (in thousand $)	Number of Experts Making This Forecast	Analysis of Responses
72	2	
73	4	
74 IQR	7	
75	9	. . . . Mode/Median
76	2	
78	2	
79	2	
	28	Mean = 74.8

Comments of experts whose third-round forecast falls outside the second-round IQR:

72: Staying with my earlier forecast; based on my experiences in marketing new products.

78: Product "X" is like product "Y," which sold $78,000 in the first year; staying with my original forecast.

79: Based on my experiences with new products; past experience and survey data from distributors.

The third-round mode and median is $75,000 and the mean is $74,800. The interquartile range is $74,000 to $75,000 and the range of distribution of all of the responses is $72,000 to $79,000.

The panel of experts are given all of the preceding third-round data and asked to make a new forecast. As this is the last round, they are not asked to explain their forecast if it falls outside of the third-round IQR. The fourth round when summarized appears as follows in table 5-4.

Table 5-4
Product X: Fourth Round

Forecasted Sales (in thousand $)	Number of Experts Making This Forecast	Analysis of Responses
73	2	
74 IQR	8	
75	12	. . . . Mode/Median
76	3	
77	2	
78	1	
	28	Mean = 74.9

The fourth-round mode and median is $75,000 and the mean is $74,900. The interquartile range is $74,000 to $75,000 and the range of distribution of all of the responses is $73,000 to $78,000.

After having gone through four rounds of the Delphi forecast you can see if the forecasts are converging and then make the final selection or forecast. We can see that the forecasts have been converging

(in thousand $)	Range	IQR	Mode	Median	Mean
Round #1	63-81	70-77	73	72	67.9
Round #2	70-80	73-76	75	74	74.6
Round #3	72-79	74-75	75	75	74.8
Round #4	73-78	74-75	75	75	74.9

The mode, median, and mean from the fourth round would lead you to go with a forecast of $75,000 in first-year sales for product "X." The Delphi method does not assure you that the forecast is correct for the actual results might differ. However, it gives you a representative consensus of the experts and my experiences, and the experiences of others, shows that the Delphi forecasts are very close to the actual results. It is a forecasting technique that does not require a computer and it takes very little time to develop a good forecast.

The Brainstorming Method. This forecasting technique utilizes the skills of experts but in a verbal rather than a written manner like in Delphi. The problem is described to the panel of experts and they are asked to give their forecasts. You must be careful when you are gathering their data to keep a free and open atmosphere for the experts to express themselves. Get every idea, suggestion, or estimate that he or she will offer. Even wild ideas and forecasts are good because they trigger the thinking of others in the group. You must do nothing in the way of actions, gestures, or comments to inhibit the free flow of information. What you want is the maximum amount of data for it is easy to later review this and eliminate information of lesser importance. When you get lots of estimates and comments the odds improve that you have within them the correct forecast.

You must be very careful not to judge or criticize any of the inputs for this will stop the flow of data. Only after you have gotten all of the data should you begin to judge and evaluate its merits. At this point you can take many suggestions and combine them into a few good ideas and forecasts. When using the brainstorming method, be a good scribe; listen and record the inputs and discuss it later. You cannot be critical while being creative. Suspend all judgments until all comments have been recorded. An ill-timed comment can influence the open and penalty-free environment. Members of the group will then give you what they think you want rather than their honest opinions. The brainstorming method is very effective when properly conducted. Accept all inputs including impractical suggestions for these later might prove to be very worthwhile. I have found the brainstorming method to be very effective in forecasting and it has resulted in good decisions. Those who have found it not effective must in part blame themselves for usually they have biased the inputs through their actions or statements.

The Task-By-Task Method. This approach in estimating is extremely effective. The forecasts prove to be very accurate and it is a self-fulfilling methodology. You begin by discussing each task with the individual who will perform it and you request his or her estimate. You have an idea based on your experiences as to the time required to perform the task. You measure this against the estimate of your employee. Often he or she will underestimate rather than overestimate. We all think we can do things faster than we do. You must then negotiate your employee's estimate down or up to a reasonable number. It then becomes his or her estimate and not a number edicted by you; hence, it becomes self-fulfilling. Let's look at how this process works. Our first employee is John and we want him to write programs "P1, P2, P3" for project "CAST."

John: [P1]   John estimates eight or eleven days. If eight, we know it is light and we discuss it with him in order to have him increase it to what we feel is a more reasonable estimate, that is, nine days. If eleven days, we endeavor to negotiate it back with John to about nine days. You will know what employees overestimate or underestimate. Most people underestimate; hence, we miss target dates for installation of a project and it comes in over budget in costs. We after a discussion agree on ten days.

John: [P2]   We repeat the preceding process for this program and mutually agree on seven days.

John: [P3]   The negotiation process is done for this program and we agree on three days.

The estimated-time requirements for programs P1, P2, P3 to be done by John appear as follows:

Days:	*10*	*7*	*3*
John:	P1	P2	P3

Total = 20 days

Our second employee is Mary and we want her to write programs P4 (twelve days), P5 (four days), P6 (four days). Our third employee is Paul and we want him to complete program P4 (eight days) and write programs P7 (six days) and P8 (six days). Our fourth employee is Jean and she will write programs P9 (eleven days) and P10 (nine days). The estimated times required for Mary, Paul, and Jean are arrived at in the same manner as was done with John, that is, on a task-by-task approach. When the process is finished you have a schedule that appears as below. This schedule can then be given to each person on the team and he or she knows exactly what is being done, when, and by whom. You will notice that Mary must finish her work on P4 in twelve days so that Paul can put eight days in on it to complete it. This will get all of the ten programs done in twenty working days per person, with no interruptions this would be an elapsed time of twenty working days for the team of four programmers. You will also notice from the schedule that while Paul is waiting for Mary to do her twelve-day portion of P4 he is doing P7 and P8. You should give this schedule to higher-level management as well as your people for it shows how your forecasted time requirements were determined and it also shows how you will use your resources. It becomes an excellent vehicle to communicate up and down in the organization and it facilitates scheduling and control. (See figure 5-2.)

The task-by-task method is sometimes called the transactional approach for it focuses on the individual work assignments or tasks of each person working on a given transaction or operation. Through the open communi-

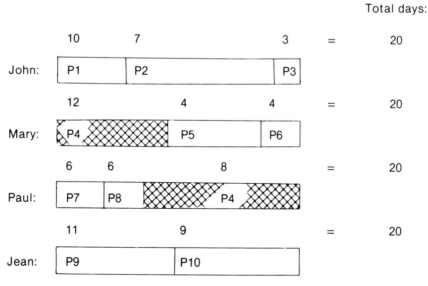

Figure 5-2. Forecasted Programming Time: Project CAST

cation fostered and the negotiation of the estimates it gives an accurate forecast. It can also be used to adjust estimates that have been arrived at through other forecasting techniques.

The Script Method. The script or scenarios method is an approach that uses personal insights and judgments to construct a big picture that prophecies future events. It is not a scientific approach in that the facts available can be interpreted differently by people as they subjectively try to in a qualitative manner establish broad parameters based on past events. It is not a costly method of forecasting and can be done without the use of computers. It helps long-range planning and is effective in forecasting the sales of new products. The method requires that you write a script that forecasts the scene as best you can at this point in time for a future event. For example, if you were in the brokerage business you need to prepare for handling increasing daily volumes of transactions. The script you would build might cover the next ten years (figure 5-3). You

Time period: T_1 _____ T_5 _____ T_{10}

T_1 (time period T_1 is today) and T_5 and T_{10} are five and ten years, respectively, in the future. The daily volume of transaction that you handle today (T_1) is N_1, and for time periods T_5 and T_{10} you estimate N_5 and N_{10}, respectively. Your script now appears as below:

Time period: T_1 _____ T_5 _____ T_{10}

Volume of transaction: N_1 N_5 N_{10}

Figure 5-3. The Script Forecasting Procedure

must now picture the environment that your service systems (providing services to all customers) will operate in for the forecasted periods of T_5 and T_{10}. You begin this visionary forecast by identifying all of the conditions present in the current environment. These are all of the current driving forces (growth) and restraining forces (constraints) in your business and service systems. Any factor that will impact your service system must be identified in the script. These are shown in figure 5-4 as X_1's for Environment under T_1 and all assumptions applicable to T_1 are shown as O_1's for Assumptions.

You now include in your script how you see the conditions in the environment for T_5 and T_{10} and these are illustrated with X_5's and X_{10}'s. All of the assumptions you have made about the environment that your service system will operate in for T_5 and T_{10} are illustrated with O_5's and O_{10}'s. Your completed script now appears as follows in figure 5-5.

Time period:	T_1 ——————	T_5 ——————	T_{10}
Volume of transaction:	N_1	N_5	N_{10}
Environment:	X_1		
	X_1		
	X_1		
	X_1		
Assumptions:	O_1		
	O_1		

Figure 5-4. Script Factors for Today

Time period:	T_1 ——————	T_5 ——————	T_{10}
Volume of transaction:	N_1	N_5	N_{10}
Environment:	X_1	X_5	X_{10}
	X_1	X_5	X_{10}
	X_1	X_5	X_{10}
	X_1	X_5	X_{10}
		X_5	X_{10}
		X_5	
		X_5	
Assumptions:	O_1	O_5	O_{10}
	O_1	O_5	O_{10}
		O_5	O_{10}
		O_5	O_{10}
			O_{10}
			O_{10}

Figure 5-5. Script Factors for Tomorrow

Now that your script is prepared you can follow it each year and compare all actual conditions against the forecasted ones. What forecasted factors, that is, N_5, X_5, and O_5 or N_{10}, X_{10}, and O_{10} appear not to be holding up? Why are they changing? Must you reforecast N_5 or N_{10}? If N_5 or N_{10} will be much greater than forecasted then you must be able to see this as early as possible in order to plan for a bigger and better system. You can periodically keep asking many questions about time period T_5 and T_{10} in an effort to fine-tune your forecast. For example: What volumes will be handled? How much usage of data and what computer memory is needed? Are people with the required skills available? What are the costs and benefits of the system? Are we building the wrong system? What kind of hardware and software is required? Are the economic factors, that is, inflation rates, interest rates, and so forth, changing? Are there legal, political, or social changes? You use the script as a structure to periodically evaluate the possible accuracy of your forecast. It is an inexpensive method of forecasting and can utilize the judgments of many experts in building a visionary scene and script.

Time-Series Analysis

This forecasting technique uses the data that has been gathered over a number of years to statistically make projections. If you were just to use the raw data as it is, the quality of your forecast would be poor because buried in the data are many seasonal and cyclical patterns. Time-series analysis enables you to focus on the trends and how fast they are changing. Both the trends and the rate of changes are isolated in the data. You then separate the trends in the data from the cyclical patterns. Once you have determined the effects of the cyclical patterns over a short period of time and factored in the rate of change in the growth rate of the trends you are ready to make the forecast. You must first perform a time-series analysis of the data.

The time-series-analysis technique functions on the basis that the patterns existing in the historical data will carry over into the future. If you are doing a short-term forecast (under a few years) the patterns might not have much time to change to any significant degree and your forecast can be accurate. However, your long-term forecasts will not be accurate unless the patterns in the data are stable and there are stable relationships between the factor to be forecasted and other relevant factors. A few ways of forecasting with time-series analysis are described briefly next. For further information consult the references shown in the bibliography.

The Moving Average. This is one of the most frequently used forms of time-series analysis. You develop points which are the weighted or arithmetic average of a number of consecutive points of the series. The intervals used might be periods of weeks, months, or years. What you endeavor to do is to choose these points in a manner that will lessen or eliminate the effects of cyclical patterns or other forms of irregularity in the data. This forecasting technique works best when you have many years of history about the factor to be forecasted and other relevant factors. If you are using this technique to prepare a short-term forecast, it can be accurate and reliable. However, its value as a forecasting tool decreases the further you forecast into the future.

Exponential Smoothing. This technique is very similar to the moving-average approach to forecasting; however, you give more weight to the more-recent data points as they are more representative of the current trends and the rate of change in these trends. Your forecast becomes more accurate as you take into consideration seasonal variations in the time-series of the data and compute these in your projection. Frequently, an extensive amount of mathematical computation is required when performing exponential smoothing; although simple forms of this forecasting technique do not require a computer the more-sophisticated versions can require much time to run on a computer.

Although this forecasting technique is accurate for short-term projections it is not accurate for long-term forecasts. Just like the moving-average technique exponential smoothing works best when you have a number of years of historical data to better handle the seasonal variations. Also, as for the moving-average technique you can make a forecast with exponential smoothing quickly, often within a day.

Trend Projection. This technique fits a trend that might be a trend line to a mathematical equation. Trend fitting can also be performed with curves, the most common of which are the s curves. The trend line or curve is projected into the future by the mathematical equation. There are many variations to this technique. Some simply look at the slope of the trend line or curve whereas others use logarithms for more-accurate projections. You will find that trend projections give reliable and accurate forecasts in both the short-term and long-term periods. However, to get a high-quality forecast you need as much historical data as you can get with a minimum of five years as an effective starting point. Also, like all of the other time-series-analysis techniques you can develop a good forecast within one day.

Causal Models

This forecasting technique also requires much historical data wherein you must carefully identify the relationships that exist between the factor that you are going to forecast and all of the other related factors. This is a very sophisticated tool for forecasting as it requires that all of the associated causal relationships be expressed mathematically. Often you use the results obtained from the time-series analysis that you performed; all of this data is built into the equations or models that are to be used. When data is needed but it is not available you will need to make assumptions about the relationships. Don't forget to monitor closely what happens in order to validate your assumptions or, if necessary, make new ones and issue a revised forecast. It is common to issue revised forecasts because assumptions often are changed as you learn more about the changing business conditions and economic environment. Because the technique is sophisticated in handling many relationships as well as predicted factors and forces, it often helps you to clearly identify turning points in your business. This will enable you to revise and fine-tune your short-term forecasts and make more accurate long-term forecasts. Some ways to forecast with causal models are described briefly next. For further information consult the references shown in the bibliography.

Regression Analysis. This is a complex statistical technique for forecasting. Large amounts of data are processed in the calculations; however, the computer makes this easy for you. It is a very accurate forecasting technique and the results are very reliable. It examines the movement in the factor you are forecasting and the other relevant factors. Why do many managers shy away from this forecasting technique in favor of subjective, less-scientific methods? Generally it is because plotting a trend line and projecting it by a visual examination is easy if you assume that the trend will continue in the same direction and at the same rate. This does not require you to look at the causal relationships of the variables; therefore the foundation of your forecast is not as solid as with regression analysis.

In regression analysis you look at the explicit functional relationships between one or more independent variables (the factors relevant to the factor you are forecasting) and the dependent variable (the factor you are forecasting). The dependent variable is then hypothesized and estimated and compared to the values forecasted for the independent variables; you project the value for the dependent variable. In order for the regression analysis technique to give you an accurate forecast, there must be a constancy between the structural relationship of the independent and dependent variables. The regression-analysis technique predicts more accurately than many of the less-scientific techniques because it uses a systematic approach to forecasting. It begins by taking those independent variables (related factors) that influence the dependent variable (the factor you are forecasting) and performs a statistically based forecast. Your dependent variable might be sales and your independent variables might be disposable personal income, savings, and interest rates. This technique is good for forecasting profit margins as well as product sales. Regression enables you to analyze a considerable number of independent variables and search out those that have predictive or explanatory characteristics. When you analyze more than one independent variable the technique is known as multiple-regression analysis.

Regression analysis is a good technique when you are foreasting not further than a few years into the future as beyond this the results are not very accurate. As in time-series analysis, you need a minimum of a few years of historical data to establish good statistical relationships for this technique to be reliable. Many large companies today are making increased use of regression as a forecasting tool because the computer can digest and massage large amounts of data quickly. Whereas in earlier years it took many hours to perform the regression-analysis calculations by hand today with programmed regression routines the results are obtained quickly. Once you have built your forecasting equation you can test many independent variables quickly on the computer for all you need to do is to modify your equation by changing some of the independent variables.

You will find that regression analysis is a powerful forecasting tool; however, some biases can affect the accuracy of your forecasts unless you handle them properly. One is that the independent variables are not truly independent of each other. This is known as multicollinearity. For example, in the earlier discussion we correlated sales (dependent variable) with disposable personal income, savings, and interest rates (independent variables). Since savings and interest rates might have shown a strong association with each other in the past, you cannot measure the extent of their separate effects on sales. You can correct this possible source of inaccuracy in your forecast by dropping one of these two independent variables, that is, either savings or interest rates. A second bias is when the independent variables (disposable personal income, savings and interest rates, and other independent variables) affect the dependent variable (sales) but the dependent variable does not affect the independent variables. This is one-way causation and your regression-analysis forecast will not be as accurate as if you introduce two-way causation—often known as simultaneity—in your regression equation. You can do this very simply by introducing into your equation other independent variables—for example, income levels or prices—which influence sales (the dependent variable).

Regression analysis is a scientific approach to forecasting. However, even though it uses a precise statistical method it cannot eliminate risk and uncertainty about the future. Forecasting still remains much of an art and you must always apply good judgment to your projections.

Econometric Models. Econometric models are quite complex and are generally expensive to develop. The models are made up of a series of regression equations that contain either behavioral equations or identities. The behavioral equations contain parameters or values that are estimated simultaneously. The identities are defined and the internal (endogenous) variables are determined within the series of equations although you specify the external (exogenous) variables.

Your first step in forecasting with an econometric model is to construct the model by specifying a number of behavioral equations or identities and determining their functional relationships. In each equation you are specifying how given sectors of the business or the economy are going to behave. Next you estimate the parameters or values for the behavioral equations; this is often done by using the regression-analysis technique previously described. Now you must enter into the model the external values; this is used to forecast the internal values through simulation of various future conditions and projecting the results.

Are econometric models good forecasting tools? They are very good for both short-term and long-term forecasting and for identifying turning points in your business or the economy. They will help you to forecast profit margins, product sales, and growth of product lines. Also, you have the capability through simulation to look at many possible courses of action and determine how they might affect your forecast. However, you must use great care in constructing your models. If you leave out key behavioral equations or identities or give incorrect importance to their relationships, you will not get an accurate forecast. Also you must use great care in how you extrapolate from the past and project this data into the future because sometimes the structure of your business as well as the business world and economy change and it is not always possible to measure the degree of change immediately. As you enter into the model the external values, you must be careful in how you specify them as well as the assumptions that become the foundation of your forecast.

Input-Ouput Analysis. This forecasting technique is based on the premise that industries are related: The output of some industries become the inputs to other industries. For example, the output of the steel, rubber, and textile industries become inputs to the auto industry. Input-output analysis uses input-output flow tables. You construct an output table showing all of the related industries vertically by rows and horizontally by columns. When you want to determine the distribution of output for an industry, you read the row for that industry in the table and the inputs to the industry can be read in the columns for that industry. This will show you how important each of the industries are for the output of each industry's goods. You can look at your own industry and determine how many dollars of sales can be expected by each of the related industries that use your products. This method of analysis enables you to develop more accurate forecasts because it shows the interindustry flow of your goods or services in the marketplace. It also helps you to understand the flow of inputs required to obtain given outputs in the industry. When you convert the dollar amounts in the output table into percentages you have a direct-requirements table that shows what the relative importance of each industry is as a supplier to an industry.

The important product in performing input-output analysis is the construction of the direct-requirements table. A considerable amount of effort is required to develop the tables used in input-output analysis. Also, extensive work is required to apply the tables to your business and use them properly in forecasting. The input-output analysis technique is not reliable for short-term forecasting but it can be accurate in making long-term forecasts as well as forecasting turning points in your business. You can use this technique to forecast product sales and project the growth trend of sales. However, at least a decade or more of historical data is required to develop meaningful interindustry relationships. It becomes very expensive to develop and correctly use input-output analysis.

In using this technique to forecast, you should realize that the dollar value of production by industry is based on the prices that prevailed during the year when the data was gathered. You should recognize that even though there might be no changes in the real flow of the inputs or outputs that changes in prices over a period of time will cause changes to appear in the dollar flows. Endeavor to factor in an allowance for this condition. Using an adjustment for changes in the rate of inflation is a good approach. Also, the tables assume that when the output of an industry increases its inputs increase in constant proportions and this is not always a sound assumption. If the assumption is not valid then the growth of an industry might not have the same effect on the interindustry relationships as you forecasted using input-output analysis. Although you can use this technique to forecast local, regional, or national markets for your products you will find that it is an expensive forecasting tool. Additionally, the very rigid structural assumptions that accompany the development of the tables and their correct application reduces its value as an accurate forecasting tool.

Forecasting Business Activity

As a manager you should know some of the commonly used forecasting methods that will help you to use the forecasts made by other people. Some managers need to make forecasts of demand for their product lines and as these are often based on business conditions it is necessary to know how business activity can be forecasted and measured.

Gross National Product (GNP)

Managers must make guesses about the future in order to make product line, pricing, production, and financial decisions. One of the most common approaches is to measure business activity by looking at Gross National

Product (GNP) which is a measurement of the market value of final goods and services produced in a given period. It represents the summation of consumption, investment, government spending, and net exports. GNP as a measure of business activity can be determined by measuring either the sum of the amounts spent on all final goods or by the total incomes that accrue to the owners of the resources. Forecasting the future is done through analysis and projection of the fluctuations of the components of national income. One of the best sources of national-income-accounts information is the monthly publication by the Commerce Department entitled "The Survey of Current Business." This publication also contains other important data concerning the state of the national economy.

Macroeconomic Models

The foundation for this method of forecasting rests on the assumption that business activity is governed by demand. Therefore the question is how you forecast the total (aggregate) demand. In order to do this you must break GNP into its component segments, forecast each segment, and sum the results. The major segments are: federal spending, state and local government expenditures, residential and commercial construction, capital spending on plants and equipment, consumption, inventory investments, and import/export analysis. These segments are interdependent so you must verify the data carefully and often make an adjustment in a segment to keep it in balance with your forecast of another segment. You will find that you will be making a number of adjustments in the segments before you are finished. You can use simultaneous equations as a tool to manage the interdependency of the segments.

The segment that has the least interdependency is federal government spending for it is largely planned in advance in accordance with proposed and enacted legislation.

You will find it very difficult to gather data on all of the spending by state and local governments. The trends generally are upward due to increased spending on social programs.

Forecasting residential and commercial construction is made more difficult because you must first forecast monetary conditions, which play a major role in changes in construction expenditures. These conditions include interest rates and the availability of credit; in recent years these have changed their levels frequently in short periods. You should analyze residential and commercial construction contracts awarded. Look at the number of new family formations, housing starts, and vacancies in commercial buildings. Try to determine if the interest rates and down payments are heading lower and whether loans are easier to get. Residential construction can be very seasonal in nature—not quite so for commercial construction—and you should correct for this when you forecast. Also, the two forms of construction are not always parallel in movement. Residential construction can fall off but the slack in the economy can be taken up by high levels of commercial construction.

Your accuracy in forecasting changes in capital spending on plants and equipment rests on your ability to analyze business conditions and growth. As sales and profits move to higher levels, business plans are generally modified to provide for more new plant and equipment. This is particularly true for industries that have old plants and obsolete equipment. Given the ability to finance expansion, with a good outlook for business replacements should reach new high levels. You can use surveys of business-investment plans to analyze past investments and intentions to invest in plant and equipment. You can extrapolate trends into the future and give them a faster growth rate if it appears that new orders for durable goods are increasing. These new orders mean higher-level sales; this could result in more production, which might require new plants and equipment.

In order to forecast the consumption segment of GNP you must first estimate changes in income. Investment in plant, equipment, and inventory coupled with federal, state, and local government spending will produce changes in income. However, just estimating income is not enough for a good forecast. Changes in tax structures and tax rates will affect income and cause changes in the resulting levels of disposable personal income available for consumption or saving. What portion of the disposable personal income goes into consumption or savings rests on many factors, some of which are the results of monetary conditions whereas others are psychological in nature. You must look at the attitudes of consumers for their levels of expectations strongly influence their expenditures. Consumers are more willing to purchase big-ticketed items of durable goods such as automobiles and furniture when they are optimistic and do not fear threatened with a loss of their income or a recession. If levels of installment debt are low you can predict consumers might be more willing to take on debt in order to consume goods and services at higher levels. Consumers, you will find, show a more stable and consistent pattern of spending on the nondurable goods that are consumed in a short-time period. You can forecast these expenditures quite accurately by doing trend relationships or regression analysis on historical data.

Forecasting the investments in inventory can best be done by analyzing the ratio of the levels of inventory to sales. Recent recessions gave rise to considerable amounts of inventory being liquidated. Effective executives today manage inventory levels carefully, usually with the assistance of computerized programs. It can be costly to run out of inventory and lose sales; however, an excessively large inventory increases storage expenses and interest charges. Also, there is the added risk that competition might, with a technological breakthrough, produce and sell a better product, thereby taking your markets and leaving you with shelves filled with finished or semifinished goods. Expectations of improving business conditions generally result in increased investments in inventories.

The last component segment of GNP forecasting that we will look at is estimating how much exports will exceed imports and how this will affect business conditions. Import and export figures are provided by the government and appear in newspapers. You can make a more-optimistic forecast when there is an excess of exports over imports for this condition results in larger investments in plant, equipment, and inventory. If you sell in foreign markets, a strong export position is inducive to growth. You will find that estimating how much exports will exceed imports and how it will affect the economy and your business is difficult. You will need to study the growth of foreign economies and factor in such items as the affects of tariffs and protectionism on foreign trade. Protectionism is increasing very rapidly around the world, and its impact on free trade will hurt the growth of the economies of many countries over the next decade.

It is not easy to forecast with macroeconomic models. You will find that from year to year prices—both domestically and in foreign countries—are far from stable. You must adjust for this and modify your initial forecasts. You also will find that the changes you make in one component segment of GNP forecasting will generate errors in other segments; therefore, each segment is generally forecasted with an assumption that changes in expenditures from one time period to another will be small. When significant changes that do not fit your assumptions occur, you will find that they cause large errors in your forecast.

Indicator Forecasting

Just as you can observe changes in levels of both the GNP and national income and forecast the future, you can do the same with other economic measurements that reflect changes in general business activity. There are a set of indicators that measure behavior that historically precede, coincide, or lag changes in GNP and the business cycle. These are known as leading indicators, coincidental indicators, and lagging indicators. You will find that the leading indicators often identify in advance the turning points in the business cycle. This is helpful in helping you to forecast business activity. The coincidental indicators help to confirm for you what the turning point was at that given identified point in time for they move in agreement with the changes in the business cycle. The lagging indicators confirm to you at a later date that the turning point was actually that specific time that you identified in the data. These indicators provide some insights into the future performance of the economy. To the extent that they are correct, they will help you to develop more-accurate forecasts. However, you should not rely too heavily on indicators for forecasting as they often give misleading signals. Sometimes indicators turn down many months before a peak is reached in the business cycle and often they turn up in a recession only very shortly before the upturn. Because of the misleading and conflicting signals that are sometimes given by leading indicators, the National Bureau of Economic Research has developed a method called the diffusion index. What this does is to determine the percentage of the members of the indicator series that are moving upward. When all are moving upward the index is 100 and when all are moving downward it is 0. This shows the extensiveness of the expansion or contraction. The diffusion index provides a measure of how extensive is the forthcoming change in business activity.

Although the indicators approach will help you to develop better forecasts, you must be aware of some shortcomings. The leading indicators are worthwhile only if there are no major changes in the structure of the economy. Should structural change occur the amount of time by which they lead changes in the business cycle might significantly be shortened or lengthened. Also, you will find that the indicators give signals regarding changes only a handful of months before the actual changes occur. Another weakness is that the indicators will signal a change in business activity but will not indicate the magnitude of future changes.

Survey Methods

You can improve the accuracy of your forecast by conducting surveys of attitudes and plans of business leaders and consumers. Ask questions that will help to measure their attitudes toward future investment or consumption. Find out what manufacturers' expectations are for investing in plant and equipment, building inventory levels, and increasing sales. Although this data indicates intentions and expectations it will help you to make better forecasts.

You will find surveys of consumer attitudes to spend helpful; however, plans to buy goods can change quickly with changes in attitudes. Therefore, both must be analyzed. Monetary conditions can dramatically affect consumption and investment attitudes and buying plans; therefore use surveys of consumer intentions to help you forecast but be alert for sudden changes. You should try to utilize all sources of information that are available to you. Keep an open mind and look at all segments of the economy and their interdependency. Weight data from one segment against another and adjust your projections if necessary. Track the actual results as to how each segment of the economy performed as opposed to how you forecasted it and look for reasons to explain the difference.

Forecasting the Short-Term Growth of Your Business

The bottom line is that managers are more concerned with forecasting the short-range growth of their business and the increased market share of their product lines than the long-range growth trend of the economy. There are two steps that you should follow in forecasting the growth of your business. First, estimate what are the production needs of other firms that use your goods or services. You will find that the input-output analysis technique discussed earlier is helpful in this matter. You must determine what firms will use the products of your industry and in what quantities. Do a local and regional analysis of this data by product line and sum it into a national-demand schedule. Now adjust for changes in market structure as well as changes in trends and growth rates. Second, estimate total producer and consumer purchases at the national level and estimate what share of this market you can obtain. Forecasting what share of the market you can take is not an easy job. Many variables must be considered such as how much advertising you will do, how you will distribute and price your products and what will be your levels of quality and service. For each regional area you should look at population and demographic data and the associated consumer's buying power. Your analysis of consumers'-attitude surveys will help you to be more accurate in forecasting how personal disposable income will be spent and how it will affect the demand for your goods and services. You arrive at the market potential of each product line for your company by summing the total amount of purchases that you have forecasted for each of the markets served by your company.

Once you have forecasted demand for your business you must measure this against your ability to price your goods and services at a profitable level and to produce sufficient quantities to meet the needs of the market. You must be sure that you have adequate capital and skilled resources on hand to either enter a new market or to increase your present share of the market.

Forecasting Social Changes

Social changes can have very profound effects upon your business. They will affect what you can buy, produce, and sell. Consumer goods that were popular yesterday are no longer in demand today. Changes take place in our cultural values and social needs. There is no model that you can build that will take into account new behavioral relationships and increased pressures for environmental adjustments. We see increasing demands for more convenient and time-saving goods and services. Increased importance is being placed on more leisure time. Greater importance is given to living a better life today and being less concerned with tomorrow. Many companies thrive by capitalizing on this philosophy. The Puritan work ethic of all-out commitment to the job and saving for tomorrow seems to be declining. These cultural trends must be recognized when they are applicable to your business for cultural values and attitudes help to determine how consumers spend their monies.

Forecasting Technological Changes

You really need a crystal ball for this area of forecasting. However liberal you are in your forecasts you will probably be far too conservative. You can begin by taking the status quo in a given technological area and extrapolating a trend into the future or ascertaining future needs and projecting what is required to attain these goals. However, technological breakthroughs generally are not the result of some overnight miracle but the sum total of many trial-and-error experiences that have been ground out through hard work and much expense. It is not easy to forecast when and how these breakthroughs will appear. You cannot do this with any accuracy; therefore you should attempt to determine the probability of a technological change occurring and estimate how it might affect your business. Be realistic in what you estimate for technological changes are still more evolutionary than revolutionary. Man's first flight at Kitty Hawk was many decades before his flight to the moon. More than half of the products and services that you offer today will hardly be profitable in their current state ten years from now. You must strive to develop new product lines and offer new services; however, generally these will be changes in greater performance of your products at lower prices, higher quality, and broader applications. A totally new product and concept occurs in some businesses like pharmaceutical only once in seven to ten years. Most companies grow by doing what they are currently doing only by doing it better. However, do not be the first to try the new technology, nor the last to lay the old aside. The things that you did to achieve success today will not be the profit makers in tomorrow's markets.

Forecasting Sales

When you forecast sales you are making short-range projections of the market; this includes the effect of competition in each market. Your sales forecast is actually an assessment of how each of your competitors will do in the marketplace. The sales forecast is very important to the company for from this forecast you can project costs, revenues, and profits as well as manufacturing and purchasing requirements. Also, you can estimate personnel needs and begin the required hiring and training.

Forecasting sales has one of the longest histories of any type of forecasting. Because high-level management has great interest in sales they will review these forecasts closely for they are the driving force in the firm's planning cycle. Also, they are more judgmental in nature than most other financial forecasts. Because sales are measured as a rate of change over a period of time rather than a specific event at a given time, you must predict what changes are taking place. Further, you must determine what will be the outcomes and when they will be realized. This is difficult for unlike other types of forecasts, sales forecasts do not have many interdependent variables that have direct cause and effect relationships that lend themselves to scientific forecasting. There is a difference between a sales forecast and a sales goal. The former becomes self-fulfilling for once you have issued the sales forecast all of the activities of the firm are aimed at achieving the numbers. Hence, when you make the forecasted sales level it is not a measure of how accurate your forecast was but a measurement of how efficient the company was in manufacturing and marketing the products or services. You will find that long-range sales forecasts are less self-fulfilling than short-range for the company is less able to achieve higher levels of sales just by goal setting.

One way to forecast sales is to collect estimates from your sales force. You can begin by getting individual estimates from each sales representative and then compile these and have them reviewed at different levels throughout the company. When you do this, you are building your sales forecast from the bottom up. The advantage in this approach is that each piece of the forecast comes from the person who is closest to making the sale. As many people submit estimates and different levels of management review, adjust and smooth the data the sales forecast should not contain bias by the participants. One weakness in this approach is that it becomes a self-fulfilling prophecy in that each salesperson contributing to the forecast or each sales manager handling the data establishes sales goals based on the numbers. These goals now become performance measurements that affect salary and commissions, and therefore the numbers lose the characteristics of being a forecast.

Another way to forecast sales is to collect estimates from your customers. This approach avoids any bias being built into estimates for unlike the sales force the customer has no income stake in the accuracy of the final sales forecast. Also, because of this customers, to the best of their ability, should give you accurate information about their intentions to buy your products or services. Should your company have many customers, this can be a costly and time-consuming approach to forecasting sales. However, if your customer set is small because you manufacture and/or sell only specialty-type products or services with a limited market it can be a good sales-forecasting technique.

You can forecast sales using judgmental factors or sophisticated techniques such as the previously discussed time-series analysis, regression analysis, and input-output analysis.

Areas of Forecasting

Your sales forecast plays a central role in the organization's planning function for it forms the foundation on which many other forecasts are based. Your company must look at the marketplace and identify needs that are not being met. You must determine if your line of products or services should be expanded to meet these needs. If your company has an aging line of products or services it is important that you quickly and accurately assess what is your business and where are you going. You must forecast the growth of your current products or services as their growth will be very dependent on the growth of the markets.

Only after you understand your markets and have forecasted sales can you begin your manufacturing forecasts. This is an easier forecast to make than others because it is built on your accepted sales forecast. The manufacturing forecast is a schedule of production activities that will provide sufficient amounts of products or services to achieve the levels established by the sales forecast.

In order to determine the profitability of the company it is necessary to forecast prices and all costs for the products or services. Unless you have forecasted prices and costs you will react rather than proact to market changes. If prices begin to fall you might plan to implement cost-cutting programs to preserve profit margins; if costs increase, then raise prices.

Having performed the preceding types of forecasts you can now forecast cash flow. This forecast is important in making financial plans to cover the operating expenses of the firm. It also will indicate if excess funds are available and these can be invested in expanding your products or services or offering new ones. You can project your investment plans into the future only after you have projected cash flow. If the cash-flow projections indicate a shortage of funds then the company can explore methods for raising the needed monies.

In order to keep growing, a company must invest in research and development activities. Forecasting the funds needed is difficult for often the amounts are large and tangible results are hard to assess. Also, difficult to forecast are the staffing needs of the organization. You will only be able to forecast these with accuracy when all of the other forecasts mentioned previously have been done.

Judgmental or Scientific Techniques

Forecasting is still more of an art than a science. Whether you use judg-mental or scientific approaches, the quality of your forecasting is deter-mined by how accurate and useful are the results. A scientific approach con-sists of a series of orderly steps that have a high degree of replicability be-cause of explicit theoretical relationships. The outcomes should be about the same regardless of who does it and when they do it. However, you can use a judgmental approach to forecasting in a systematic manner. When assumptions are documented and forecasters have similar experiences with the data, the forecasts should be similar. Even scientific forecasts can be less than satisfactory if poor judgment is used in the interpretation, evaluation, and application of the results.

Scientific-forecasting techniques have in the past been too involved and expensive and many smaller companies have not used them. Today there are people available with the skills required to develop models and possessing the ability to interpret the results correctly. Also, computer costs are falling rapidly and technological developments have put at your fingertips vast amounts of data. Many firms run forecasting models on time-sharing systems or microcomputers and greater attention will be given in the future to modeling as a forecasting technique. However, the ability to handle larger amounts of data with greater precision will not always give you a more-accurate forecast.

Many firms use a number of different forecasting techniques. Often, one technique is the primary tool for forecasting and the others are used to check on the reasonableness of the results. You might, for example, use a consultant to forecast sales of your products and then compare the results with a forecast that you have made from input-output analysis. The results of one technique might be used as a check on the other or you might through a weighting approach use both. However, don't fall into the trap that by combining many scientific forecasts it will result in a more-accurate forecast. We must not forget the importance of judgment. The bottom line is that it is the experience and judgment of the forecaster that gives accuracy and credibility to forecasts. Even scientific forecasting techniques rely heavily on the experience and judgment of the forecaster.

Finally, you must not ignore the differences in cost between judgmental and scientific-forecasting techniques. Almost without exception scientific forecasting is much more expensive than judgmental forecasting. When you decide on what forecasting technique to use, you must consider the expense of the detail or accuracy that is afforded to you by scientific-forecasting techniques.

6

Financial Strategies

Whenever you undertake investments that produce greater returns than the cost of capital, you grow the business and create greater values for your firm's shareholders. The formulation of a good financial strategy is an important part of your corporate-planning activities. It requires an evaluation of the financial strengths and weaknesses of your company relative to competition. Also it requires that you begin planning by establishing objectives that have measurable goals. Provide for feedback in an iterative manner so that changes can be made when required. Your plan cannot be static; it must change to reflect changes in risk, the cost of capital, and how the sources of capital affect the capital structure and the future cost of capital.

Each proposed investment and its associated level of risk must be evaluated and you must make effective financial decisions. This is described under Financial Decision Making. Those projects or ventures that increase the value of your firm and help to accomplish the objectives outlined in your corporate strategy are selected. Now that you have selected and ranked the proposed investments you must allocate funds among the alternative investments. This is discussed under Allocating Funds to Investments.

Financial Decision Making

There are three major phases that you must go through in order to make a good financial decision. In the first phase you must carefully identify and quantify all of the associated costs and benefits and perform a cost-benefit analysis. The second phase requires that you assess the risks involved in the proposed project or venture and evaluate how they affect your ability to stay within the estimated costs and to achieve the expected benefits. In the third phase you must justify the investment and the committing of the resources to the project or venture from the standpoint that the return on investment (ROI) is good or because it has an impact on the success and growth of the company.

Phase 1: Cost-Benefit Analysis

You must have in place a uniform and consistent process for identifying and quantifying costs and benefits. Costs are actual or anticipated expenditures

165

for personnel, materials and services, and equipment. You should think of costs as being all of the resources needed to obtain a benefit. Benefits are the results of any actions that help the company. Benefits are classified into three types: cost displacement, cost avoidance, or value added. *Cost displacement* is any current expenditure for personnel, materials and services, and equipment which as a result of the project or venture will no longer be a recurring expense. *Cost avoidance* is a specific planned future expenditure for personnel, materials and services, and equipment which will not be expended because of the increased productivity or efficiency that results from the project or venture. *Value added* is the dollar value that you place on gains attributable to increased revenues, improved decision making, improved managerial controls, or improvements in service and/or quality of your products. The gains might be tangible such as increased sales or less tangible like the ability to make better and faster decisions because of quicker access to more accurate data.

You should have a methodology in place for performing a cost-benefit analysis. This is a process for comparing all costs and benefits over a given period of time in order to determine the gains or loss on an investment. The cost-benefit analysis is a cornerstone in making better investment decisions. Also it will serve as an auditing tool when you gather cost-benefit data at the start of the project or venture, during its design and construction, and later when it is finished. You can compare the estimates with the actuals at all of these stages and identify causes for the differences. This evaluation will help you to forecast costs and benefits better in the future.

You must gather data for the cost-benefit analysis very carefully and validate its accuracy. In the area of personnel be sure to identify the salaries, wages, and fringe benefits of the positions involved. In the area of materials and service look at supplies, operational costs, systems-support costs, and all items purchased outside of the company.

When you do a cost-benefit analysis it is important that you use formal procedures. There are five reasons why this is important. First, it assures you that all proposals are going to receive uniform treatment. This uniform treatment comes about because you have established criteria for making selections and all functional groups rank their investment proposals using the same standards. Also, the use of formal procedures helps to see that the very minimum amount of information needed to make a good financial decision is at hand.

Second, a formal procedure is necessary to evaluate the economic feasibility of a project or venture. You have a methodology whereby you can look at the proposed investment and weigh the profitability of using the monies there or in an alternative program. Also, a formal procedure is a structure on which you can build the business case for the project or venture and calculate the effect of the investment on the cash flow of the company.

An insufficient cash flow and loss of liquidity can quickly slow the growth of your company.

Third, you establish a method for ranking each proposed investment with other alternative uses for the funds and you prioritize within the list of those projects or ventures that have received approval. The method is used by all divisions and departments to select only those programs that meet the goals of the company while providing the best ROI.

Fourth, you wil find that formal procedures maintain an organized way of looking at a make or buy decision. Only when all costs and benefits are treated in a uniform manner are you in the position to wisely decide if there is a cost advantage in doing the job within the organization or buying it from a vendor.

Fifth, a formal procedure assures that all elements of cost and benefits are collected in a disciplined manner. When forms are provided for gathering the data there is less chance that elements will be overlooked and it is easier to verify the accuracy of the information. Also the forms show what is to be delivered and who the responsible parties are.

When you are estimating costs and benefits, use ranges. If you do not and the actual figures miss by only small amounts, your forecasts get criticized. Some managers develop three sets of estimates. One is the best case, another the most likely, and the other the worst case. In order to accurately estimate costs and benefits over the life of a project or venture, you must forecast what changes will occur because of business growth, organizational changes and technological developments.

The purpose of performing cost-benefit analysis is to provide meaningful data for effective financial decisions. As these decisions drive the implementation of your financial strategies you should support them with a statement of the assumptions that underlie your estimates of future costs and benefits. Often this results in getting faster authorizations for making capital expenditures.

You must be careful when you are estimating costs and benefits for a proposed new system that will replace a current system. The proposed system is only cost effective if it does all that the current system can do but at less expense. Also look for better utilization of equipment to collect and massage data faster and to provide you with the ability to use this to run models and simulate changes in the marketplace. On-line computers have helped airlines, hotels, railroads, and car/truck rental companies to process vast amounts of data quickly. Banks, insurance companies, and investment firms have improved performance and accuracy because large amounts of data can be processed rapidly. Japanese plants have reduced production costs while improving quality through the use of computerized robots. Almost all of these users of computers have enjoyed the added value of better planning and control over normal day-to-day activities.

Many managerial financial decisions are for investments in information-management systems. Areas here that should be examined for possible benefits are any calculating and printing tasks. Any step that improves accuracy and speed of handling data as well as reduces the per-unit cost of an operation has some benefits. Look at all record-keeping tasks and try to standardize them as well as automatically collect and store the data in useful form. At the same time, provide a greater degree of security and privacy to the files. Look at record-searching jobs for often benefits can be found in these areas. The faster retrieval of data, improved ability to access and change the data base, and better auditing procedures often are beneficial.

The ability to restructure the capabilities of a system can produce worth while rewards. This is the ability to move about large files of data as well as to create new files by merging pieces of other files. Also there are benefits in having the ability to simultaneously change entire classes of records. Often there are significant benefits to be found in doing simulation and performing complex and simultaneous calculations. Your ability to make better financial decisions is improved when you can do what-if types of exercises. The what-if variables are conditions, forces, or factors that you identify in your model and you simulate changing events and determine their outcomes. When you are better able to fine-tune a production process many benefits result from the improved controls and better allocation of resources. Look at the benefits that can arise in cost displacement when justifying an information-management system. Procurement costs must be looked at from both the purchasing or leasing of the equipment. Accompanying this are the installation costs, which include at times the modifying of the physical facilities. There are start-up costs that arise from installing needed communication lines. Costs increase as it becomes necessary to hire and train people. If the project or venture involves computers, then programs must be written and documented. During the life of the system there will be maintenance costs.

Before we begin to assess risk and apply it to the cost-benefit analysis we should look at two aspects of cost and benefit considerations that are often passed over lightly.

Cost-Benefit Criteria. Four types of criteria require our attention. The first is to maximize the benefits for given costs or to minimize costs for given benefits. In this approach the incremental differences in costs or benefits are often not fully reflected, and produces unreliable estimates. Because this type of criteria focuses on fixed costs it often doesn't consider whether or not a substantial benefit can result from only a small increase in cost. The trade-offs might be marginal; however, other times they are not and must be considered. Also, it doesn't fully consider the value of money over a period of time. You will soon see in this chapter that this is an important element in making financial decisions.

The second is to maximize the ratio of benefits to costs. As cost is the denominator in this equation, the criteria is sensitive to any small changes in costs. This being the case, it can give unreliable results. Also, sometimes it is difficult to determine if a given element is a cost or a benefit. This is particularly true if it is shared over functional groups in the company. To one group it could be a cost whereas to another group it could be a benefit. Like the first criteria, it doesn't fully consider the value of money over a period of time.

The third type is to maximize the net benefits. In this criteria the value of money over a period of time is applied to costs and benefits. Costs are subtracted from benefits to produce net benefits; these are expressed in present value figures. In this chapter we will see how net present value (NPV) figures are calculated and why they are important.

The fourth is to look at what a project or venture yields. This type of criteria gives you a percentage return on the investment, which allows you to rank alternative proposals and also to compare their yields with other types of investments. In this chapter we will also look at how this yield or internal rate of return is calculated.

Most managers use the third and/or fourth type of criteria described previously in making financial decisions. We will see how they do this in examples that follow in this chapter. Once you have selected the cost-and-benefit criteria to be used, then apply it to all proposed investments from functional groups and include the figures in the requests for allocation of funds.

Quantifying Intangible Benefits. When looking at cost- and benefit-figures you will find that costs are usually underestimated and benefits overstated. Also, costs are difficult to control and benefits are difficult to achieve. Assessing benefits is a more-difficult and time-consuming task than estimating costs. It is difficult to quantify some benefits and the tendency is to write them off as being intangible. This is dangerous because often they add up to large amounts and can play a large part in building a good business case for a project or venture.

One way to assign some dollar amounts is to ask the people who will benefit from the project or venture to give you their best estimate. Ask them what it is worth to them and get them thinking by suggesting some numbers. Look at the experiences of other firms and go to the trade journals.

When it is difficult to estimate the value of a benefit, you can sometimes relate it to an activity that can be measured. For example, one benefit from the proposed investment might be a reduction in employee turnover. You can begin to quantify this by looking first at what the cost of employee turnover is to the firm. Determine how much it costs to hire and train a person to the level where the turnover is occurring. If the cost to do the hiring and training is five-thousand dollars per person and the new investment can be seen as reducing turnover by five people and benefit can be seen as twenty-five thousand dollars.

You also can use logical conclusions to quantify benefits. This is an application of the what-if approach. For example, what if we don't invest in this proposal to better control inventory? The inventory will grow by X dollars; Y dollars will have to be borrowed to finance it; at today's interest rates it will cost the firm Z dollars. If the interests costs can be avoided they can be considered as a savings. Another example is, what if we don't implement this proposal? Backorders (or outages) will increase by U dollars, resulting in V dollars of lost sales; at today's profit margins this will be W dollars of lost income.

Look for different places in the company where benefits can be shared and estimate their value to the group. If another part of the firm is receiving goods, services, and information more quickly because of the project or venture, then this has a value to them and should have a subjective value assigned.

Phase 2: Cost-Benefit with Risk

The second phase of financial decision making requires that you associate risk with costs and benefits. Profits are the results after expenses have been taken from revenues; therefore all benefits that increase revenue and/or reduce expenses improve profits. However, there is a need to classify each benefit by a level or degree of confidence by which risk can be managed. The ability to achieve benefits depends on two risks. The first is in regard to time, for often benefits are realized much later than estimated when the cost-benefit analysis was performed. The second risk is that the total benefits are never attained. You can express the level or degree of confidence that you have in benefits by placing them in a confidence matrix. Risks that you cannot allow for in this table are the risks that the actual costs far exceed the cost estimates and the project takes longer than expected.

The confidence matrix establishes three degrees of confidence: that is, high, medium, and low. Attaching one of these degrees of confidence to a benefit is often quite subjective. Often a portion of the benefit is assigned to each of the three unless it is apparent that with certainty only one applies. If too much is assigned a high degree of confidence you might overstate the position that you make for the proposal; however, assign too much to the low degree of confidence and you might be discounting the building of a good business case.

You perform the cost-benefit risk-level assessment by building a table that shows each of the three benefit classes (cost displacement, cost avoidance, and value added) down the side and the three degrees of confidence (high, medium, and low) across the top. You build such a table for each year of the life of the project or venture. When all of the benefits have been built into the table you select, based on your risk profile, a cumulative amount of benefits which on a year-by-year basis for the project forms a table of estimated cash inflows. This table shows the stream of total annual benefits from which you subtract the stream of total annual costs—also year-by-year—to arrive at the net benefits for the life of the project on an annual basis. These figures are then subjected to present-value-calculation procedures in order to determine the ROI.

Phase 3: Justifying Investments and Committing Resources

The third phase of financial decision making requires you to rank all proposed investments so that you can intelligently select those programs that are in the best interest of the firm and show the greatest returns on the monies invested. Three basic considerations influence every investment decision. First, consider what impact the project or venture will have on your business. Will what you are going to do improve the profits and accelerate the growth of your firm? Will revenues improve, will you increase your share of the market, can you lower expenses, and are you able to offer a higher-quality product or provide better service at lower prices? How will the proposed project or venture help your organization to meet or exceed the short-run and long-term goals of the firm? Are you more flexible in your posture to meet changing markets and economic fluctuations? How visible will the impact of the proposed change be to employees, customers, and shareholders? Unless it is perceived as being positive and worthwhile, it might never get off the ground.

Second, you must determine how successful the project or venture will be and will it be accepted readily in the organization. Are resources available, are the required skills on hand, and do you have higher-level-management's support? If you undertake any program with any of these critical elements missing you are courting a high risk of failure. Your organization will measure your performance on the quality of the product that you delivered, was it on time and within the budget? Effective managers deliver benefits early; often for with each passing day conditions change, and what looks great today is not applicable tomorrow.

Third, you must select very carefully where you are going to allocate funds and in many cases this is where the ROI is highest. You must look at the ROI on each proposed investment and rank each so that only the best are chosen. Financial justification is built on four methods for evaluating investments. They are as follows: the payback method, average rate of return, net present value, and internal rate of return.

The *payback method* measures how long it takes to get back through the cash inflows the initial capital investment. In table 6-1, which would you select: investment A or investment B?

Table 6-1
An Investment Decision

Investment: Investment amount:	A $50,000		B $50,000
		Cash Inflows	
Year 1:	$25,000		$15,000
Year 2:	25,000		15,000
Year 3:	20,000		20,000
Year 4:	20,000		20,000
Year 5:	—		40,000

Using the payback method you would select investment A as the initial investment is recovered in two years as opposed to investment B which is three years. The payback method favors the investment where the initial investment is recovered quickly. This would be important to you if liquidity is a factor in your business or where you want to minimize risk by recovering the initial investment as quickly as possible. The latter might be of significance if the investment is being made in an unstable political or social environment or where technological innovation is proceeding at a whirlwind pace. The payback method is simple to use and understand; however, it does have some shortcomings. One disadvantage is that it does not consider the time value of money. A dollar received today is of far greater value than a dollar received in the future for money has earning power that increases with time. The payback method does not recognize the time value of money and does not consider the timing of cash inflows and cash outflows. Also, this method fails to consider the cash inflows past the payback period and in investment A this was forty-thousand dollars, whereas in investment B it was sixty-thousand dollars. There are two other points to consider. First, the payback method does not measure a rate of return on the invested monies; therefore you cannot compare it with your firm's cost of capital in order to determine if the project or venture is making money. Also you do not know what the yield is on the appropriated funds and you might be investing monies in programs that can't begin to compete with alternative investment opportunities. You might get your initial capital investments returned quickly; however, if they have not resulted in growth for the company they have been sterile activities. Preservation and retention of funds is a conservative approach and at times is justified; however, growth comes in taking risks and managers are paid to do exactly that. Second, the payback method concentrates on only the initial years of the investment and does not look at the opportunity to reinvest the monies at even higher levels of return.

Also the payback method is short-run in focus and it does not consider the fact that a long-term investment is at the time a far better use of the funds. Few corporate strategies are built around allocating funds to programs and activities that are short-run in nature where the emphasis is on how quick the funds come back rather than how productive they have been for the firm.

The average-rate-of-return method, or accounting-rate-of-return method, measures on a percentage basis the return on the invested monies as averaged over the life of the investment. Table 6-2 shows how the average rate of returns are calculated for investments A and B:

Table 6-2
Example of Average Rate of Return

Investment: Investment Amount:	A	B
	Cash Inflows	
Year 1:	$25,000	$15,000
Year 2:	25,000	15,000
Year 3:	20,000	20,000
Year 4:	20,000	20,000
Year 5:	—	40,000
Total cash inflows:	$90,000	$110,000
Total investment:	− 50,000	− 50,000
Total net proceeds	$40,000	$60,000

Now the average proceeds per year can be determined.

Total net proceeds:	$40,000	$60,000
Number of years of investment life:	÷ 4	÷ 5
Average proceeds per year:	$10,000	$12,000

The average rate of return can be determined as follows:

Average proceeds per year: Total investment:	$10,000 ÷ 50,000	$12,000 ÷ 50,000
Average rate of return:	20.0 percent	24.0 percent

Using the average-rate-of-return method, you would select investment B as its return is 24 percent as opposed to investment A, which is 20 percent. This method, like the paypack method, is easily understood and easy to use. Unlike the payback method it does consider the cash inflows beyond the payback period and over the entire life of the investment. It does give you a rate of return on an annual basis; however, like the payback method it ignores the time value of money.

The net present value (NPV) method measures an investment by discounting back to the present time the cash inflows over the life of the investment to determine if the NPV values equal or exceed the investment. If it does, the venture is profitable. The NPV method recognizes the time value of money; this means that time must pass before a return on an investment can be realized and the time value of money is the opportunity cost of money. It is what the money might have earned had it been invested in an alternative venture with comparable risk. An example will show the concept of the time value of money. If you put $100 in an investment paying 10 percent interest per year, at the end of the year it will grow by compounding to $110 when the $10 interest is credited. Think of the $100 as the discounted present value of the $110 because the $100 is the result of discounting the $110 at 10 percent. This 10 percent is called the discount rate. Present value of $1.00 tables show for each year of life of an investment, by (discount rate) percents a number called the discount factor which when applied to the future cash inflow determines its present value (what it is worth today). In such a table the discount factor for one year at 10 percent is .909091. Applying this to the preceding example the $110 returned to you one year from the present is worth $100 now. The calculations are $100 × .90901 = $100. For simplicity, in examples that follow the discount factor will be shown only as three digits. The discount rate is provided by your financial people and will be specified to equal or exceed the cost of capital. The terms *hurdle rate* or *cutoff rate* are often used in place of the term discount rate and they mean the same thing. The following example shows how the net present values are calculated for investments A and B (see table 6-3) using a discount rate of 10 percent.

Both investment A and B have positive net present values and are acceptable proposals; however, investment B has a higher net present value. When the size of the investments are about the same, you rank the ventures in the sequence of decreasing net present value and select from among the highest. However, when the size of the investments differ it is good to divide the present value of the cash inflows by the present value of the investment (cash outflows), and the resulting profitability index is used to determine the ranking of the ventures. The equation for calculating the net present value is

$$ \text{NPV} = \frac{R_1}{(1+dr)} + \frac{R_2}{(1+dr)^2} + \ldots + \frac{R_n}{(1+dr)^n} - I $$

In this equation R_1, R_2, and so forth represent the cash inflows; dr is the discount rate (equal or exceeding the cost of capital); and n is the life of the project or venture and I is the investment.

The net-present-value method contains advantages that are not in the payback method or average-rate-of-return method. First, it takes into

Table 6-3
Example of Net Present Value

Investment: A
Investment: $50,000

	Cash Inflows		Discount Rate at 10 Percent	Present Values
Year 1:	$25,000	X	.909	= $22,725
Year 2:	25,000	X	.826	= 20,650
Year 3:	20,000	X	.751	= 15,020
Year 4:	20,000	X	.683	= 13,660
Present value of cash inflows:				$72,055
Present value of investment:				− 50,000
Net present value:				$22,055

Investment: B
Investment: $50,000

	Cash Inflows		Discount Rate at 10 Percent	Present Values
Year 1:	$15,000	X	.909	= $13,635
Year 2:	15,000	X	.826	= 12,390
Year 3:	20,000	X	.751	= 15,020
Year 4:	20,000	X	.683	= 13,660
Year 5:	40,000	X	.621	= 24,840
Present value of cash inflows:				$79,545
Present value of investment:				− 50,000
New present value:				$29,545

consideration the timing of the cash inflows and quantifies the time value of money. Second, it permits comparison of alternative investments with different years of life and considers all cash inflows over the life of the venture. As stated earlier the discount rate must be known in order to calculate the net present value; however, as this is readily known in the firm it is not a problem. The internal-rate-of-return method measures the yield of an investment. It is that interest rate that equates the investment (cash outflows) with the cash inflows to a present value of zero. Table 6-4 shows how this method is used to calculate the yields for investments A and B.

The yield for investment A falls between 30 percent and 31 percent as shown in the following example and the yield for investment B falls between 27 percent and 28 percent as shown in table 6-5.

The equation for calculating the internal rate of return is

$$\text{IRR} = \frac{R_1}{(1+x)} + \frac{R_2}{(+x)^2} + \ldots\ldots\ldots + \frac{R_n}{(1+x)^n} - I = 0$$

In this equation R_1, R_2, and so forth represent the cash inflows; n is the life of the project or venture; I is the investment; and x is the unknown. As the

Table 6-4
Example of Internal Rate of Return: Investment A

Investment: A
Investment: $50,000

	Cash Inflows		Discount Rate at 30 Percent	Present Values
Year 1:	$25,000	X	.769	= $19,225
Year 2:	25,000	X	.592	= 14,800
Year 3:	20,000	X	.455	= 9,100
Year 4:	20,000	X	.350	= 7,000
Present value of cash inflows:				$50,125

Note: This exceeds the $50,000 investment so a higher discount rate should be used.

	Cash Inflows		Discount Rate at 31 Percent	Present Values
Year 1:	$25,000	X	.763	= $19,075
Year 2:	25,000	X	.583	= 14,575
Year 3:	20,000	X	.445	= 8,900
Year 4:	20,000	X	.340	= 6,800
Present value of cash inflows:				$49,350

Note: This is less than the $50,000 investment so the discount rate is too high.

equation has one unknown, you can solve for the value of *x*. There will be some value of *x* that will cause the sum of the discounted cash inflows to equal the investment, making the equation equal to zero. It will be that value of *x* that is the internal rate of return (yield). The solution of *x* is the internal rate of return.

Table 6-5
Example of Internal Rate of Return: Investment B

Investment B:
Investment $50,000

	Cash Inflows		Discount Rate at 27 Percent	Present Values
Year 1:	$15,000	X	.787	= $11,805
Year 2:	15,000	X	.620	= 9,300
Year 3:	20,000	X	.488	= 9,760
Year 4:	20,000	X	.384	= 7,680
Year 5:	40,000	X	.303	= 12,120
Present value of cash inflows:				$50,665

	Cash Inflows		Discount Rate at 28 Percent	Present Values
Year 1:	$15,000	X	.781	= $11,715
Year 2:	15,000	X	.610	= 9,150
Year 3:	20,000	X	.477	= 9,540
Year 4:	20,000	X	.373	= 7,460
Year 5:	40,000	X	.291	= 11,640
Present value of cash inflows:				$49,505

You should rank the investments in the order of decreasing rate of return and then select the investment only if the yield exceeds some prescribed hurdle rate such as the cost of capital to the firm. The internal-rate-of-return method reflects the impact of the timing of cash inflows and quantifies the time value of money in the same manner as the net-present-value method. Also, it includes all cash inflows over the life of the venture. This method considers the profitability of the investment over its lifetime. However, it assumes that all of the cash inflows will be reinvested immediately in other ventures with the same yield. This is not always possible.

Net Present Value (NPV) or Internal Rate of Return (IRR)

We have looked at four methods for evaluating investments: payback, average rate of return, net present value, and internal rate of return. Of these, only the net present value and internal rate of return use discounted cash flow and only these objectively give a true value to money over a period of time by measuring a project or venture in present cash value. You must realize that to reflect current conditions, the discount rate that is used is equal to or exceeds the cost of capital. Should the cost of capital change because of the method of capitalization then you must recalculate the cost of capital and perform new net present value calculations. The internal rate of return also uses discounted cash flow but it solves for a discount rate that provides a net present value of zero. Which technique should you use for evaluating investments? The net present value is the best to use for the three following reasons:

First, the net present value technique permits you to use different discount rates in future years. When you do this you can factor in economic changes such as inflation, price changes, and increasing risk. When you use internal rate of return you evaluate the project using only one discount rate.

Second, the net present value technique better facilitates evaluating projects or ventures that have different life cycles. For those that have a long life you can use different discount rates and reflect more accurately the environment.

Third, you will find that due to the analytical process that there are times when the internal rate of return technique either gives vague or ambiguous results.

What do you do when you have more projects that are excellent investments than the amount of the capital available? You should rank the projects in descending order based on their net present values and allocate funds accordingly. Managers often use more than one method to financially justify where funds should be allocated. The net present value is the primary vehicle for selecting projects or ventures and the internal rate of return is used to see if the yield exceeds the returns that are available in alternative forms of investment.

As the discount rate used in the net present value method is specified to equal or exceed the cost of capital there must be an understanding as to what is the cost of capital for your firm. How is cost of capital determined? A company in order to acquire investment monies draws on a number of different sources that make up the capital structure of the firm. The capital structure has as its individual components the following: debt, preferred stock, retained earnings, and common stock. Each of these sources of capital have different degrees of risk and associated costs. The first step is to identify the cost of each component of the capital structure and relate it to the proportional amount that it is of the capital structure. The result is a weighted cost of capital. All of the information that you need to perform these calculations can be found in your firm's balance sheet as included in the annual report.

The cost of debt (bank loans and bonds) is their stated interest rates less the income-tax deductions allowed because of these interest expenses (a tax shield). You are concerned with what new debt costs you; therefore the costs of borrowing in the past are irrelevant to the decision process now being made on new investments.

The cost of new preferred stock should reflect the selling costs by the brokers to your firm. If there are no selling costs then your firm will receive the market price of the preferred stock; however, if there are selling costs your firm will receive less than the market price. The cost of new preferred stock is calculated as follows:

$$\text{Cost of new preferred stock} = \frac{\text{Preferred dividend}}{\text{Price of preferred stock—selling costs}}$$

$$= \frac{\$8.50}{\$59-\$2} = 14.91 \text{ percent}$$

Preferred dividends are on an after-tax basis for they are paid out of earnings after taxes.

The cost of capital obtained through retained earnings can be assigned as the rate of return shareholders require on your firm's common stock. This is because retained earnings when reinvested internally in the operations of the company will not cause a change in the current stock price provided your firm earns the required rate of return on its investment. If the firm earns more or less, the current stock price will rise or fall. You might think of these monies as being the same as proceeds from the sale of stock because the funds are owned by the shareholders. However, should your firm hold the retained earnings and not reinvest them internally your firm is paying an opportunity cost that is equal to the profits lost to your firm by forfeiting the use of the monies.

The cost of capital obtained from the sale of new common stock will, because of the selling costs by brokers to your firm, be higher than the cost of capital obtained through retained earnings. The calculation requires a factor for growth. This factor is your best estimate of future annual growth of earnings, dividends, and stock prices. The cost of new common stock is calculated as follows:

$$\text{Cost of new common stock} = \frac{\text{Dividend}}{\text{Price of common stock} - \text{Selling costs}} + \text{Growth rate}$$

$$= \frac{\$2.50}{\$50-\$5*} + 6 \text{ percent} = 11.56 \text{ percent}$$

*Selling cost assumed to be 10 percent of stock price.

Once the cost of the individual components of the capital structure have been determined a weighted average cost of capital can be calculated as shown in the following example. The amount of capital for each source has been taken for the example company from the balance sheet and the cost of the bank loans and bonds have been arbitrarily assigned. The cost of the new preferred stock and the new common stock are those shown in the preceding calculations. The common stock and retained earnings have been shown as a single entry and where applicable a 50 percent income-tax rate has been applied. See table 6-6.

Table 6-6
Determining Cost of Capital

Type	Amount	Component Cost	Component After-Tax Cost	Proportion (Percent of Total Capital)	Weighted Cost of Capital
Bank loans	$ 3,000,000	17.50%	8.75%	3%	.26%
Bonds	11,000,000	9.50%	4.75%	11%	.52%
Preferred stock	9,000,000	14.91%	14.91%	9%	1.34%
Common stock and retained earnings	76,000,000	11.56%	11.56%	77%	8.90%
Firm's weighted average cost of capital					11.02%

Interest Rates and the Cost of Debt

If you are able to forecast what the interest rates will be when your company enters the market for funds you will better understand the firm's cost of capital and make more effective financial decisions. This is a difficult forecast and you can approach it by determining the cost of risk free instruments and then adding to this some factor to allow for risk. What is the cost of risk free investments? Weekly sales of U.S. Treasury Bills establish the risk-free interest rates. As these are the safest form of all investments they set the minimum interest rate for all forms of securities.

Interest rates reflect the price for money; this is established through supply and demand. When the demand for monies goes up, so do the interest rates. Two factors affect the level of interest. First, the inflationary pressures and availability of money that accompany changes in the business cycle drive up interest rates. There is an inverse relationship between interest rates and the availability of money. Every time the money supply is expanded or contracted, pressures arise to decrease or increase the rate of interest. In order to forecast changes in interest rates and develop sound financial strategies, you should understand what the Federal Reserve policies are doing to the money markets. Should the policy be to increase the money supply, then interest rates should fall. Should this program go too far, then the resulting expansion of money supply will generate inflationary trends and the increase in demand for credit will push interest rates even higher. Now an interesting psychological force takes over for as consumers see an erosion of the purchasing power of their money they demand more through credit and then interest rates climb. The costs of their loans climb and they need more monies to settle their debts. When recession sets in, the demand for goods and services should decline, the economy should contract, the demand for monies to invest in plants and equipment should decrease. This should reduce the cost of money or interest rates. Recessions have recently had only a minor affect on reducing costs, prices, and inflationary pressures. There are too many fixed supports such as minimum-wage laws and guaranteed work-and-wage schedules. With each passing year, the floors get set higher and become more rigid.

Second, you will find that the seasonal and random effects of interest rates have a very small impact on your cost of long-term financing. This is because they primarily influence the cost of your working capital. What else should you look at in establishing a financial policy? Two areas require your attention. First, you must focus on how long the capital will be invested in the project or venture. Second, you must evaluate what impact it will have on the risks confronting your firm and the associated interest rates. The longer the life of the loan, the higher the interest rates. Why is this? It is because those who have invested the monies have doubts about the future and demand a higher rate of return on their investments to offset the risks.

A financial strategy used by many managers is to borrow monies just for the length of the life of the project or venture. This helps to keep down long-term borrowing, and when new investment opportunities arise they can be financed easier and often without an increase in the interest rates. When a company has a large amount of long-term debt, then new borrowing is often available—only it is at higher interest rates for the lenders associate higher risk with the company. You will find that as you take on bigger projects, the overall risk of the company increases and usually the cost of debt increases.

Aspects of Debt and Equity Costs

As debt is a lower-risk instrument to investors than equity, it is generally less expensive. Another characteristic of debt is that the interest is tax deductible and provides you with financial leverage. Table 6-7 provides an example of financial leverage. Situation A uses both debt and equity financing. The debt provides the financial leverage. Situation B uses only equity financing, and as it has no debt it has no financial leverage.

As equity is a higher-risk instrument to the investor than debt it is generally more expensive. The cost of debt is explicit and it is determined; however, the cost of equity is more implicit and must be derived. You can determine the pretax cost of debt if your company has both short-term and long-term debt by simply taking a weighted average of the interest rates. You can derive the cost of equity by adding the present percentage yield of your stock to the estimated average annual percentage increase in earnings per share and stock price over the next two years. For example, if the current price of your stock is $60 per share, the current dividend is $6 per share, and the estimated average annual percentage increase in earnings per share and stock price is 7 percent annually, your cost of equity is $6/$60 + 0.07, or 0.17 or 17 percent.

How Capital Structure Affects the Cost of Capital

The discount rate that is applied to your net present value calculations is the cost of capital. This is a function of the capital structure of your company. When you develop a financial strategy you must know what changes will be brought about by changes in the cost of capital and how this will affect changes in your capital structure. Over the years different theories have been popular regarding what is the best capital structure. In the past, it was

Table 6-7
Financial Leverage

Situation A		Situation B
Capital Structure		
$1,000,000 debt at 10 percent	No debt	
$1,000,000 equity (20,000 shares)	$2,000,000 equity (40,000 shares)	

Condition I: Stable Earnings before Interest and Tax position.

$200,000	Earnings before Interest and Tax	$200,000
100,000	Interest	None
100,000	Earnings before Tax	200,000
$5	Earnings per Share before Tax	$5

In the preceding the $100,000 interest is a tax shield in Situation A and with only half as many shares outstanding you have less dilution of the stock and more control of the company.

Condition II: Earnings before Interest and Tax grows:

$400,000	Earnings before Interest and Tax	$400,000
100,000	Interest	None
300,000	Earnings before Tax	400,000
$15	Earnings per Share before Tax	$10

In the preceding the Interest as a tax shield in Situation A through financial leverage resulted in a higher Earnings per Share before Tax. When your company is growing and Earnings before Interest and Tax are up, then financial leverage works for you and debt is good.

Condition III: Earnings before Interest and Tax falls:

$100,000	Earnings before Interest and Tax	$100,000
100,000	Interest	None
0	Earnings before Tax	100,000
0	Earnings per Share before Tax	$2.50

In the preceding the fixed obligation of the Interest in Situation A resulted in a lower Earnings per Share before Tax. When your company is not growing and Earnings before Interest and Tax are down then financial leverage works against you and debt is a handicap.

considered wise to have an equal balance between debt and equity financing. The thinking was that both the cost of debt and equity remained fairly constant given a reasonable range of capital investments. Should either one increase dramatically the cost of both would rapidly increase. Due to the effect of taxation the cost of debt financing was less than equity financing. As the ratio of debt to equity financing increased the cost of debt decreased until a point was reached where the cost of debt reversed and started to increase rapidly. If you perceive the future as being one of good growth and higher profits, then the tax shield of debt is a great advantage. However, should the business decline and profits fall then the repayment of principal and the interest costs might become a burden that you cannot manage. Many firms that have overextended their growth and taken on too much debt have found sales, revenues, and cash flows falling; debt requirements could not be met. They sold off good assets to make interest payments, and in doing this caused earnings to fall even more. Remember, it often takes only a small decline in sales to result in insufficient cash flows. You must look at each capital investment to see if it can meet any potential debt requirements. If there is a high degree of risk in the product or venture you should not be using debt to leverage growth. Most new and speculative firms in the field of high-technological development raise their funds through equity. As profits grow and cash flow improves, you are then better able to use debt with less risk to the company. If your debt/equity ratio is low you can use debt to give you financial leverage. A wise approach is to alternate the use of debt and equity for this utilizes leverage, helps keep interest rates lower for the firm, and doesn't go overboard in diluting the stock and losing control of the business.

Allocating Funds to Investments

How you plan your capital expenditures has an important effect on the competitive posture of the company. In order to forecast accurately the results of your investments it is necessary to know what cash flow will be produced for each investment opportunity. The investment is justified when it returns more than the firm's cost of capital. Almost every firm has more investment opportunities than available capital. Effective managers understand the needs of the business and have in place a program for capital budgeting that is in harmony with the corporate strategies. To implement the program requires an in-depth knowledge of the markets and the product lines. However, you must go further than knowing what business you are in for you must define what business you will not enter. This will help you to avoid investing in projects or ventures that are not in keeping with the missions of the firm.

Your shareholders, customers, employees, and competitors anxiously watch how your company spends its funds. It indicates the direction of the business, through the activities in which funds are allocated, and the rate of growth, through the amount of capital expenditures. It is corporate strategy that gives meaning to capital budgeting. You should not allocate funds in a spontaneous manner and then build the corporate strategy around these investment opportunities.

Some managers look at each piece of the budget as a separate entity or operation, and in doing this often the total returns to the firm are not maximized. What happens is that a good business case is built for individual investments; however, when the benefits of all of these are summed the total is less than if the funds had been put into an alternative program of investment opportunities. Also an alternative program might better have filled the firm's long-term objectives. Focus first on the firm's objectives and goals, and then select the projects or ventures that will accomplish them and allocate funds accordingly.

The ultimate responsibility for the total allocation of funds throughout the company rests with higher-level management. Once the functional groups in the firm are given their capital budgets, they are responsible for the effective use of the monies. Functional management decides where, when, and how the funds will be spent but it is always within the framework of meeting the objectives as outlined in corporate strategy. The accountability for managing the budget always rests with the managers of the functional groups. When investment proposals originate in a functional group they generally are self-serving to the interests of those that nominate them to higher-level management. Effective allocation of funds requires that the officers of the firm set the direction for capital spending. This is important for only they can see alternative uses for the funds beyond the scope of what is proposed by the functional groups. Also, separately justified independent projects or ventures—when all of the capital expenditures are added together—might cause serious problems. One problem could be that the monies to complete all of them in a given period of time might critically affect cash flow. Another problem might be that the combined result is a concept, product, or service that is far too revolutionary for the current marketplace. Many firms have suffered financial losses because what they offered was too far ahead of its time. Know your customers as well as your markets. Buyers of new automobiles are historically conservative and motor companies have often introduced new-style changes that were not readily accepted. Also, you can have a problem if you go heavily into a program that has commendable long-term goals yet it captures so much of your resources that you lose flexibility in your operations. If you cannot adjust quickly to new technological developments or pressures from competitors you can soon lose your market share. Funds should be allocated only where they work best on a collective basis for the firm. You must help those whose investment requests were denied to realize that the needs and benefits were greater in those organizations that received the monies. This is a difficult task when funds are allocated to investment opportunities with lower returns on the investment. Often more important than the financial case is the impact that the capital expenditure has on the business. The impact to the firm is high when it comes to retaining market share or increasing market penetration, meeting competitors prices, and maximizing revenues and/or profits. How you allocate funds in the short-run can have a profound effect on the long-term success of the company.

An effective way to allocate funds is to look at your entire product line and determine for each product how much investment is required to achieve a specified long-term return. However, it is higher-level management that directs and controls the firm's product offerings and allocates funds to each product line based on market forecasts.

One way that you can allocate funds is on the basis of the expected cash flow. Cash flows start low but rise rapidly as the profits from new products or services grow. Often you must decide if a large up-front infusion of funds will be sufficient to build a strong cash flow quickly or if a continuous commitment of funds over a long period of time is required. Such a decision can play a major role in the establishment of pricing policy. The pharmaceutical industry is constantly faced with this decision. Large amounts of research-and-development dollars go into the development of a new product. Often the expenses continue for many years while the markets are built and the product improved. Do you price high and recover the costs quickly and invite competitors to step in because of the high profit margins? Or do you price low and recover the costs over many years and with low profit margins discourage competition and substitute products?

You must also determine when a product will reach a level of sales where some profits are available for reinvestment in other new products or services. In slow-growth industries the development and marketing of new products can often be financed on the profits achieved from the present product mix. However, in high-technology industries your competitors might leap-frog your most-profitable product or service with a better one before you have the cash flow needed from it to be used in developing and marketing other products.

Another way that you can allocate funds is to distribute them among products in a manner that keeps risk well-balanced and diversified. All products have risk; even your stable and mature products are subject to the risk of obsolescence or changes in buying habits. However, you still invest in these to offset potential losses on the new fast-growth but high-risk products. You can put all of your eggs in one dynamic single-product basket but it can be very risky, even when you watch it carefully.

Also, you can allocate funds by forecasting the remaining life of the product and using this as a guide for investing more monies. This is not an easy forecast; if industry capacity builds faster than demand then allocating funds in that product or service can result in large losses. On the other hand, many mature products have continued their impressive growth because investments were made in improving the product or service and developing better marketing approaches. Unfortunately, your forecast of growth can be self-fulfilling for if you feel that growth is declining you invest less in the product or service and this results in its demise. Some products are in themselves not a good investment; however, they might improve the value of other products. You should allocate funds to these when the collective returns are more than the firm's cost of capital.

How well you manage capital budgeting is the key to where your firm will be in the future. All too frequently, funds get allocated to projects or ventures because they serve a political purpose at the time. Also, when the capital budgeting process is not integrated with corporate strategy then intelligent trade-offs in the uses of funds are not made. Where is the firm going and what is it trying to accomplish? When you answer this, you know where to allocate funds.

Allocating Funds to Dividends

We have in this chapter discussed two fundamental financial decisions you must make, that is, where to raise funds and where to invest them. Your third decision involves allocating funds to dividends. Your financial decisions on investments were focused on such objectives as: (1) the direction of the business, (2) profitability, and (3) rate of growth. Your financial decisions on dividends focuses on the objective of maximizing the market price of your stock. This requires a decision whether or not to declare a dividend. Understand that the purpose of a dividend payment is to increase the wealth of the shareholders. Therefore you should declare a dividend only when the sum of the final market price of the stock and the dividend will be greater than the market price of the stock at the time you made the dividend decision. Declare and pay a dividend if the amount of the dividend will be greater than the decline in the market price of the stock because of the payment. The bottom line is what will be the market price of the stock after the dividend payment. The market price of the stock might rise when you declare the dividend. However, this is not sufficient reason to take this step if the sum of the final market price and dividend will not be higher than the market price at the time of dividend declaration. Upon the payment of a dividend, the market price does not always decline by the same amount. When current shareholders and potential shareholders perceive the dividend payment as an intelligently planned way to increase their wealth through stock ownership, they will not sell. They might even buy more and thus raise the price of the stock.

As the payment of dividends is a use of funds the shareholders must perceive that these were used wisely. The source of these funds have an opportunity cost in that they could have been used for other purposes. Everyone must understand that by not using the funds for these purposes—but for dividends—it has not harmed the growth and profitability of the firm. In fact, it might help to more easily raise equity capital should it be needed in the future. Should additional financing be required to pay dividends then you must realize that this could affect your cost of capital and the discount rate used to financially justify the allocation of funds to the investments.

Lease-or-Buy Decisions

Many managers see leasing as a good source of capital for financing capital-equipment needs. Even if you don't own the equipment its use can result in profits to the firm. Also, when equipment is leased rather than purchased it can reduce costs, hedge against inflation, and preserve your line of credit and working capital for other purposes. Perhaps the greatest benefit your firm might enjoy from leasing, if it can't use the tax benefits generated from owning equipment, is through the tax-oriented lease. In this arrangement the lessor claims the tax benefits that result from owning the equipment and through lower lease payments passes these on to the lessee.

Leasing works in the following manner. First, the user, who is the lessee, makes a selection of equipment and resolves such issues as pricing, delivery, and installation. Once the sales contract is signed, the lessee signs a lease agreement with the lessor. Second, after the lease is signed, the lessee assigns the buying rights to the lessor. The lessor now buys the equipment. The lessee signs off on the delivery of the equipment, the lessor pays the bill, and the leasing agreement takes effect. The rentals that you as a lessee now pay are net to the lessor for you must pay all maintenance, service, insurance, and taxes. Third, when the lease expires you as a lessee have a number of options. You can renew the lease, buy the equipment (often with a credit for the rentals), or return the equipment. The options you select determine how the lease is classified for taxing and financial accounting. There are three basic forms of leasing.

The first is the lease for tax purposes in which the lessor claims ownership and gets all of the tax benefits. The lessor takes all of the deductions for depreciation; if you are the lessee you can take all the lease payments as expenses. The investment-tax credit can be taken by the lessor or, if agreed on, can be claimed by the lessee. At the termination of the lease the lessor owns the equipment. This type of lease is known for tax purposes as a true lease.

Second is the leveraged lease. In this form of leasing, the lessee selects the equipment and signs a lease. Like in a nonleveraged lease the lessee must pay for maintenance, service, insurance, and all taxes. However, this form of leasing is quite complex because many people (the lessee, the lessor, and a long-term lender) are involved, there is a great deal of paperwork, and many complex legal issues arise. In the nonleveraged lease the lessor provides all of the capital; however, in the leveraged lease the lessor provides less than half of capital and the balance is provided by the long-term lender who is generally an institutional investor. This long-term lender takes very little risk for an assignment is put on the equipment, lease, and lease-rental payments. Even though lessors put up less than half of the capital they can still claim all of the tax advantages that go with ownership. However, the lessor's tax-shelter benefit is greatly offset by high risk for the long-term lender has first lien on everything.

Third is the conditional sale. As lessee you get all of the ownership and an option to renew or purchase based on what the fair-market value of the equipment is at the time you exercise the option. As lessee you own the property and can depreciate it for tax purposes. You can claim the investment-tax credit and deduct for tax purposes the interest portion of the rental payment. In this nontax-oriented form of leasing the lessor must treat the situation as a loan. Therefore as the lessor does not retain ownership and keeps the investment, tax credits, depreciation, and tax benefits a low leasing rate cannot be offered like in the true lease.

What is the best course of action for you? Should you lease or buy? Look at all alternatives for capital financing. Internal funds might be best. Perhaps you might add debt or equity financing to your internal funds to meet the growing needs of the business. It might be better to capitalize on the economics of leasing. You can only choose the right course when you compare the costs and benefits of each and see how they fit in with your present financial position. We have seen earlier that the net-present-value technique for financial decision making is realistic and effective. You should use this approach when comparing the cost of capital equipment acquisitions through leasing or other methods.

Your decision to lease or to buy depends on your tax situation and financial posture. If you have a limited amount of working capital on hand and if other investments offer greater returns, then leasing can be a wise approach for financing capital-equipment needs. On the other hand, if you have a large amount of working capital and if other investments offer a low rate of return, then purchasing can be your best course of action. Whether or not you can use tax benefits is important. If you cannot use the tax benefit that comes through the purchasing of equipment then leasing can be a wise choice.

The primary advantage of leasing over purchasing is its low cost. The lessor passes on the tax benefits to the lessee through low rental rates. Additional benefits are as follows: improvement in cash flow; establishment of specific future equipment costs (this permits you to forecast future cash needs); coordination of payment schedules with seasonal and growth patterns of your business; avoidance of the need for an initial down payment as leasing generally covers all financing; retention of capital that can be used to grow the business; avoidance of the dilution of ownership if equity financing is required and avoids the interest and principal payments that arise if debt financing is required. However, as good as all of these advantages seem, leasing might in the long-run cost you more than purchasing if you have tax benefits through ownership.

7

Strategy Formulation

Strategy formulation is a problem-solving process whereby objectives and goals are developed for the firm along with policies and programs needed to accomplish them. It is a carefully prepared plan to achieve an end. It is synonymous with strategic planning. If you are to make effective decisions regarding the use of the firm's resources in the future then all managers doing this in the company must approach it systematically. This is accomplished through strategic planning.

Corporate Strategy

Corporate management is responsible for the formulation of the firm's strategic thrust as documented in the strategic plan. The strategic plan is a road map for managers to follow. It is creating the future of the firm. It begins by identifying the opportunities and risks in the business and sets forth crisp directional statements. It is a structured and comprehensive approach to assessing the future. The purpose of corporate strategy is to identify critical issues and to decide what to do about them. This entails asking questions. What is our business? What should be our business? What will our business be in the future? When do we want to be in that business? How will we get into that business? When you answer these questions you can develop long-term objectives and goals for the firm that will remain relatively unchanged. However, the strategies for attaining these objectives and goals do change. They should change because the environment in which you conduct your business changes. These changes arise because of new directions in the economy, legislative and regulatory acts, and technological developments.

Strategic planning is concerned with the direction and thrust of the firm particularly in areas such as products, markets, customers, and growth. The firm's objectives are realistic statements that often can be quantified and usually prioritized. They generally address newness in the nature of the business regarding concepts, capacity, and products. The objectives can be ranked in order of their importance to the firm, that is, what is vital to survival, or what is needed for growth, and so on.

Strategic planning looks at long-term changes and conditions as they relate to short-term activities and decisions. It often begins in an informal manner with officers in the firm talking about what they see as future issues and needs and how they can be met. The issues can be opportunities, or they might be problems that threaten the very life of the firm. These issues become the very heart of a structured and well-defined strategic plan. Just as there is uncertainty when you forecast future events there will also be uncertainty when you lay down a plan to address the issues and achieve the firm's long-term goals. This means the plan must be somewhat flexible for the goals will not change but the strategies will change with the changing business world. You must reassess periodically all alternative options for each issue.

Strategic planning requires more than filling out forms. Accompanying discussions must focus on the critical factors that mean success or failure to the business. Talk about the strengths and weaknesses of the company particularly as they affect your competitive posture. Strategy is concerned with issues at different levels in the organization. At the corporate level, it addresses the nature of the business and its rate of growth, the effects of technological developments, and the acquisition and allocation of capital through the capital-budgeting process. At the divisional level, it addresses the product line on a product-by-product basis in order to increase market share and improve profits. Also, under the capital-budgeting process the funds must be allocated where they can return the most on the investment and grow the business.

Strategic planning produces a set of mission statements that are communicated to the functional groups in the company. The mission statements outline the long-term objectives and direction of the company. They provide a foundation for making effective decisions and allocating the firm's resources. Strategic planning requires good insights and opinions from all levels in the organization.

Types of Planning

All planning is not strategic, there are also tactical and operational planning. Strategic planning is business planning that addresses the long-term needs of the firm. It is more than a sophisticated information-management system or a complex corporate-financial model. These are tools for doing strategic planning; they are not themselves the strategic plan. The strategic plan sets forth mission statements that are specific and simply defined. One major company has six mission statements. Mission statements often address the following important areas: marketing, manufacturing, service, quality, administration, and social responsibilities. For example, a marketing mission might be: Sell the product line worldwide to meet all market needs and to fulfill the business volume plan established for each country. The strategic-planning function is a cornerstone for managing the future.

Tactical planning is the implementation of the strategic plan by divisions. Each division builds their own tactical plan. Rather than addressing business planning, as in the strategic plan, it addresses resource and adminstrative planning and focuses on the measurements and controls required in these areas.

Operational planning is the implementation of the tactical plan at the departmental levels. It looks at how products and services are controlled, how data about quality and service levels is collected and analyzed, and how changes should be managed. It addresses the control function through task planning and it produces the expected results through technical planning. It is concerned with what must be done and where and when it must be done to meet the tactical plan and the established measurable targets.

Strategy formulation requires looking at the values of high-level management and the levels of competence in the firm. The aims as expressed in the strategic-planning process might be in the right direction; however, if management places a low value on them or the organization can't accomplish them, then there is high risk of failure. In large multinational companies the functional strategies require a planning process that takes all of the ideas and looks at the synergistic effect on worldwide operations and interdivisional relationships. You must document carefully the dependencies of functional groups on each other, particularly in marketing and technological development. What new products and services do we need to offer and when? Where will the research and development be done, that is, what countries, what locations? Who will be our new customers? What levels of quality do they expect in our products or services?

Benefits of Strategic Planning

Strategic planning is a discipline that forces high-level management to look closely at the firm's future: This is perhaps its greatest benefit. It makes corporate management responsible for setting the direction of the business. Another benefit is that it establishes formal procedures whereby functional groups can focus on new concepts, products, or services. Managers then ask questions, which is strategy formulation, rather than search for answers to resolve problems, which is tactical planning.

Other benefits come from the improvements in communication. On the peer level, executives discuss issues and options on an informal basis and then communicate them formally through the mission statements. Vertically, the channels of communication between corporate management and the managers of functional groups improve. This is because much ambiguity is removed in the decision-making process because measurable targets have been formally assigned. Also, the communication improves between managers in divisions and departments for they must work closely together to provide the data and insights so necessary to the strategic-planning process.

Without good strategic planning, you are not going to make effective decisions and you will not move the firm in the correct direction at the right pace. Without a comprehensive and coordinated strategic plan in place, functional groups do what is self-serving rather than what is in the best interest of the company. Strategy formulation is directed by the chief executive officer, but it is not formulated by him or her. No one person, regardless of great abilities, is capable today in the fast-changing and dynamic business world to identify all issues pertaining to the future and to independently develop strategies to handle them.

Implementing Strategic Planning

The targets that come out of the mission statements are very specific in nature and term. Usually they are expressed as profit objectives. In the manufacturing area, for example, the objectives relate to costs and in the marketing area to revenues. It is the responsibility of each functional group to develop strategies to meet their assigned objectives. Each objective has quantifiable targets. These are built on forecasts for the plan period and results are measured against them. The objectives should be accompanied by assumptions about how possible economic, environmental, and business conditions will create opportunities and problems. Make an assessment of the risk, develop an action program, and assign resources for the plan period.

Strategic planning forms the foundation on which established policies, practices, and procedures can be applied to make better decisions. Often there is little interdependency on the decisions made in one group with decisions made in another; therefore all are able to readily attain their targets. This is not so if concurrent decisions in the organization cause conflict because needs and interests are going in different directions. It is because of this that strategic planning is done on a total-company approach.

Where do you find the issues that are addressed in strategic planning? They are both external and internal to the organization. The external ones are found in the economy, domestic and international markets, and regulations of governments. Customers, distributors, suppliers, and investors all have changing needs and value. The internal issues revolve around such areas as organizational structure, working conditions, and competency levels. The focus is on people for it is through them that managers help the business to grow and remain profitable.

Strategic plans should be reviewed on a periodic basis. Measure what was attained against what was expected monthly. Of particular concern are the revenues attained and actual expenses versus the targets. Look at the bigger picture and reexamine the issues quarterly. Have they changed? Are changes being effectively communicated? Is there resistance to the strategic plan or its implementation?

Resistance to Strategic Planning

New directions and approaches often result in changing the nature of work and how it is performed. Most people need time and education to adjust to changes. They must perceive that the targets and activities that come out of the strategic plan are not threats but ways for them to do a better job and gain recognition, rewards, and promotions. If a person has a large ego he or she might need a greater involvement in the process and be encouraged to contribute inputs into the development of the strategic plan. Often strategic planning results in organizational changes. All levels in the organization should be encouraged to take a positive attitude toward the process. Get many people involved in the process for a vested interest in a program usually leads to a higher level of commitment. The results of strategic planning should not be perceived as a threat to anyone's rights and status in the group. It should be seen as a sound business approach for identifying future issues and implementing new ideas to benefit the company and each employee. Corporate management will be more effective and the operational units will still retain their authority to make decisions.

Sometimes the approach taken to strategic planning has a lot to do with the levels of resistance that are generated. If you use too many sophisticated computer-planning models all levels of management can develop concerns about the results and not use them. Make it known that planning models are only tools to be used to help to better analyze and evaluate data. Making effective decisions is still a human process based on opinions, facts, history, experience, and judgment.

Organizing for Strategic Planning

The responsibility begins with corporate management. They must establish long-term objectives to improve the profits and growth of the business and measure managers according to their results. Unfortunately, most managers are measured on short-term results. It is the quick bottom line that counts, so programs that produce results here are put ahead of those that have often far-greater returns but in the future. Corporate management should think further about this matter for much of the recent spectacular growth in Japanese business is a result of putting the emphasis on the long-term accomplishments and not the short-term.

Strategic planning is often done by a staff whose sole task is to control the planning activities; they report to corporate management and do not do the actual planning. Planning is done by the functional groups; the strategic-planning staff offers advice and guidance on how data should be collected and presented. Often they help the group to establish goals and measurements. The strategic-planning staff presents ideas and plans developed in the organization to corporate management for use in the construction of the firm's strategic-planning document.

Strategic planning can also be done by a committee composed of executives from the various functional groups, that is, manufacturing, marketing, finance, and so forth in the firm. They meet at periodic intervals and usually have a much-larger role to play than a strategic-planning staff. They have a strong hand in the actual formulation of strategy. They develop mission statements, issue objectives to the divisions, and even offer guidance in the preparation of the budgets.

Weak Links in Strategic Planning

Corporate management will develop a sound strategic plan but often it is not followed in the organization. Frequently this is because it is weak in content. The plan often becomes an exercise in form over substance. When this happens decisions are made outside of its framework, targets are not taken seriously, and measurements are not applied. It becomes a paper exercise to satisfy the chief executive officer. A lot of effort goes into strategic planning; therefore it should be treated as a signed commitment by all levels of management to the stated objectives. This is a contractual obligation and not just a promise of best effort. Failure to deliver by any manager should be reflected in his or her performance evaluation.

Why are strategic plans sometimes not taken seriously? Often it is because the plan just is not good. Unless a plan is creditable, managers will not commit to it. There are many reasons why a strategic plan might not be realistic or accurate. Frequently it is because of poor inputs of data and assumptions. Data is often collected in a superficial manner and assumptions become hastily drawn conclusions about conditions. Often history and experience is discounted or perhaps totally neglected. Sometimes there is no attempt to quantify the degree of risk involved in the alternative solutions. Insight can be gained here by looking at the performance of the organization with similar issues in the past. Was the performance good? If not, can it be better now and if so then why? If the issues are new, then the risk of failure increases.

Sometimes the forecasts on which strategic-planning volumes are based are not reliable. Perhaps the wrong forecasting technique was used or the data was incomplete or inaccurate. Often strategic planning consists of nothing more than taking last year's plan and increasing all of the volumes by a given percentage. This is a fast and often-foolish way to prepare for the future. The figures will be more realistic and accepted quicker if they are developed by building them up on a product-by-product basis by customers by markets. Targets are often set from plan to plan with little concern about the actions and events that must take place in order to produce the expected results. For example, if you need high-competency-level people to meet next year's targets and it takes time to hire and train these people, then you had better get to work on it quickly. Resources must be in place when they are needed.

Often strategic plans fall apart because they have not addressed unforeseen contingencies and there is no program for handling them when they arise. You should look at the key areas in the strategic plan and try to anticipate what major events might take place and how they could impact the organization's ability to meet the objectives. Make three cases: the best case, the most-likely case, and the worst case. Attempt to determine what the outcomes might be for each of these and list the options available for handling each condition. It is very much like driving a car in a defensive posture. When you approach a traffic situation that might cause problems you mentally review many what-if types of events and you decide how you will manage them should they arise. You don't wait until the problem occurs to think of a quick solution, which is emotional and often wrong.

Strategic planning often neglects to address the truly critical issues, opportunities, and problems of the organization. Therefore it does not force everyone to think creatively about new products and services. The end result often is the development of the plan rather than establishing a program to deal with future events.

Analyzing the Market

To be effective, strategy formulation must include an in-depth analysis of your competitors. This is most important for it helps you to understand what moves they might make in the future and how they might react to any moves that you make. Doing a competitor-analysis study is a lot of hard work for much data must be collected and a large part of it is not readily available. You should begin by asking many questions. Who are the dominant forces in the market? What share of the market do they have? How do they increase their share of the market? Are there only a few big competitors, or are there many small firms? Is entrance into the market easy or difficult? Do the competitors offer a broad line of products and services? What are their bread-and-butter products? How extensive and effective are their research-and-development programs? Are they the leading edge in technological development? How large a sales-and-service force do they have? How do they market their products? Getting answers to these questions is not easy; however, answers are available in newspaper articles, trade publications, press releases, annual reports, and comments made by their marketing force. In some firms the accounting and financial staffs do the analytical work whereas in others a special type of commercial analysis staff has the responsibility.

Once information about competitors is at hand the analysis gives particular attention to these three areas.

Objectives

Compare current objectives with future objectives for it might indicate a change in their strategy. This could help you to anticipate their entering new markets or introducing new products. Also, you might get signals of changes in their pricing policies. Should you be planning some strategic changes, knowing what you do about competitors will help you to be better prepared to anticipate their reactions and manage them when they come. The future objectives might indicate a change in their financial needs and show to what degree they are willing to take risk. Try to identify their major aims. Are they trying to capture the specialty markets? Do they want to be known as the leader in technological development? Are they trying to break into foreign markets? If so, why, when, and how? Are their marketing policies and programs, organizational structure, and managerial controls changing?

Beliefs and Values

Every organization, including your own, sees itself fulfilling certain roles. Like an individual, in order for an organization to achieve its objectives it must have a self-image equal to the role. How the competitor acts and reacts is often based on the assumptions it makes about itself (self-image) and assumptions about other firms, including yours, in the industry. Do competitors see themselves as the price leaders in the industry? If so, they might induce price wars to fulfill that role.

Much can be learned about the positions of competitors and their role in the industry through their actions and public statements. Comments from their marketing force will indicate how they see their role in the marketplace: for example, high-quality products and service, low-cost producer with low prices and special discounts, leading edge in technology, and aggressive moves to increase market penetration.

You can examine the past practices of competitors for clues as to where and how they manufacture, the kind and amount of research and development that is performed, and marketing-and-distribution approaches. Over the years, these practices generally remain unchanged. For example, one major food chain has their vendors deliver directly to each store whereas their major competitor has their vendors deliver to central warehouses from which they deliver to their own stores. Both have stayed with their respective approach for a great many years.

Financial Health

An analysis of each competitor's strengths and weaknesses, their future programs for growth, and their capabilities in the industry are important areas in doing a systematic analysis of competitors. However, the financial health of the firm will be the catalyst and driving force that will eventually determine their direction and rate of growth. A very-detailed study is required to do a good financial analysis. The competitor's sales by product must be forecasted, revenues projected, expenses (identified by type) deducted, and net profits determined. Look carefully at planned investments and how the funds will be acquired. Study the sources and uses of funds as shown in the annual report; if it is not there, then construct it from the balance sheet. This will permit you to construct a pro-forma income statement and a pro-forma balance sheet to analyze the financial characteristics of the company. Look at cash flow and the major business ratios that show liquidity, indebtedness, activity, and profitability for each competitor.

Growth through Expansion

An important element in strategic planning is the generation of growth through internal and external expansion. Internal expansion is an enlargement of your firms's facilities and operations. Often you need to do this because demand is increasing for your products and services. Also, you might be introducing new products and entering new markets or expanding current one. Internal expansion is financed using retained earnings as the source of funds. External expansion, financed through debt or equity, is going outside of the company and making an acquisition or merger of another established company or buying the rights to products. If you buy the company, everything is in place: manufacturing, marketing, servicing, and even the customer base. With this approach you begin to recover your investment immediately. If you buy the rights to old products you benefit from their established reputation, and with new products you avoid costly development efforts. However, it is now your marketing force that is responsible for selling the product. That means they should understand it very well.

When you make an acquisition or merger with another company you gain more than just rights to products. You acquire the patents and trademarks and all of the technology, manufacturing, and marketing that accompanies them. You own all of the established plants, laboratories, distribution systems, and service centers. Also, immediate financial gains are often available through tax-loss carry-over situations, investment-tax-credit conditions, strong cash positions, and an established earnings base. It can be seen from all of these benefits that buying an existing company, given a reasonable price, is the fastest way to grow your business.

If your strategy calls for external expansion, then should you use acquisition or mergers? It all depends on your goals. If you want the acquired company to remain a separate entity, but become a part of your company and operate as either a division or subsidiary, it would be an acquisition. You would buy the company with cash or some of your stock and you would own their stock. Often there can be consolidation of assets for tax advantages. This acquisition approach should be considered in strategic planning, particularly when you want to gain fast entry into a market with new and usually high-technology types of products.

If you want the assets and liabilities of the other company to become part of your company it is a merger. Usually you buy the company through an exchange of stock. The company that has then merged with your company no longer exists as a business entity. The changes brought about by a merger can be extensive within the organization so their impact on the strategic plan should be watched carefully. Often there are tax advantages to a merger but in many cases the merger is made in order to become more efficient and more competitive. There are different forms of mergers. Horizontal mergers are a form of expansion in which a company takes over a similar company. For example, one retail-chain company merges with another retail-chain company. Vertical mergers are a form of expansion in which a company takes over another company that either supplies it with materials to be used in production or takes the production as a semiprocessed product and continues processing it to produce a finished product. For example, a company manufacturing aluminum wrappings mergers with a company that supplies aluminum. Conglomerate mergers are ones in which a company in one industry takes on a company in another unrelated industry. For example, a chemical company dominates an automobile company through the holding of its stock.

The success of external expansion rests upon many factors. Future earnings must be high enough to meet interest payments on debts and dividend payments on stock if either or both are used for financing. Also, the company that you acquire must fit into your strategic plan if you expect to accomplish your intended objectives. With many conglomerate mergers in the past this was missing and losses ran high. Also, the company that is acquired must provide a high return on investment and contribute substantially to the growth of the business.

Most companies rely on both internal and external expansion. The direction taken can have a significant impact on the future of the company. Therefore include in the strategic plan the direction and extent of expansion.

Multinational Corporations

Formulating a strategy for doing business in a foreign country is difficult, but even more complex is the strategic-planning process. Strategic planning requires both short-term and long-term forecasting. This is not easy for foreign markets because of political, cultural, social, environmental, and economic factors. Multinational corporations take great risk whenever they invest in countries where there is much political and economic instability. However, the opportunities are profitable for the economic needs are great.

The business climate is changing in many developing countries for in the past the complaints were that the multinationals were exploiting them; the complaint now is that they are being neglected. They want to apply technological developments and feel that not enough help is being given to them. However, in many of the lesser-developed countries they have only a small need for it; as technological advances move so swiftly they fall further behind the developed nations. What are multinational corporations to do about this when they are building their strategic plans? Most multinationals invest large amounts of monies in foreign countries in order to establish a market or increase their share of the existing market. Look for applications in business where technology can be applied and through educational programs help with the implementation. I am familiar with one country where this was done at the highest government levels. Selected government employees spent one year in classrooms learning and applying the most-advanced tools in computer technology. Now not only will the government of that country be more effective, but it will be able to encourage and lead companies to become more efficient. Often multinational corporations enter a foreign market because the manufacturing costs are lower due to lower labor costs. However, this is rarely as attractive a reason to enter as the potential for profits in the markets.

Multinationals face problems other than the use of technology in foreign countries. There is often a concern that the multinational corporations are avoiding currency-and-exchange regulations, pricing controls, and tax laws. In a rapidly changing world that is full of risk, there are two important objectives in strategic planning. First, produce the highest rate of profit possible for the firm. Second, assess and manage risk wisely. The risk is the potential political turmoil versus what you perceive as an opportunity to make profits. Your strategic plan should provide a mechanism to measure and evaluate political risk. It might be that you assign some of your own people to closely monitor events in the country, or you might use foreign-affairs consultants and/or sophisticated computerized models.

Try to avoid the types of problems that some multinational corporations have encountered because of their practices. Don't engage in the practice of manipulating transfer prices between the parent corporation and subsidiaries in an attempt to avoid taxes on the foreign investments. Also, try to fill corporate-management positions with local employees rather than expatriates. Those who are native to the country can speak the language, can negotiate better with the unions, know how to handle relations with local governments, and have the cultural insights needed to understand politics, law, and the business climate. Fluency in the language of the country is important today for many foreign countries require that only their language be used for all correspondence. This also applies to contracts and all forms of sales literature as well as product instructions and labels.

Using local employees to fill management positions has many other advantages. It is very expensive today to send employees overseas to work because of high living costs and tax disincentives. Also, labor relations can be difficult for expatriates to handle in some countries. Labor disputes are often not handled conventionally. In some countries dissident employees have taken management hostage and held the plants instead of engaging in collective bargaining to gain wage increases.

Some of the things that you should consider in formulating a strategy for doing business in a foreign country are as follows. First, realize that each foreign country has special situations, customs, and culture. Second, recently the approaches to marketing in foreign countries have taken many sophisticated forms and are becoming increasingly more competitive. Third, be prepared to deal with governments who might very closely monitor your contracts, projects, and profits. Fourth, in some countries the best way to gain access to the markets is through joint ventures with local partners. Select them carefully. Fifth, it is advisable to provide adequate insurance on the company's assets and earnings. Sixth, as the people employed are of different nationalities you must establish effective channels of communication between headquarters and the local overseas offices. Seven, recognize that there will be many problems that will arise from factors that you have no control over: for example, foreign taxation, currency fluctuations and exchange controls, and inflation.

It is one thing to see and understand the complex problems that face a multinational corporation in doing business overseas; however, it is another to formulate an effective strategic plan to handle future issues and events. Reach for the highest rate of profit possible but only conduct business in those areas where you can live with the risk.

The Financial-Service Industry

This industry today is going through traumatic changes. A host of companies are moving into the industry and are getting very involved in providing many forms of financial service. Why have so many companies made the financial services a major part of their strategic plan? There are several reasons. First, it is a business that can be entered at a very low cost. Second, the firm's profits can be greatly increased because of the commissions and the gains from the large float that these funds generate.

Companies enter this business through either the internal expansion route or the external expansion methods that have been discussed in this chapter. Some will be successful; others will fail. Some of those that fail will do so because it is a new business that they will not understand. Also, because the organizational structure and management philosophy is quite different it will not be easy to integrate an acquired firm into the acquiring company. Not having established sound objectives and goals or poor strategic planning will also be a cause for failure. The financial service industry has for years been going through great structural changes. The trend has been toward offering a wide selection of financial services. In the past some of these financial services were provided by only a small number of firms. Today, however, an increasing number of firms are moving into some form of financial service. For example, mutual-fund accounts offered by brokerage houses are now offered through financial institutions. Almost every type of financial institution, insurance company, large corporation, brokerage firm, or pension fund is aggressively entering the financial-services arena. They are offering many types of services; some are offering more than they can handle. Competition is intense and growing at an unbelievable pace. Only the strongest will survive; many of the new entrants as well as some of the established institutions will fail.

Those who are now in the financial-service industry or are about to enter it will need to be very good at both short-term and long-term forecasting. In addition, they must effectively build these forecasts into a sound strategic plan. Such a plan will need to provide the mechanism to offer a broad type of financial services. The trends show increasing uniformity in the industry as to what is offered and how it is offered to corporations as well as individuals. The many mergers and acquisitions that are sweeping the industry furthers the trend in the uniformity of services. Insurance companies and large corporations are merging with or acquiring brokerage firms. One large brokerage house recently acquired a financial firm and entered the field of mortgage banking. The traditional role of banks, insurance companies, and credit organizations will soon give way to companies that provide all of the financial services needed both by corporations and individuals.

The financial-service firms not only offer uniform programs but they are expanding the scope of their offerings rapidly. The offerings are so extensive that a great many financial consultants are busy providing professional guidance in selecting the services. Many of the financial-service firms have not only a great business at home, but they are moving aggressively into foreign countries. Customized packages are prepared to meet the needs of any market.

The efforts of the federal government to deregulate the financial industry has increased competition between the commercial banks and the savings-and-loan associations. It intensifies even more now as they move into new markets such as money-market funds. Almost every financial-service firm is trying to penetrate the markets of others. Has strategy been carefully formulated or is it a follow-the-crowd approach?

To make the scene even more exciting many foreign banks have been moving into the home markets of U.S. financial-service firms. It is a strong thrust; in just the past few years, they have doubled their share of the market. How have they been able to do this? In part it is because they have a lower cost of capital because they do not have to comply with the reserve requirements of the Federal Reserve as do the U.S. financial institutions.

Perhaps the strongest competition to the financial-service industry will come from the large corporations. Some already have professional staffs that handle investments. They have lots of capital and close contact with other firms and individuals. Many already are experts in handling pension funds, making acquisitions, and raising funds through commercial and private instruments.

In formulating strategy for the financial-service industry some basic structural changes must be recognized. First, the trend toward uniformity in offerings and approach will accelerate, for example, insurance companies, commercial banks, large corporations, pension funds, brokerage firms, and savings-and-loan associations will continue to offer a wide scope of financial services. Second, strategic planning will provide the mechanism for greater product differentiation in the offerings. Third, there will be an ever-increasing number of new firms entering the business. Fourth, competition will increase at a fever pitch. The service that is offered must be carefully chosen or costs will rise and profits fall. Fifth, deregulation of the industry will continue. It might only be a matter of time before the restrictions that now separate commercial banks from brokerage firms will be gone.

In addition to allowing for the structural changes taking place in the financial-service industry, strategic planning must also look at the technological changes. The problems of money management have given rise to the electronic transfer of funds. This permits monies to be moved quickly by computers; it is increasingly being used for the depositing of pay checks to banks, in automatic-teller machines, and to improve the flexibility of transfering funds between institutions and accounts. Financial-service firms that are not including the new high-technology methods in their strategic planning will lose market shares.

Strategic planning must consider the structural and technological changes as discussed earlier. However, there is a third area of change: That is the future markets for financial services. Just as foreign banks have moved into the U.S. markets, many major U.S. banks have expanded their overseas operations. The strategic plan must provide the mechanism for integrating the firm's financial services into a worldwide system.

The financial-service industry must keep pace on the domestic markets to increase profits because of the large corporations with their in-house financial services. They will intensify the pressures that the financial-service industry will face because they will become more aggressive in their head-on attacks to secure a major position in a very profitable field of business. The opening statement of this section is quite true, that is, "This industry today is going through traumatic changes." Where then do the smaller financial-service firms go for future business? They must turn to the small- or medium-size corporations or individuals.

The importance of strategy formulation is perhaps more vital to the survival and success of the financial-service industry than any other industry.

With changing organization structures, changing markets, rapid technological changes requiring large amounts of capital, multitudes of new offerings, increasing competitive pressures from foreign banks and large corporations at home, economic changes, the demise of fixed-rate mortgages and the rapid acceptance of variable rates in mortgage lending and elsewhere, and changing federal and state regulations the only possibility for the financial-service industry is to improve return on investment and increase innovation and flexibility. Each firm in the financial-service industry must know when, where, and how to compete. Small firms cannot go head-to-head with a vast array of services in broad markets that are the domain of the larger firms. The small firm will need to be selective in their approach. When competition rises and profits fall, even the larger firms will need to become selective if they hope to increase profits. Those in the financial-service industry who do their homework well will survive and prosper. Those who do not will become the victims of mergers and acquisitions. This is now only a small wave, but it will get very large.

If you are in the financial-service industry the years ahead are ones of great challenge. Frustrations? Yes! Problems? Yes! Risk of failure? Yes! However, the greatest opportunities in the industry lie ahead for both small and large firms. Big firms will grow larger through mergers and acquisitions. Small firms can be very profitable if they specialize, selectively seek new markets, and keep on top of the technological developments.

Your corporate strategy will require a monthly review of the strategic plan. The strategic plan relates long-term changes to short-term activities. It is doubtful that you need to change your objectives and goals, but you might want to realign your strategic plan.

Diversification

A company must continuously change and grow if it is to stay in the industry. Very few firms can stay with only their original products and services and still improve profits and grow. Many firms grow first by developing new products; second, by developing and entering new markets; and third, by increasing their market share by a deeper penetration in the present market. The fourth approach is by diversification. This can be more difficult than the other three approaches. Problems come because the company is usually entering product lines and markets where it has no experience and perhaps only a little knowledge. Current strategic plan is based on a long-term marketing strategy for established products. The characteristics and performance levels of the products are known in addition to who the customers are and what their needs are. However, diversification brings unfamiliar products and new markets. New marketing skills might be required and perhaps new manufacturing techniques must be learned. Sometimes new manufacturing facilities must be built and new distribution systems established. Diversification usually requires large amounts of capital and results in significant changes to the financial posture and organizational structure of the firm. Most firms grow by using one or a combination of the four approaches. They provide for this in strategic planning.

Why should a company diversify? With most firms it is essential to future growth. If you cannot develop new products and new markets and it is difficult to increase profits with your current products and markets, diversification should be considered. This is often done for a combination of reasons. If you have not spread your risks or are failing to keep up with technological developments you might look for other product lines or markets. Sometimes diversification is used as a means to invest earnings if the new direction means a better return on investment than could be achieved with the current products. Diversification is often used even when the preceding reasons do not apply and when growth appears good for the firm. This usually occurs in high-growth industries. The firm is not growing as fast as the industry, even though their growth is good; therefore corporate management looks for activities outside the scope of the current business in order to improve profits. If the diversification still lies within the character of the industry the risk can be managed. However, if the firm diversifies into an unfamiliar business to push up the growth curve many problems could arise.

Diversification can also protect the company from unforeseeable events. Most of business planning is directed at the foreseeable events; however, an unforeseeable one like a major technological breakthrough in your industry might be devastating to your firm. As you cannot plan for the unknown you might put the mechanism in the strategic plan to move into broader product lines, improve your technological base, or enter a new growth business. For example, the silk industry was thriving until synthetic fibers appeared; within a short time it died and with it many cities. In fact, one city (Paterson, New Jersey) had so many silk mills it was known as "silk city" and it took many years to recover.

Economic change and technological developments move at such a rapid pace that few firms, including large ones, can afford not to consider diversification. This applies even when the future looks good for the company. There are many examples where the nature of a business turned quickly: that is, railroad passenger and freight business was lost to the airlines and trucking, and the radio and movie industry was given a back seat to television. Most successful large companies today provide far different products and services than they did in their early days. In many cases only the company name is the same.

There are three primary purposes for diversification: first, to increase profits and improve the growth curve of the company. Often a company will set an annual rate of growth as a target. When this target is missed, one course of action is to diversify the nature of the business. The second is to improve the stability of the firm. Diversification might help to increase revenues even when the business is good and it could help to hold the revenues up when business turns bad. Third, it might make the firm more flexible and better able to handle future unforeseeable events. A carefully planned merger or acquisition might give you a better technological base or advanced products. Diversification should follow the long-term objectives of the firm. It should also maintain the character of the company, that is, if the firm has a reputation for quality, then don't put its name on shoddy products. Diversification is not an end in itself; it must contribute to profits of the firm. Although many business ratios can be applied to measure the profit potential of a diversification, the most-important test is the return on investment. In its simple form this is a ratio between the capital invested in producing the earnings and the net earnings after tax.

The process of diversification generally follows these steps. First, search out areas for diversification that fit in with the long-term objectives as defined in strategic planning. Second, identify what opportunities are present and then evaluate how and when they will improve profitability and growth of the company. Third, propose the plan for diversification to higher-level management for approval and authorization of funds. Fourth, once the diversification has been approved it must be worked into a revised strategic plan.

**Strategic Planning for an Information-
Management System**

In some firms there is inadequate strategic planning for the development
and implementation of an information-management system. The ever-
increasing number of crises that arise week after week because of incomplete or inaccurate data often forces management to react by directing
that small projects be done quickly to modify and improve the present procedures. These projects are usually not very effective in the long-run and
much valuable time and important resources are wasted. The user executives become more frustrated and dissatisfied and eventually force a formal plan for managing information to be built. Because developing a good
strategic plan is difficult, most managers' first impulse is to allocate
resources and design the information-management system by projecting a
growth trend based on the firm's past expenditures for computer services.
Avoid doing this because it is a superficial approach that ignores the real
issues of what are the users information requirements. This approach also
frequently lacks a clear definition of the objectives of the information-
management-system organization. Also it often omits policy statements
regarding the allocation of resources to the information-management
system.

When formal strategic planning for an information management system
does not involve the users, the program developed often focuses only on the
needs of the information-management-system organization or their perceived needs of the users. The information-management system that is then
developed becomes an extension of the current one and new creative computer applications are not identified or implemented. The firm does not
benefit from the strategic plan because it serves only the needs of the
information-management-system organization. Even when a new informa-
tion-managment system is proposed if the users have not been involved in
its design and development they will not appreciate its benefits, nor will they
be committed to making it a success. Don't discount the ability and value of
the users to help in planning a long-range information-management system.
Go directly to the user executives and interview them to define their business
needs and information requirements. While you are getting their insights
and involvement, you can request commitments for the resources required.
It is important to document all of these discussions for often new creative
computer applications surface and data will be needed later to justify them.
High-level management will need to appreciate the benefits to the firm and
realize how the organizational goals will be accomplished. Without a clear,
concisely documented package you cannot expect corporate management to
fund the development of a new information-management system. All too
often inadequate planning produces an information-management system

that does not yield the higher-quality information needed to help high-level management make more effective decisions. Weak implementation often results from a long-range plan that is cluttered with far too many functions. Frequently these functions are not even interrelated. Often they cannot be integrated into the current information-management system, and to implement them as a new information-management system can require many frustrating years of effort. During this period of implementation few benefits are realized by the company and the firm's competitive posture in the industry might suffer.

It is the chief executive officer who defines the missions of the firm and it is also his or her responsibility to establish the mission of the information-management-system organization. The responsibility rests at this high level because the computer is vital to the growth of the business. The strategies and objectives for the information-management system must be carefully defined. The system must provide all of the required data needed to support the strategic objectives of the firm. Include in the strategic planning for the information management system the policies covering personnel and equipment needs, funding, and functions performed by the information-management-system organization. The strategic planning is an interactive process for corporate management must continuously define the changing information needs of the firm and assess the capability of the information management system to meet them. Once the objectives have been established for the information-management-system organization the funding needs can be determined. Management should base the information-management-system budget on what is required for the various services provided by the system and not on whatever charges the users will pay.

The strategic plan for the information-management system provides resources for both short-run and long-run projects. Therefore all potential projects must be identified and given a priority ranking by management. The method of ranking follows the guidelines as provided in the formal strategic plan for the information-management system. Resources are then allocated accordingly to meet the firm's strategic-information-management-system objectives. Some of the projects will be the development of new information-management applications whereas others will be modifications and improvements to existing applications. It is, however, the primary function of the information-management-system organization to develop new computer applications that will benefit the entire firm and not just the functional groups only.

When necessary, you can build creditability quickly through short-term projects. This might be important in order to retain high-level management's involvement. Often the small information-management-system projects can be completed quickly, thus providing the users with immediate benefits. However, these should not be given priority over the larger projects when the latter are vital to increasing the firm's competitive posture or helps the firm to meet the information requirements of federal, state or regulatory agencies. Also the information-management-system strategic plan should consider those new projects that arise because of corporate management's strategic need for more accurate decision-making information. In the formulation of the strategic plan for the information-management system it is important that it be driven by the needs of corporate management, the user executive community, and the information-management-system organization. It is the firm's strategic objectives that determines what new technology is to be implemented in the design of the information-management system. Information-management systems often fail because the reverse approach is used and starting with new technology a complex information-management system is designed around it which is not required and cannot provide significant benefits to the firm.

It is the responsibility of the user executives to define their information requirements to top management so that the strategic plan meets the functional groups objectives as well as the firm's current needs and long-range goals. The inputs required to formulate strategy for an effective information-management-system strategic plan must therefore flow upward from the user executives in the functional groups as well as downward from corporate management to the information-management-system organization.

Developing new applications for the information-management system usually requires a large commitment of resources; hence these projects should be subject to the approval of the corporate-computer-systems steering committee. When formulating strategy to implement the information-management system, include as part of the strategic plan the establishment of a corporate computer systems steering committee. The chief executive officer has the responsibility for the establishment of this committee for it can be an effective decision-making group in the successful development and implementation of the right computer applications. The chief executive officer is responsible for the development of the corporate strategic plan. This is controlled through the corporate-computer-systems steering chief which under his or her authority approves and prioritizes the new computer applications required to meet the strategic-statement objectives.

Strategic planning for an information-management system must provide for assessing at given periods the efficiency and effectiveness of the system. Therefore develop measurement tools for the functions performed by the information-management-system organization. One point of measurement would be the completeness and relevancy of the documented objectives of the information-management system and their attainment. Evaluate the clarity of the policy statements of the information-management-system organization and how they are communicated in the firm. Assess the degree of accuracy with which the costs and benefits of new computer applications under the information-management system are estimated. Define the elements of risks confronted in the information-management-system projects and determine how well they were managed. Provide in the strategic plan a procedure for doing a postinstallation study to compare the actual with the estimated costs and benefits of the information-management-system projects. Be sure that the strategic plan for the information-management system is targeted at the most profitable utilization of the computer resources for the firm rather than the information-managment-system organization. In some firms the strategic-planning efforts have focused on only the needs of the information-management-system organization. The systems often fail because they provide little assistance to corporate management in making more effective decisions.

A Corporate Strategy for New Ventures

A new venture is often quite loosely organized. It can take two forms: either an entrepreneurial venture or a new business sponsored by a compnay. New ventures are important for the growth of the firm as most companies—either large or small—must keep searching for new opportunities as changing technology or changing tastes cause some products to become obsolete.

When the entrepreneurial type of new ventures fail it is usually due to lack of capital and experience or poor management decisions. You would expect that the new ventures sponsored by corporations would have a higher survival rate, but for all of the resources that they devote to the new product or service they do not do any better. In fact, in the long-run those entrepreneurial-type new ventures that do survive are generally more profitable than the corporate new ventures. Both forms of new ventures lose money in the first few years and on average require more than five years to become profitable. It generally takes more than ten years before a new venture reaches the profit levels of a mature business. Why is it that many major firms lose large amounts of monies on their corporate ventures and are not as successful as entrepreneurial ventures in their efforts to develop a new business? Two reasons that stand out above all others. The first is the lack of corporate management's long-term commitment to the business. This often first surfaces in the strategy formulation where the mission statements do not clearly define the objectives. The risk of failure is increased more with an inadequate commitment of capital investments and the lack of measurable goals to monitor performance. As the level of performance is generally low during the first few start-up years, this must be expected and the new venture should not be deprived too early of its financial resources. The growth of most firms often rests on how succesful they are in developing new businesses. You might be able to conduct a merger or acquisition to get through another firm new products or services but most companies form their own corporate new ventures.

In any new venture there is risk due to uncertainty. Reasonable targets must be established and when they are missed you must quickly take corrective action. An individual running an entrepreneurial venture can easily do this; however, large firms often move slowly through a tangle of bureaucratic procedures and perform an extensive rational analysis of the causes and effects of the problems. The asset to the firm of being able to do in-depth analysis slows down the decision-making process and it becomes a liability that dooms the new venture. Strategic planning for a new venture requires guidelines to facilitate the taking of prompt and firm measures when situations arise. The strategic plan must provide for management by objectives whereby goals are set and progress measured. It also must provide for management by consensus whereby strategy conferences can bubble ideas about the new venture up to corporate management.

Most executives in large corporations do not like uncertainty. There is predictability and security in having a well-entrenched position in the market with successful products and services, and efficient distribution system, and effective controls. The corporate environment through its institutionalized approach often constrains managerial aggressiveness and the quick decisions required to manage corporate new ventures. This is the second reason why the entrepreneurial ventures often outperform the corporate ventures.

There are some things to think about that can help to lower the risk of failure and improve the performance of corporate new ventures. First, it is going to take time to generate success with any new product or service. You should be prepared in the strategic plan to allow at least five years of poor earnings; during this period the activities must be adequately funded. Second, if you are getting into the new venture through a merger or acquisition you must analyze the other business very carefully. Are the products or services ones that your firm can understand and manage? Do they fit within the long-term strategic plan of your corporation? Often on the whim of an officer a company will embark on a new venture that will contribute very little to the growth objectives of the firm. Third, put the new venture under the control and authority of an entrepreneurial type manager. He or she must be willing to take risks, make quick and often-intuitive decisions, be creative, and a hard worker. Such a person might need to be brought in from outside of the firm as even an offer of high compensation is generally insufficient inducement to entice one of your present managers into this high-risk job. This entrepreneur must be highly self-motivated. The incentives must be quite different from those you apply to other types of managers. Provide for these incentives within the guideline of the strategic plan. Fourth, when possible keep the cost of failure as low as possible. There is always the tendency to reach too far for fast growth. Without skilled people experienced in the business, committing ever-larger amounts of money to the new venture may not guarantee its success. In the strategic plan define critical points in the development of the new venture where you can measure the results and then invest more funds if needed. Fifth, when support and commitment is required from user executives, corporate management, governmental agencies, and customers be sure that it is secure. Look for creative ways to develop the appropriate environment and structure within the firm for the new business. This requires a rigorous analysis of each proposed venture.

How are you going to manage the new business? For example, will it be a licensing company and sell rights or franchises? Should it be spun off as a separate company? Will you make it a division of the company? It is not uncommon to find that as the new venture grows a different structural form might be required. You might start it as a division and then spin it off later as a separate company. Also, the form of reporting might change with growth and the responsibility might be to corporate management or to a group of senior officers rather than a division manager.

Most new ventures start off on a small scale. As most large companies do things on a large scale they require management to use different styles and managerial philosophies when they move into a new small business. This must be defined in the strategy-formulation process and covered in the strategic plan. This change in managerial approach is not easy for most firms for much of their success is due to the largeness of scale by which they do their marketing, distribution, and production. The benefits have come from the economies of scale in these activities and now smallness must be made efficient and effective. As a solution some large corporations establish special organization groups to function like the small-venture business. This requires in the strategic plan a different approach to measurements and controls. Each company must formulate its own strategy in how it will manage new ventures. Some companies have been very successful in expanding their internal based diversification into new-venture businesses. They use the strategic approach of developing new products and services within the organization and growing them into small companies. For this to be successful, the strategic plan must provide an environment that encourages and rewards innovation and technological development. Other companies have had good success by looking outside of the firm for new businesses. They have looked for products and services that complemented their own and with synergistic results accelerated the growth of the entire corporation.

8

Managing Information

There is a Japanese proverb that goes "A frog in a well cannot describe the broad sea." This proverb warns against allowing the mind to be cloistered. So it is when we manage information for there is a tendency to limit technological developments to improving current methods for handling records, files, and large data bases rather than creatively looking for new applications.

Creativity in Managing Information

We are all familiar with the procedures used in many hotels for handling wake-up calls. You dial the front desk and leave your room number and wake-up time with the operator, who usually manually registers it and then calls you at the proper time. This is only a small piece of information to manage for each person but in a large 1,700-room hotel this collectively is a lot of data to handle on a recurring daily basis. On my most recent visit to Japan, I was impressed with how the modern hotels have creatively computerized the managing of this information. At no point in the process is any personal interaction required; rather, the computer automatically handles the transactions. For example, the wake-up-call service is computerized by dialing the number 71. You give the time based on the 24-hour clock; for example, 71-0820 for 8:20 A.M., 71-2315 for 11:15 P.M. To reset you dial 71 + your desired time; if you wish to cancel you dial 79. The computer registers your instructions and as soon as you complete the dialing a recorded message on the telephone says in Japanese and English "Your wake up call has been registered." At the correct time the telephone is activated by the computer and you receive the following call in Japanese and English: "Good morning. It is time to get up. This is a prerecorded message." This pleasant and effective procedure for managing information demonstrates uncloistered thinking.

Information-Management-System Design

You cannot successfully manage information without a system whose design addresses three levels: that is, strategic, tactical, and operational (see figure 8-1).

Strategic level: Planning and Control
- Corporate Strategic Planning
- Systems Design
- Information-Management-System Planning and Control

Tactical level: Planning
- Management
- Development
- Services
- Resources

Operational Level: Control and Operations
- Control: Development and Maintenance
             Services and Resources
- Operation: Development and Maintenance
               Services and Resources

Figure 8-1. Information-Management-System Design

You design an information-management system from the top down and begin with the strategic level. At this level the strategic plan is developed along with the required controls; these are passed down to the tactical level. Management at the tactical level produces a project and a service plan, which are passed down to the operational level. Operational-level management translates these in programs and schedules that can be both measured and controlled. Let's now look at each level in greater detail.

Strategic Level: Planning and Control

Management's objective at this level is to develop the information-management-system strategic plan. The process begins by defining the missions of the firm.

Corporate Strategic Planning. In the first step—corporate strategic planning—you begin the strategic planning for the firm by defining the mission of the information-management system. These are published along with a statement of policies for controlling the strategic plan. Now you define the processes required for conducting the firm's business and then describe the information requirements, how the data flows, and how it must be managed. With the information needs identified the structure of the information-management system can be defined and designed.

Systems Design. The second step—systems design—starts with an analysis of the nature and characteristics of the applications and their required data that accomplish the mission statements. Define the input data and its output forms. Examine how the data will be processed, the technological structure of the required system, and how it will interface with current systems. Seldom do you have the time and resources needed to develop and implement a completely new information-management system. Often, information requirements are defined only when a need arises because of problems and/or changes due to the growth or nature of the business. Therefore information-management systems usually develop in an evolutionary fashion. In this process applications and data must be carefully structured so that they can easily be integrated into the framework of the existing information-management strategic plan.

Information-Management-System Planning and Control. It is in the third step—information-management-system planning and control—where you can construct the strategic plan which is the cornerstone of the information-management-system structure. This plan addresses how the system will be implemented so that the corporate mission statements are accomplished through the strategic objectives of the functional groups. Management approves these strategic objectives and prioritizes them. Establish how the strategic plan will be controlled and pass it down to the tactical level for planning.

Tactical Level: Planning

The purpose of management at this level is to address four areas of planning necessary to facilitate the implementation of the information-management-system strategic plan at the operational level. These four areas are management, development, services, and resources.

Management. In the first area, management planning defines the information needs of the organization as related to the strategic objectives passed down from management. A methodology is established and standards and procedures for implementing the information-management-system projects are defined and published. Included therein are the measurements needed for monitoring the progress of the projects. A plan for assigning resources and responsibilities is prepared for the projects that support the information-management system. Estimates of costs and benefits are made, work schedules are developed, and management's approval is obtained. In order to track performance and progress, a procedure must be announced for collecting and summarizing data for each project. Comparisons of accomplishments against expected results are made and reported to strategic-level management.

Development. The second area is development planning, which identifies the applications required and defines the data flow. A tactical application plan is prepared or the current one is updated. Also, a tactical-data plan and tactical-system plan is developed for managing the information. The latter plan addresses the equipment and programming needs as well as the resources and facilities required. Now that these three tactical plans have been developed you can prepare the tactical-project plan. The functions covered in the tactical-project plan are vital to the success of the information-management system for they focus on auditability, recoverability, accountability, security, and service levels. The specifications of the projects are defined, resources allocated, and measurements and controls published. When justified, the funds are approved and priority schedules established.

Services. The third area addresses services; planning here relates the strategic plan, tactical information-management-systems plan, and tactical project plan to the service-level needs of the organization. Many plans and service agreements are developed or updated. One of your first steps is to develop a marketing-service plan. Define the markets and the levels of service required and provided. Now that these have been identified and related to the functional groups, it is possible to forecast data volumes and price the services sponsored by the information-management system. Now develop and negotiate service-level agreements and promote the services provided by the system. Consolidate the many service agreements in a total service plan that satisfies all of the firm's information requirements. To provide adequate support to the program you should develop a recovery plan. Unexpected problems should not degrade the performance of the system for even the shortest period of time. To effectively handle these situations examine the environment in which you run the information-management system. Try to anticipate what problems might arise and build a contingency plan. Test this plan to be sure that it will work when it is needed. Monitor the effectiveness of the recovery programs and report the results to management at the strategic level. Also, to support your total service plan it is necessary to do security planning: Define the security operating environment, identify the security requirements, and develop a total security program. Finally, as part of services planning define the auditing requirements of the information-management system, and establish effective auditing procedures.

Resources. The fourth area is the planning of resources. The project plan and the total service plan is used to quantify the need for monies, people, equipment, and facilities. Information requirements and service requirements can be used to forecast volumes and load demand on the equipment. Relate this to capacity and document any variances. Also, the information derived from the project plan and total service plan permits you to determine staffing and assess skills in the organization. Determine the number of people required to support the total service plan and compare this to your table of organization. Hiring and training must be planned and not performed impulsively and reactively. When the previous information has been developed you can determine the financial needs of the organization and develop the budgets required to implement the information-management system. Budgets are the result of continued refinements and analysis which are predicated on given assumptions and certain conditions. Choose the most-likely budget and document it for each functional group. This is an interactive process in which project planning, capacity planning, and skills planning provides feedback to the budgeting process. Also each step in resources planning provides feedback to the other three planning areas: that is, management, development, and services.

The outputs of the four planning areas—that is, management, development, services, and resources form the basis for the tactical plan. This plan now passes the corporate missions and objectives established under strategic planning to the operational level where policies and procedures are developed to implement the programs. Tactical-level management approves and publishes the information-management-system tactical plan. The implementation of this plan at the operational level is monitored and adjustments made as required.

Operational Level: Control and Operations

The operational level in the information-management-system design consists of two areas; both are based on the project plan and the service plan that are produced in the tactical level. One is the area of control, and the other is operation.

Control: Development and Maintenance. In the operational area look at the controls required for development and maintenance projects. The first step is to make an assignment of the project with responsibility and appropriate authority vested in one person. For this, select a project leader who will get the users involved in the design of the information-management system. Also, obtain the full support and commitment of user management. Now identify all tasks to be performed and schedule the work; all deliverables from the system are to be identified and the date when they will be ready. Define how they will be tested. To more effectively control resources and performance divide a large project into smaller component modules. This also estimates costs and benefits easier. The detail project plan is passed up to management at the tactical level for review and monitoring.

Once the project is underway, operational-level management must follow its progress and adjust the plan when required. Check points are established where the results are reviewed and management is advised of the status. Define all unresolved problems and examine all alternative solutions. At critical decision points in the development of the project, review the make/buy decision that was made earlier. Perhaps a vendor's package now looks more attractive or the costs of modifying it might be lower than when it was first evaluated.

It is important that you retain control over the project requirements. All requests for changes must be written and approved by management. Evaluate what impact the requirement changes will have on the system and either accept or reject the request. If the changes are accepted, then publish a revised project plan. If rejected, let this be known to avoid unnecessary efforts. When the project is finalized, document the results and compare it to the project plan, service plan, and tactical plan. Explain any variances to tactical-level management.

Control: Services and Resources. In the operational area define the service controls required in the system. Use as a basis for the control of services the project plan and service plan produced at the strategic level and that were molded into the tactical plan at the tactical level. The elements are the service level and agreement plan, workload and capacity plan, and the information-management system plan for the applications and projects. A workload schedule is developed at the operational level for production and distribution; included in this are all of the required maintenance activities with standards for measurement. This workload schedule must satisfy the service-level agreements made with the users, and any differences must be renegotiated. Publish this schedule so that management understands what is to be done and how it will be measured. Next get written management approval.

The production and distribution schedule accompanied by measurement standards serve as a basis for evaluating how well the resources are managed. Analyze performance and note problems and how they were resolved in a problem log. This information is worthwhile in developing improved procedures to eliminate weak links in the information-management system and increase effectiveness in the recovery programs. All problems and how they were resolved are reported to tactical-level management. Examine the service that has been provided under the information-management system and match it for compliance to the service agreements. Variances and their reasons are identified and reported to tactical-level management; they always are interested in knowing the level of service provided by the system as well as all new requests for services.

The project control performed in the development and maintenance area provides feedback to the tactical plan. The control there over change requests is important because, if it is not properly handled, both the level of service and resource utilization can be greatly affected. With insufficient resources you will finish the project later than the planned completion date and perhaps far over the monies budgeted for the project. A worse case is that the change requires skills that are not readily available and the project fails. Define the resources needed for a project early in order to allow time for training and/or hiring. Not only should you get approval for the resources but you should get the resources in place quickly. Make management aware of how they are being used as this type of status reporting is critical to keeping them secure for the project.

Operation: Development and Maintenance. First, define the design and programming efforts required for the new applications as well as what is needed to improve or modify the current applications. Now design the external needs of the project. In this step you define the requirements, nature, and characteristics of the reports and computer-terminal screens to be produced for the users. Once these have been approved in writing by management, you can focus on the internal design or how the required computer programs will be written. Once this is approved the writing or coding of the programs can get underway and the programs can be individually tested when completed. Now all of the programs are integrated as a package and all are given a systems test for the application. When the results get the approval of your quality-assurance group, the application is ready for installation.

When you are improving or modifying existing applications in an information-management system or buying programming packages from outside vendors, some different steps are involved. The application requirements are defined and matched against the deliverables provided by current programs or offerings provided by vendors. Performance levels must be acceptable and any changes must be negotiated with the users. If corrections are needed, amend the agreement for the purchase of the vendor programming packages and secure management's approval. Test all improved, modified, or purchased programs to determine reliability and performance levels. Integrate these into the information-management-system operating environment and monitor performance.

You cannot install new equipment or improve facilities without doing a detailed requirement analysis. The demands of the user community help to define the equipment that is needed and the required system network. Now you must do the physical planning for the installation and develop an effective system-recovery procedure. All of the new equipment must be tested and integrated into the current system prior to a complete-system test. Provide a status report on the performance of the system to tactical-level management.

At the operational level you must make provisions for maintaining the information-management system. Carefully examine the cause of each problem and record how it was resolved and how effective the solution was. When a problem is solved, the fix must be tested prior to installation and measured against the service-level agreement. Publish instructions to help others who might encounter the same problem. Finally, after the informa-tion-management system is installed it might need a fine-tuning and balanc-ing to help it to reach its highest level of performance.

Operation: Service and Resources. Develop a methodology and publish standards and procedures for the production and distribution jobs run in the information-management system. Clearly define how jobs are to be sub-mitted, what input is required, and how the jobs are to be run. Establish schedules and formats for both input and output data. Develop a procedure for monitoring the progress of the production activities against the work schedules. Also, publish emergency production procedures in the event that the production run does not execute properly in the system. Be responsive to changes and require that all data used in the information-management system be in computer-readable form; also, all input must be validated and recorded. All output should be in the form requested by the user and recorded and checked for accuracy and proper distribution. Monitor the distribution tasks just as you do the production tasks and match the results against the distribution schedule. You should establish emergency distribu-tion procedures and set aside resources for these situations. Also, you must establish procedures to publish the distribution status of the information-management system.

It is important at the operation level to provide information about the user-support services offered by the information-management system and the resources available to assist the users. Help the users to write small pro-grams and to use program products that can be run on the system. Suffi-cient resources should be available to help the functional groups to produce quick reports and perform simulation or modeling exercises when needed. To grow the information-management system and encourage new uses, a marketing program for the services must be developed that will encourage its use for new applications. Evaluate all requests for new services and pro-vide them quickly once they are justified. Offer a broad list of services and promote them with a strong public-relations program.

The final service area to be considered in the operational level is all of the administrative support necessary to manage the information-management system. A vital element for the success of the system is ade-quate education and training. Educate the people in the organization on the benefits and services provided by the system; establish a training pro-gram to improve the skills of those involved in the management-information system. Document all of the education and training plans. Monitor the progress of each person, and as his or her skills change record them in their skills profile. The skills-profile base serves as a means to manage resources as well as to provide directions for building career lad-ders for people in the organization.

Also, at the operational level provide for collecting data on the performance level of those involved in the information-management system and evaluate this against the manpower plan and work schedules developed in the tactical-level planning. Report the performance results to tactical-level management planning so that the implementation of the tactical plan at the operational level can be measured.

One last big area requires attention: That is the financial administration of the information-management system. All of the charges for the system must be calculated and distributed on a simple, fair basis to the users. Included in these charges must be all of the expense of outside contracts and vendor costs. All of the supplies, equipment, and facilities costs must be reported and considered in the user's fee for the information-management-system services. Accounting procedures must be in place that provide the tactical-level management planning with a complete picture of the financial status of the information-management system.

Office Automation

One of the growing problems faced by most firms is that of office operations. This work involves the managing of information, and its volume and value to the business grows each day. Managing information in an office environment is quite different than it is in the factory environment. In the factory the payback on the investment comes very quickly; however, in the office the benefits are realized more slowly. Also, training is required to apply computers to office problems; this is an expense to the organization.

For many years, the productivity gains in the office have been lower than in all of the other business functions of the firm. Many corporations find that the office costs are more than one-half of all of the total operating costs. What makes the office environment so different from the factory environment? One reason is that the tasks performed in the office are knowledge work, and managing the knowledge worker has never been easy. The work involves handling large amounts of information and using it to make decisions. These activities are very difficult to measure; therefore productivity standards are hard to establish. Even when you establish performance levels it is not easy to gauge each person's capability. A good performance as the result of great effort by one person might only require a moderate amount of effort for the super-achiever type. How do you manage the latter type? The secret for effectively managing the knowledge worker is to manage information better in the office environment. An efficient organization cannot keep allocating more and more of the firm's total resources to office operations when returns fall and expenditures climb.

One of the greatest challenges to a manager is to better manage information in the office operations. What is one of the keys to this problem? It begins with getting your people to work more efficiently—and not just harder. You can improve productivity by using the technological tools that are now proven effective in automating office activities. Unfortunately in most corporations the office operations have been the last functions to receive the benefits of the computer. In the manufacturing environment more than ten times as much capital has been invested compared to the office environment in making available more-productive tools for each worker.

Both the cost and the size of computers have come down drastically in recent years. You must now bridge the gap between your less-than-efficient methods of managing information in the office and the increased productivity possible through new computer technology.

Personal Computers

The recent remarkable technological strides in office automation can be seen in the rapidly growing use of personal computers. They are small, inexpensive, and powerful; they can lighten the burdens placed on the large computer systems. They can shorten the amount of time required to implement new applications because the lengthy data-processing studies can be avoided. Often these studies have been needed to understand the users requirements and to help to justify financially the system. Now a much-shorter study can be performed to justify and implement the computer for the user of the personal computer knows better than anyone how he or she can profitably use the system. With a personal computer accompanied with excellent program packages available at the nearby computer store a user can quickly and at very low cost address the information-management problems in his or her office. Most computer stores offer a wide range of programming packages; therefore a computer user does not have to write his or her own programs. Not too long ago these packages were not easy to use; they did not run well under some operating systems and they were not well-documented. It was difficult for a user to modify the packages to meet their specific needs. Now it's a different ball game: The packages are well documented, easy to use, and easy to change. It is no longer necessary to rewrite a program each time you want to do a different task. Programming packages are flexible, and the programs talk to each other. The data used in one program and the results can be entered into other programs; this was not always possible with earlier personal-computer programming packages. The technological advances are not abating for now new programming products are available that integrate many separate programming packages into a single program which will perform a multitude of tasks. You can develop stimulation models and express the results in graphic form or written reports. The data is passed back and forth rapidly between programs with no programming changes required.

As a manager you are a decision maker. The personal computer will answer your needs for a tool to access and massage data, compare information, and prepare reports for corporate management. You want your employees' productivity to increase. Your managers want your productivity as a manager to increase, also.

Word Processors

The meteoric rise in the use of personal computers in the office environment has been exceeded only by word-processing systems. The growth in this area of the office environment has been separate and distinct from the growth of data processing. In the past little attention was given to clerical and secretarial activities. Letters and reports were edited and retyped: errors were corrected, changes were made, and new errors introduced. In an interactive process it was done over and over again. Some large corporations established dedicated functional groups of highly paid typists and operators to improve productivity; often the expense incurred wasn't offset by benefits. Why? Often, the errors were typing errors, and in retyping new errors were introduced. Then either the output was sent on at a poor-quality level, or the job was re-done or abandoned. Also, a very minor change in the content of the text might require the retyping of the entire letter, report, or document. If retyping was required the costs skyrocketed; however, if the author ignored the change in order to restrain the costs the communication was often less than desired and misunderstandings resulted in even greater expenses in the long-run. Finally, when numerous original documents were required a secretary had to type multiple copies of the same letter or report. This was time-consuming and resulted in a loss of quality.

How do you solve these problems? The solution is easy if you capture all of the material on computer media and massage it as much as is required. Word processing allows changes to be made only on command and where applicable and the rest of the information remains untouched. There is no need to retype the letters, reports, or documents for it is done by the computer with no new errors being introduced. The productivity of your secretaries improves at an unbelievable rate. Does your productivity improve? Yes! When you have a target date to meet, the benefits from word processing help you to meet this deadline. Often jobs are completed within schedule only to miss the target date due to typing delays. Reduce the time required for typing and you narrow the gap between the target date and delivery date.

Word processing owes its success to the computer. Recent computer advances have driven down the costs of both the equipment and programming needed to perform word processing. Whereas in the past a single dedicated system was required to support these activities, now many word-processing applications can be supported at many remote locations whereas other major systems are being run from the central processing unit. Also, the whole function of word processing has risen to a high-attention level in many corporations and high status is given to the word-processing work station. Corporate management recognizes that it is an effective way to raise the quality level of office work while greatly reducing costs. Changes can be made quickly on the commands of the author, verified, approved, and communicated throughout the organization.

The new world of word processing is offering a whole new approach to the office environment. Word processing has been married to many new communication techniques, which has given birth to electronic mail. This approach to managing information takes the word-processing-created information and distributes it electronically throughout the organization. This technique allows many people to study a situation and make a composite decision quickly and implement it at many locations. You can author documents and communicate them around the country to other managers. The information can be changed, approved, and distributed to a central site for printing—all through the computer. Less time is required for meetings and telephone conversations as the dialogue takes place over the computer screen. All of this increases office productivity with less interruptions to work schedules.

You can go beyond integrating word processing with computers. You also can integrate word processing with data-base systems; this greatly improves office productivity. Should you have a letter to write to a specific group of customers, you can pull their records off the data base. Then you can take the standard-type response and add to it the specific information taken from the data base needed to respond to the customer situation. The result is a personalized letter that is accurate and produced quickly and at low cost. This is a far-more-effective response to a customer than a typed form letter.

There are some weak spots in how the personal computer handles word processing, but they are not critical problems. Many personal computers cannot handle both large displays of graphic as well as test data. Also, some personal computers have difficulty in handling large data bases and in sharing the access to them on a departmental basis. Often this is because the large volume of documents makes it difficult to access them by name. This is further compounded because it is often difficult to locate documents based solely on their contents.

Effective Data-Base Management

Making the knowledge worker more effective through word processing provides a good return on the investment. However, a problem that often surfaces in the office environment relates to maintaining all of the files. A large amount of your corporate resources can be allocated to organizing and updating your files. Additional efforts are required to locate relevant information and send it to interested parties. In many corporations the large computers have held the massive essential files. Often the small files are not put on the computer because the benefits do not offset the costs.

In many organizations today files are kept on index cards or ledger sheets and updated manually. Records are classified under one subject or heading and little cross-referencing is done. With only a single key to locate a file it is difficult to find a file by any other key or identifier. Searching a file is not only very difficult but time-consuming and expensive. The shortcomings in these systems can be solved through computers and data-base-management packages.

Data-base-management packages can be run on personal computers. They enable you to file, sort, and retrieve vast amounts of information and to print and distribute it quickly and at low cost. The information in the data-base-management record contains all that must be known about a customer, employee, or vendor in a single source. Each of these records have fields of data that serve to answer the inquiries of the users. These fields permit three types of transactions to be performed through the computer. The first transaction facilitates the creation and maintenance of files. Electronically you can create, delete, or modify existing records. Once the fields are established it is easy to add new files and the users of the data-base-management packages can search through any records in the data-base file.

The second transaction allows you to retrieve certain records based on the criteria that have been established. You can specify a required-skills code and request a listing of all people with a given number of years of experience and education in that discipline. The computer does a very fast search and in seconds will display or print for you those few out of thousands of employees who meet your criteria. This ability to manage information is important when you are assessing the hiring and training needs for the organization and planning work schedules.

The third transaction is the ability to generate reports on the data that you have retrieved from the files. The user of the data-base-management packages can define the fields of information that is required in the report and specify the format or layout of how it will appear. Many program packages are available that facilitate sorting the data and performing calculations when required. The data-base-management packages, when run on personal computers, can significantly improve the performance level of office workers. Staff people can have faster access to up-to-date information and present to their managers more accurate and timely reports. Managers must also be able to reference the data-base files and pull from them on the computer the information required to make more-effective decisions. However, the benefits of data-base-management packages do not stop here for the results of the searching, sorting, and calculating activities can be passed to the word-processing work stations where reports, forms, documents, and letters can be prepared. To further manage the information in the office environment more effectively, you should integrate the data-base-management packages and word-processing activities into a communication system that will distribute copies of the materials produced to people at even the most-remote geographical locations.

The attractiveness of word-processing and data-base-management packages is not unflawed. One problem is that the methods for building and searching the files allow little flexibility in the instructions used. However, this shortcoming can be corrected by using menus to help the users to select the functions to be performed and to provide the instructions to do them. A second problem is the high cost involved in establishing the large data-base files. Records in paper form must be entered through electronic methods into the data-base files; also they must be entered accurately. Soon a third problem arises: The data-base files and word-processing files become very large. As many personal computers utilize diskettes, many might be required to do the job. One way to handle this problem is to use fixed-disks files with their far-greater capacities. This increases the costs, which however, are soon offset through higher productivity in the office.

Spreadsheet Packages

For years, large computers have been a valuable management tool when used for financial modeling. In analyzing business situations you often need to evaluate alternative courses of action prior to making a decision. Entering various assumptions into a financial model permits you to handle many variables quickly. As the different scenarios are simulated, a large amount of computer capacity is required. Before the development of the spreadsheet packages this was difficult to do on personal computers. Now the spreadsheet packages provide in their programs the capabilities of the large computers, only at a much lower cost. Also they are quickly understood by the personal-computer users. The range of functions is very broad: You can use the packages to perform financial justifications, forecasting, profit-and-pricing analysis, and cash-flow analysis. You can project income statements and balance sheets into pro forma statements that will improve your ability to make better financial decisions.

The spreadsheet packages begin with a blank grid of rows and columns on the personal-computer screen. You enter data into this table just as you would post it to a ledger sheet. Once you have completed the table the personal computer, as you instruct, does the required calculations. This allows you to test many what-if type of situations; by changing and massaging the data you can immediately display the results. Sometimes all of the spreadsheet cannot be displayed at one time on the screen; therefore you divide it into sections and display these as needed. Once you are satisfied with the displays, you can format the results and print reports.

The spreadsheet packages permit you to pass the data back and forth between spreadsheets. You can make a change on one spreadsheet and instruct the personal computer to make adjustments on other spreadsheets. This function can greatly simplify the managing of information. Also the capabilities and flexibilities of the spreadsheet packages will save you much time because they can automatically and accurately do many calculations with only a few simple instructions.

The spreadsheet packages can be linked to word processors, data-base packages, and communication systems. The results of the spreadsheet calculations can be printed within a word-processing report and distributed to users at many locations. Also, you can take the spreadsheet results and through graphic packages prepare exhibits for corporate management.

Computer Graphics

The use of graphics on the personal computer to present and summarize information for decision makers is one of the fastest-growing activities in managing information. Prior to the current technological advances most graphs were prepared either through large computer systems and plotters or they were drawn manually. This process was costly, time-consuming, and full of errors. Now that many managers have personal computers or terminals in their offices, it is quick and easy to express data in graphic form.

Computer graphics is one of the most powerful tools available to you as a manager because large volumes of tables and reports are too time-consuming to analyze and summarize. Decision makers often need to focus on the big picture and look at trends and directions rather than a wealth of detail data. Often a graph in a report is required to convey a point clearly. Computer graphics digest and display information quickly; a graphic comparison of data can be easily understood. Also, the costs of computer-graphic packages are rapidly declining while their capabilities are increasing. Graphic programs are available that permit you to combine many different formats into a single chart. Also colored charts and graphs displayed on the screen can be most dynamic and effective. Many graphic programs provide menus from which you can select a variety of ways to format, label, or frame the charts. However, most printers are built for printing text; and when they can print graphic materials the quality is often not as high as you require.

Data Communications

You can classify business communications as either internal or external. Managing both forms of communication is important; however, as less than 25 percent is external it is the handling of information internally that is of primary concern to the organization. When you receive late or inaccurate information you are less effective in planning and making decisions. When you do not receive information regarding the corporate mission statements or your functional group's objectives and goals you cannot develop a sound strategic plan. Unless there is feedback regarding employee performance and the quality of the products and services being produced you cannot fine-tune the organization to make it more efficient. When you are managing people and activities at remote geographic locations, you lose control of the operations if you do not get timely information. Soon you become a reactive rather than proactive manager.

Effective managers know that they must stay on top of external as well as internal business conditions. You need information about the economy, competitors, legal requirements, and legislative changes. The success of the organization and your success often rest heavily on how quickly you can get accurate information and evaluate its impact on the business.

What forms of communication are required to effectively manage information? One of the most common forms is mail; the cost compared to other forms of communication is low and it accommodates many different forms of material. However, often it is slow; overnight mail delivery helps to correct this problem but it also increases expenses. You might turn to telegrams, cable, and other forms of wire and or satellite communications, but your costs will rise. These vehicles best serve short pieces of material and are best when used to transmit data or text.

Another form of communication is the telephone; this can be fast but also is very costly. Also much time can be consumed if the parties are not reached and return calls are required. Leaving a message is not without risk for if it is written down incorrectly misunderstandings can arise. When calls are made over a number of time zones, it might be difficult to find a mutually agreeable time period. When many people must take part in the conversations conference calls can be inconvenient and costly to arrange. Even after all of these problems are overcome, the best that you can do is to exchange verbal information.

You can use another form of communication to manage information: that is, a meeting or conference. A face-to-face discussion can be very productive; however, it can be costly and time-consuming if the participants must travel any great distance.

There is a another way to communicate and manage information effectively: That is through data communications. This form of communication helps to avoid many of the problems discussed earlier. Data communication is simply one computer talking with another. It will not replace the three forms of communication described previously but it will serve as an alternative approach for making each of these three forms more productive. If you are going to use the new tools for handling information in the office, you should consider the benefits provided by data communication. One of the best vehicles for handling data communication is the personal computer. Personal computers can pass their stored data back and forth to each other quickly, accurately, and at low cost.

How can you use the personal computer to promote better data communications? We have discussed how word processing, data-base-management packages, and communication systems combined with spreadsheet packages and computer graphics can effectively manage information. Within the organization you can use the computer for electronic mail and transmit and receive data from remote locations. Graphs as well as text material can be passed across time zones without any human interactions because the computers can automatically call each other and talk.

But there is something more that you can do to put the technological advancements of data communication to use. Your personal computer has the ability to talk with your large computers; it can ask for data and copy it into the files of your personal computer. Later, you can retrieve this data and use it in your business. However, your personal computer can reach out in many directions. It can pull data out of your company's own private data bases and it can also retrieve data stored in public data bases. You can subscribe to a growing number of services provided by firms who manage public data-base files. There are a multitude of uses for this information. Research costs can be reduced, market surveys can be analyzed, and your competitive posture in the marketplace evaluated.

The benefits of the technological advancements in office automation have also added some new concerns. The great capacity that you have to generate volumes of data often causes more to be collected than is needed. An overload in information makes it difficult to sort out what is relevant. There are some problems when the communication channels between computers get clogged, and data is not always passed efficiently. Data communications will play an ever-increasing role in managing information in the office environment. Don't sell short the impact that it will have on the decision makers. Effective managers are good at handling information.

Computerized-Automated-Manufacturing Systems

One of the most dynamic and productive uses for the computerized managing of information is in the area of factory automation. Technological advancements have moved at great speed and the early tape-coded instructions that controlled machines have been replaced with sophisticated computer systems that almost run the factory. Many of these systems seem expensive, but on closer examination you will find that they have a terrific payback in higher levels of productivity and quality. Many of the computerized-automated-manufacturing systems can run 24 hours around the clock if needed, with little supervision, and with great flexibility to change and control many different production processes.

In many manufacturing processes there is a considerable amount of time spent in setting up the machines for a particular production run. Then a given volume must be produced and the machine tools taken down and new ones set up for the next type of product. This procedure is very expensive, and at the same time much flexibility is lost because you cannot quickly and on command shift to a different volume or type of product. With automated manufacturing systems you have this flexibility and you can fine-tune production with sales or orders. Also you gain economies of scale without having to produce a large volume of only a few types of products. If you have many different models of a product or many different types of products you can closely control the inventories of semi-finished or finished goods. A production line designed for large volumes can be efficiently used for small volumes when run under the guidance of a computerized system. Also because of the great flexibility provided by computerized automated manufacturing systems you can build small rather than large plants and still keep production costs down. These smaller plants can be located closer to the markets, thus reducing your distribution costs.

When you can manage your production line with only a few simple computer commands you can change production runs at a moment's notice. The concept of computerized management of the factory environment is not new; however, its benefits have been discounted. Japanese manufacturers have implemented automated-manufacturing systems using industrial robots with great success. The quality of their manufactured products has improved greatly while their manufacturing costs have declined. In some factories, entire shifts are run by computer-controlled robotic systems with only a few people to monitor the results.

The price tag to automate a factory is not low: Computer-controlled machine operations utilizing robots are very expensive. However, they are still many times less expensive than building an inefficient manufacturing facility. The maintenance work on automated-manufacturing systems is usually performed during the day shift; at night the computer-controlled machine tools produce the products almost unattended. Materials are delivered and loaded into machine-tool units automatically. After the semi-finished parts are machined, they are sent automatically to warehouse storage and when needed they are retrieved automatically for the required assembly operations.

The automated-manufacturing system begins and ends with computer programs that direct the activities. At the earliest stages when the product is developed, a computer is used to help in the design model. When the product goes into production, the raw materials and semi-finished parts are, under computer control, delivered to the work stations. They are delivered on automatic conveyor belts or carts and unloaded by robots. They are put by materials handling robots into the machine-tool units for processing. Computers select the machine tools required for the manufacturing operations and direct them based on computer-stored instructions. When an assembly operation is required, the computer is programmed to bring the parts together and to coordinate the steps. A person supervising the process can at any time change the machine tools and the volume and type of product being produced or assembled. Even the quality-control functions are computerized, and in some highly automated factories special cameras scan the finished product and inspect it for defects. Once the product has passed inspection, the robots put it on delivery belts or carts and it goes to storage or shipping.

Automated-manufacturing systems are literally exploding with technological breakthroughs. Factories are being built where the computer-controlled machine tools and robots are controlled through computerized design profiles, with production specifications residing in the data bases and computer-directed commands all being issued from remote locations. From one central site you can control the type and volume of products being produced and even change their characteristics on command. You produce only what is needed and when it is needed; you run the plant at the optimal production levels.

With such great benefits assured from computerized-automated-manufacturing systems, why are so many managers reluctant to accept the new technology? First, most managers are measured on the bottom line, which is the profit in the short-run. Automating-manufacturing processes are long and hard with large capital investments required, a high degree of risk, and benefits off in the distance. Also, many adjustments are required by the workers, and union pressures against change can be a serious drawback. Second, most managers are not aware of the technological advancements that have been made in recent years in this field. Even when they are recognized the approach is to improve a limited number of small specific operations one at a time rather than to design an entirely new approach to manufacturing. The tendency is to go with the old procedures. When new plants

are built they are carbon copies of existing plants, and no new, or few, procedures are introduced. There is risk involved in making major changes and
some managers still do not understand that they are paid to take risks.

How far have we gone in applying computerized-automated-manufacturing systems to the factory environment? Currently less than 10 percent of
the machine tools used in U.S. manufacturing are computer controlled. If
you are managing in the factory environment you must focus on implementing totally new computerized-automated-manufacturing systems. Don't keep
putting patches on the present operations. If you want to reduce labor and
material costs you must use the best tools that are available. Use the computer
to control work and material flow; get the parts to the production process
when they are needed. This will help you to keep small inventories and use as
little valuable floor space as possible. When possible, monitor all material
flow electronically and feed it back to the inventory-control system.

Manufacturing costs in the United States are rising rapidly while in
foreign countries they are falling rapidly as new sophisticated computer tools
are introduced. Automated factories and robots will reduce production costs
and raise quality. The capital investments are large but time has run out for
most manufacturers; for many, the next decade is going to be a period of survival. Implement computerized-automated-manufacturing systems with
robots and laser technology if you expect to be consistently profitable.

The Information Center

The tools for managing information in most corporations are developed in
data processing. However, in some firms data processing has not been
responsive to the needs of the users and information-managing systems
have proven to be inadequate or delivered late. Often the cause of this is
that the data-processing resources are strained beyond their limits and the
new management-information applications get a low priority. It is not uncommon in many data-procesing groups to find that more than 60 percent
of their efforts go to modifications, improvements, and maintenance of
projects rather than new applications. Also, because of pressures to get a
system up and running, some control is lost and goals and objectives
become ambiguous. As a result, many users become dissatisfied with the
long queues built for data-processing services. Your professional people
and managers need responsive computer service; and when it is not
available it hurts the decision-making activities. In an attempt to solve these
problems many firms have established information centers.

The information center is an organization that can function either
within or outside of the data-processing organization. When it functions
within or alongside of data processing there are information-center consultants who interface with the end users and help them in using the interac-

tive tools and techniques to solve their own problems. The data-processing department provides the training, computer resources, and technical support to enable the users to work with the interactive program products. Data processing works closely with the users to establish an information center that will be responsive to their needs. As a result, the data-processing department better understands the needs of the users and can be more responsive in what they do to meet requests for computer services. As the users become more effective through the information center, they gain stature with corporate management. The load is lightened on data processing, and when the projects are done correctly there is less need in the future for maintenance activities.

Users in the firm benefit from the information center through increased productivity and the ability to quickly implement new applications. Some firms have found that the off loading onto the information center has made their data-processing group more responsive for their maintenance activity has fallen to below 45 percent of their programming efforts. Through the information center only a handful of people is needed to service many hundreds of users in the organization. Also, with reduced pressures on data processing their activities are more orderly and better planned. As for the users, they express a high degree of satisfaction with the information center, and they soon exhaust its capabilities. Users find that the interactive-program products help them to make more-complete and accurate decisions in a shorter period of time. Also, on demand they can create the reports and graphs needed to support their conclusions.

The development of the information center is an evolutionary process. You look for needs of the users that cannot be handled by data processing, and you bring in the program products that can do the job. You test these against some applications that have a high priority and you advertise their success. You must provide support and service to the users and train them in the use of the products; also, new products must be evaluated. The information center has interfaces with other than the end users. It must interface closely with all data-processing people in the organization and with such functional groups as plans and control and data-base administration. Also, you must establish a close linkage with the people in computer operations and applications development. The information center must get its fair share of central-processing-unit time in order to give prompt service to the users' needs.

Mission and Objectives

The purpose of the information center is to provide tools and techniques to computer users in the organization that will allow them on their own terms and time to retrieve, analyze, calculate, and present data in a highly respon-

sive time frame. The information center teaches the users how to use the programming products themselves and thereby bypass the delays often suffered
in the traditional development processes required in data processing.

The objectives of the information center are many. First, you want
through the resources of your computer center to increase the productivity
and responsiveness of the computer users in your organization. Second, you
want to improve the decision-making abilities of managers in the organization. Third, you want to increase the productivity and responsiveness of
the data-processing group. How do you do this? Well, you decrease through
the information center the demands on them for new development programs,
new reports, changes to reports, special one-time requests, and the on-going
expensive maintenance activities. Also you are trying to give more accurate
and up-to-date information to your decision makers and their staffs.

Information-Center Services

The theme of the information center is to help the user to help him- or herself.
How do you do this? First, you set up on the computer easy-to-use programming products that help the users to retrieve and analyze data on their commands. Second, you educate users in how they can apply these tools to solve
their daily problems; they get hands-on experience with the tools under your
guidance. Third, you sit with the users and help them to apply the program
products to their most-meaningful applications. When necessary, you show
them how to write programs, but you do not do coding for them for any extended period. Once you have shown them how to use the products to solve
their problems, they are on their own. Fourth, provide all of the necessary
skills and resources required for the user to understand what data is available
to them and how it can be used in their business. Show them how they can access and use corporate data. Establish a method to manage and control the
use and preservation of the security and integrity of the information. Fifth,
you must provide whatever is needed to support the tasks that will be performed by the users. A hotline and technician must be available at all times to
resolve problems. You must have in place some guidelines, standards, procedures, and rules to plan and provide resources to meet the service-level requirements of the users. Do you know what they are?

We have looked at some of the responsibilities of the information
center, but does the user have some responsibilities also? Yes! First, they
must have an in-depth knowledge of the business conditions surrounding
their problems and an appreciation of what computer applications can do to
help them solve these problems. Second, they must provide people who are
motivated and interested in using the tools provided by the information
center to help them to make more-effective and intelligent decisions. Third,
if they want to use the computer resources they should be able to justify

their needs. Most information centers are overloaded with demands on their resources; if a user can't build a good business case then the resources should go to the more-deserving part of the organization. Fourth, the user must have a strong positive attitude. The information center will teach and hold his or her hand for only a short while during the early experiences with the product. The user must have a desire to help him- or herself to further their expertise and knowledge of what the product can do for them. The information center does not do the work for the user; it teaches and assists only. The user must learn how to use the product and then go back and teach other people in the group the same skills.

Information-Center Benefits

Let's focus on some of the more-important benefits derived from the information center. How does the data-processing department benefit? It does this first through a better responsiveness to the users needs, which builds good will. Data processing is no longer seen as the bad guy who can't get the job done but as a group who provided some service in an effective manner through the information center. The data-processing people win a better image for they are now seen as taking a constructive role. Second, experience has shown that the amount of time spent in maintenance activity is reduced in data processing once the information center arrives on the scene. Third, data-processing managers feel in general that they have a better relationship with the users. Without an information center many users begin to install their own small computer systems or use more outside time-sharing services. This approach often increases the data-processing costs of the organization with a loss of control and possible problems. The problems arise when the users get into trouble and turn to data processing to rescue them with quick fixes. Fourth, history has shown that with the information center the level of communication has risen between data processing and the user community; eash side understands the problems of the other better.

How does the user community benefit from the information center? First, we find that they are able to respond much more quickly to the changes in their environment and business problems. Second, the computer tools provided by the information center make people more productive while improving the quality of their work. Also, you will find that it gives them new capabilities to do tasks that would have been written off as impossible because of time and money constraints. Calculations no longer must be done on a calculator and reports typed on a typewriter because program products are available that will perform all of these functions at high speed and low cost. Third, it has been found that the information center has improved organizational morale. This is because the users now have improved their technical proficiencies and feel more professional in their duties.

The information center can be a part of the data-processing department, but it has been found that it functions best if it is a new operational unit reporting to the same level of management that the data-processing department reports to in the organization. In many firms the information center is very advanced in the use of efficient programming products. In time, many data-processing people will come to realize that the programming products are powerful and will themselves turn more to their use. The information center serves as a buffer for it tries to get the user as close as possible to the computer while keeping him or her away from the complexities of the computer. Whereas once data processing controlled all of the computer resources, now the user can be independent and process information on command.

Is an Information Center Needed?

There are a number of signs that indicate when an information center is needed. One is when the backlog of applications and computer-service requests are so large that data processing can't handle them in a reasonable time frame. Many firms have application backlogs double the size of their currently installed base of applications. If all of the data-processing resources were applied only to clearing up the backlog, it would take most corporations from three to five years to accomplish the task. However, even while this is being done the backlog will still be growing as new requests for computer services continue to come in. Perhaps you don't see any backlog in your corporation. If so, it is because it is invisible and hasn't been identified by the users. Also, it may exist throughout the company in data-processing satellite staffs in the various functional groups. It might not be a visible backlog because the organization is not using the computer creatively for new applications. Also, there might be no backlog because the users have given up on data processing.

The information center helps to manage a backlog of applications by providing the users with program prducts that allow the users to access data and manage the information on their own terms. This makes them more productive, and they do not have to wait for data processing to write and test programs. Many information-center users generate their own text materials, reports, and graphs in less than a day.

Another way that the need for an information center is shown is through the actions of the users. If they are using many mini-computers it might be a sign that they are dissatisfied with the level of service being provided by data processing. Also, if the users are making heavy use of external time-sharing services, it often shows dissatisfaction and can be a source of monies to the corporation when the work is brought back to the firm through the use of the information center.

One clue to the need for an information center can be seen if the users are significantly increasing the size of their programming staffs. Much of the work of writing new programs might be avoided by using the end-user products provided by the information center. Often concern arises in an organization because the development programmers in data processing cannot respond quickly to the requests from the users to do small projects. They usually cannot respond because they are committed to large projects. As user managers are very aware of what can be done on the computer, they will help to support the business case for the establishment of the information center. This is particularly true when their needs are for nontraditional computer services on their command. Often reports and graphs must be prepared quickly to aid the decision-making process or to present information to corporate management. With office costs and programming costs increasing at a rapid pace while productivity is falling, many executives question the use of the programming resources and ask that an information center be established in the organization.

Users and Their Requirements

The users of the information center are staff people, planners, researchers, engineers, accountants, and all managers and professional people who want access to their own data and on their own terms. They want to be more productive and more responsive to the needs of the business. They must make effective decisions and present the results simply and promptly to corporate management. Many secretaries and administrative people find that the information center helps them to produce more-accurate reports and text materials in a shorter period of time; none of these people requires any skill in data processing. In fact, they do not even want to get near the technical complexities that often make up the computer environment. Users want to get on the terminal to use the resources but they want it to be simple.

What are the requirements of the information-center users? First, they need information quickly and the data must be up-to-date, complete, and accurate. Second, they want to build their own files and massage the data to meet their needs. Third, they want a terminal close at hand and they want to get on it to run their applications when it is convenient. The information center must be prepared to handle a lot of unscheduled processing demands. Fourth, the user does not want to be a programmer, an application specialist, or product technician for the corporation. He or she wants to sit down at the terminal, sign on, and run the end-user product that will give him or her the calculations, reports, or graphs needed. Fifth, the user wants the information center to provide new services and at a high service level.

The information center, as we have seen, offers many benefits to the users. It also provides benefits to data processing. First, it takes from their shoulders the smaller projects and allows them the time needed to concentrate on large projects and new leading-edge applications. Second, with fewer small projects the maintenance load is reduced. Third, data processing can proact and develop long-range project plans and workload schedules without the frequent troublesome interruptions to priorities caused by having to react to urgent computer-service requests.

Just as the information center must meet users' requirements, users must meet information-center requirements. There must be a proper attitude established in the user community; they must be willing to get involved and to do the programming required for their own applications. They must learn how to use the end-user products and teach them to their own people. When problems arise they must pick up the telephone, call the hot-line number, and request assistance from the product technician. The user must also with serious intent attend the courses and seminars offered by the information center. Also, the user must submit timely requirement statements and perform the justification for the resources. The information center should help with these tasks.

Organization and Staffing

Where should the information center report in the organization? It all depends on how your data-processing group is currently organized and the role that it plays in providing computer services in the corporation. In some firms, the data-processing department is under the direction of the data-processing manager. Data processing in these corporations might provide only the hardware and systems-programming services. The efficient use of the computer services might be the responsibility of the information-systems director of a vice-president of computer services. In those environments where the scope of the data-processing department's activities are limited, as mentioned earlier, you may have the information center report to the information-systems director or vice-president of computer services rather than the data-processing manager. There is a benefit in having the information center report outside of the data-processing department for it more quickly achieves a high level of visibility, which is necessary for success. Also, it avoids contention for the resources.

Many information centers begin with only one person; he or she is the manager as well as the end-user-product specialist. Often only one product is offered to a single friendly user who has an application that can use it successfully. To retain sponsorship it is imperative that you cautiously get the information center off on the best foot. Applause is quickly needed and one early unhappy user can stop the information center dead in its tracks. As the information center matures and grows, you can gradually build the staff. Now that you have a few end-user products you can have a specialist to support each product. As more products are introduced, you can have a specialist responsible to support a number of products that fall in a given generic area of application: that is, computer-based training, file inquiry and report generation, financial planning, and so forth.

It should not be difficult for one product specialist to support over 50 end users. One large company has over 800 end users with only 4 people in the information center. As many of these end users have a good knowledge of computers and the products, the span of control is much larger than you would expect and shows the degree of flexibility that must be considered in staffing the information center. Also, as the information center staff grows a secretary is required to coordinate education and administrative-support activities. Mature information centers often require a planner and it is the duty of this person to plan for all of the computer resources needed to service the users. This includes all of the equipment, teleprocessing lines, and the physical facilities: that is, terminal rooms, seminar rooms, and so forth.

The information-center staff must have good communication and interpersonal skills. They need to have a positive attitude and must be helpful. A background in data processing is useful, and these staff members should have a good knowledge of the company's business. Product specialists are experts in helping the users to run their own application; however, they should not get involved in coding for the users. If the application requires a lot of programming and if it is a large and frequently run job it belongs in data processing and not in the information center.

Tasks and Responsibilities

The starting point for the information center is to assist the users in selecting the correct end-user products for his or her applications. Some applications—because of their size and complexities—must become data-processing projects. However, many of the smaller ones belong in the information center. This is particularly true where the quickly needed output is in the form of text, reports, or graphs. Once an acceptable application is identified, the information center can survey the available end-user products and get the best one into the information center and up and running on the terminals. You will find that there will be many users in the corporation for a given product. You should distribute throughout the organization a catalogue of the types of applications that are being run by what users in the information center; show the functional groups, their applications, and the products that they are using.

Now that you have identified the users, applications, and end-user products you must provide the end users with education courses and seminars. Develop some good on-line self-study courses so that the users can learn by doing right on the terminals. Computer-based and -assisted training is sometimes costly to develop, but it can be used by many people when it is most convenient for them. Also, it can be used over and over again, thereby avoiding the cost of a stand-up instructor in a classroom. However, keep the materials relevant to the needs of the organization and keep the course up-to-date with the changing business conditions. For the more-advanced users, you will want to develop and teach some advanced-level seminars containing workshops that apply the knowledge.

As you bring new end-user products into the information center you will need to develop and teach special seminars. Also, when end-user products change you must develop and teach update seminars. To promote the merits of the information center it is wise to present short seminars on new tips and techniques for using and applying the products. Also, put together some good end-user product overview courses that you can present to corporate management. The seminars do not need to be long sessions; for corporate management, only an hour is required. The seminars for new users can be from one-half to two days in duration. Introduce the information-center concept and explain its benefits. Show the attendees the facilities and get them on the terminal to do a few simple problems. Show them the security procedures and teach them how they can justify using the information center. Also teach them techniques to use in problem analysis and how to test their results. Shield them from the programming language and encourage them to request assistance when they run into problems.

You have another responsibility should you be the information-center manager: That is to serve as a consultant to the users. You must help them to select the best applications to be run in the information center, and you must discuss with them the end-user products so that they will select the correct one for their applications. You must work with the users to see that their programs are using the computer resources efficiently and that they are keeping adequate files and copies of documents. You must work closely with the end users to be sure that they have established good security procedures. You want to provide debug support when it is needed and give the users a limited amount of direct assistance in managing their applications. Periodically you will meet with the users and establish, if needed, a new direction in how the information center can better meet their needs. You must help them to investigate new business applications and to do some future evaluations as to the information-center services required.

Another responsibility of the information center is to arrange access to authorized data. See that proper security clearance has been given and that staff members get a copy of the file to work with; never give them the production file. You do not want any changes made to the original data and if the user wants to massage the data and build his or her own file, at least the original file is in perfect order. Help the users to solve logic problems using the file copies and, when common coding techniques have been defined, then be sure that they have been communicated to all of the users. You might have to provide design assistance to the users and give them some simple computer exercises to help them to better understand the lessons covered in the workshops. Also, you have a responsibility to provide some test files and test packages to help them to achieve high-quality outputs.

Provide as much support to the users as you can through newsletters or technical reports, complete with some clear examples. Also, get the users together for meetings where they can discuss with other users what applications they are running in the information center and what end-user products are effective for them. A few comments from happy users go a long way toward selling the merits of the information center. You will be surprised to find that in the start-up days of the information center you will be beating the bushes to find users; however, this changes very quickly and soon you will not be able to handle all of the demands. It will not be long before your problem is one of fighting for more computer resources.

The information center has a responsibility to interface with all of the other data-processing departments in the organization and to provide the maximum amount of technical and administrative support with the least-possible amount of paper work. The information center must give the highest level of user satisfaction possible with the least amount of red tape. You must make it easy for the users to register and enroll for courses and seminars. Make sure that all documentation about an end-user product is up-to-date and at hand when needed. When a new end-user product is brought into the information center, make sure that it is published to everyone on your directory of information-center users. Try to have a facility close at hand to the majority of the users so that they can walk in and get on a terminal and some help if needed.

In order to put together a yearly resource-requirements statement for data processing the information center should get from the users quarterly estimates of their computer needs. Include in this an estimate for the central processing unit, terminals, and end-user products. It is also good to get the applications that will be run by the users. A definitive explanation of these is most helpful in the promotion of the information center. Once you have collected the actual usage figures, you must match them against the estimates and define any variances. This will help you to plan for future workloads and to revise, if needed, your resource plan.

Policy Statement

You should outline a policy for using the information-center facilities. The policy statement should cover three broad areas: definition, scope, and procedure.

Definition. This area addresses the nature and intent of the information center. It begins with a statement that corporate management has always recognized the need for user involvement in managing information. The need is even more apparent now that sophisticated programming products are available as tools that will enable the users to solve many of their problems without a direct interaction with data-processing professionals. It is recognized that through the information center users can produce their own text materials, reports, and graphs and perform calculations and make more effective decisions. Also, that they can through the use of these tools accelerate the development process for new applications. Corporate management realizes that the tools provided by the information center raise the levels of problem solving by users. The information center is defined by corporate management as a concept that allows users (nondata-processing people) to write ad hoc text materials and reports and to perform calculations and simulate other financial, marketing, and manufacturing data without heavy involvement from data-processing staffs or information-systems groups. The concept also allows the user to prototype applications and model systems in a controlled environment.

Scope. The files created for the information center users are intended to be short-duration files. These files are copies of the production files, which assures that the original files will not be inadvertently destroyed or changed. Your policy statement should announce that the master files are resident at, and controlled from, the central computer site and also that the files for the information center are not intended to replace any master files or any of the functions currently being performed on the operating systems.

It is good to make a policy statement regarding what applications should be considered for the information center. To be used in the information center an application should meet some minimum requirements. First, it should not be critical to the business operation of the company. As the files are copies, may not be up-to-date, and the data might not be adequately protected and secure only noncritical applications should be run against them. Second, the applications should not be redundant to ones that are run from the master files in the normal computer processing. Computer resources and the users' time should not be spent on production operations or producing reports that are already handled under installed systems. Third, the applications should use files that are restricted in their scope; that is, they are not shared with another user group. The reason for this is that you lose the focal point for responsibility of the data. A user in building his or her own file might change or reformat the data to fit their specific needs. Other user groups with different requirements might have difficulty working with the revised data. Even worse, if they are not aware that the data has been changed they might use it as original data and make serious mistakes or incorrect decisions.

The reason for the minimum requirements mentioned earlier is to maintain the direction that corporate data processing is to provide critical data to all divisions or departments in the company and also that the sources of this data are the master files that have been designed and are maintained according to corporate standards.

Procedure. You must develop procedures for your information center that are in keeping with the rules established by your policy-and-procedures or planning-and-control group. Some of these procedures can be built around the following approaches. First, have all of the user files recorded with the programming group responsible for the physical disk storage at the users' location. This facilitates the deleting of any unused files so that additional file space can be made available for all users. If a file is not recorded as one that has been approved then it can be deleted during the normal disk-maintenance procedure. Apply this recorded and approved procedure to all user files, whether they be copies of master files or files that they have developed. Second, to preserve the integrity of data on the master files, no user-written program can directly access any master file nor perform any maintenance activities on these master files. Third, to further secure the master files for the data-processing group no information-center systems or end-user products should be allowed to access any master files directly on the main-frame computer. All information-center activities are run only off of copies or extracts of the master files. Fourth, production programs are run only by the data-processing group and not through information-center systems or end-user products. The information-center programs have been designed for use by nondata-processing people; by containing much overhead they are less efficient than the production programs of the data-processing department. Fifth, users should not perform any computer processing through the information center that is not related to the company's business. There are usually never enough computer resources to meet all of the organization's needs and inappropriate use of the corporate computer resources should not be allowed. Sixth, prototyping of production systems can be allowed if proper management approval has been obtained. However, these should not go into a production status without proper conversion and approval of data processing and authorization by corporate management. Seventh, all maintenance transactions to master files are performed only by the data-processing group; it should never come through the information center. The information center helps the end users solve their problems with products rather than through direct interfaces with data processing. Therefore the information-center product support people will assist the users in selecting languages and choosing end-user products. Remember that an information center is established to support end-user demand processing and not to infringe on the functions of corporate data processing.

Conclusion: Managers Must Adapt

The contemporary manager must adapt swiftly and correctly to the changing demands that society places on the business firm. Goals and objectives required to carry out the missions of the company can be carefully structured, but economic, political, and social forces can require them to be quickly modified. Unless you understand what changes are required and why, you can easily miss important opportunities for your organization. You must perceive when changes are needed and know where they should be implemented. How you affect the change strengthens or weakens your leadership role. The ability to control and communicate well with your staff cannot be discounted. No one can give you a formula for managing change in your firm because each organization and group of people are unique in their understanding and participation. Your success will come from the depth of your insight and the degree to which you wisely use other people's experiences, opinions, and judgments.

The rapidity of marketplace changes and technological developments requires you to continually review the firm's product lines and production facilities. The manager in a multinational company has even greater pressures. His or her changes are magnified because competition today is on an international basis. If this is your position, then you need to study and understand foreign cultures, marketplaces, political environments, tax regulations, and financial climates to retain or expand your business. At higher-level management positions, the tasks currently become more than one person can effectively handle. Risk often increases by overloading one executive with too many decision-making situations. Large firms might find it worthwhile to reorganize into smaller companies in which decisions can be made and implemented more quickly. An alternative is to have many people serving as a triumvirate in the role of chief executive officer. Clear lines of responsibility and authority can be assigned to prevent acts of omission or conflict. Close physical proximity and coordinated exchanges of insights would have a synergistic effect in overseeing global activities of the business.

In an age with increasing emphasis on sophisticated technology, it is of course required that every manager be proficient. This is important if you as a manager are to maximize the productivity of your organization; however, you must go far beyond this and understand that the job you are getting paid for is to manage and improve the talents of your people. In order to do this well, a company must have in place a broad spectrum of skills represented in their managerial team. Without a mixture of opinions, experiences, backgrounds, and judgment, dissent rarely surfaces; without this, many decisions are not as good as they could be with more discussion. A technique that will help you adapt to change is to expand this opportunity for dissent into an environment of controlled competition. When two or more groups work on the same problems or assignments, greater insights and better results often more than justify the duplication of activities. The internal competitive spirit can be rejuvenating to some people and offer them an opportunity to achieve additional recognition and rewards. With different managers of the groups, it generates additional competition that makes it a good development program for managers as well as employees.

Managers must adapt to changing relationships with employees and higher-level managers. You must understand what motivates your people to perform at higher levels and try to see that these needs are met. Rewards must compliment efforts and bonds of mutual trust must be strengthened. The lack of good relationships both downward and upward only leads to tighter and not fewer controls. You can adapt to your greater work loads by encouraging your people to accept more responsibilities. How you perceive and communicate the needs of the organization to everyone on your staff determines his or her effectiveness as well as your own. It is possible for each person to achieve many of his or her own goals while the group achieves the objectives of the organization.

A manager rarely adapts to the continuing pressures of change without some feelings of both physical and mental stress. It cannot be completely avoided; if it were, it might not benefit you, for controlled stress can be a positive force in making you a higher achiever. It is when you cannot control stress that its negative forces cause frustration, disappointment, fear, and perhaps increasing amounts of depression and loss of effectiveness. The price that you, your family, and all business associates pay can continue to spiral until you learn how to relax—both physically and mentally. Have you ever watched a cat relax? It seems like cats respond to an internal command to relax and they do so instantly. You will adapt to change and conflict much easier if you issue your own internal commands to relax. Clear the mind for a few minutes and let your thoughts drift off to a past pleasant experience or place. Picture the peacefulness and contentment of it and relive it briefly in your mind. At the same time, let your body physically fully relax. Try to let the tensions flow from your muscles while you take some slow deep breaths. For that moment put time out of your mind and unhurriedly think of past good fortunes. When and where you take this relaxation break is determined only by you. However, you must develop the sensitivity to recognize the need and say now is the time and this is the place. Your success as a manager is measured by your ability to get things done through other people; to be effective you must be relaxed.

Significant decisions are always made by great leaders who have learned the value of creative thinking and are conceptual managers and not operational managers. An effective manager puts the mathematical approach for handling the business in perspective and avoids trying to quantify the non-science areas. In some situations the sum of the parts do not always equal the whole. A concerned manager spends time on developing his or her people and recognizes that the dignity and respect for the individual has a high priority. Some contemporary managers have lost sight of this value goal and can see any means as justifying the ends as long as the latter are increased production and ever-greater efficiency. Some managers strive so hard to be efficient that they can't render an effective decision. They feel time is too valuable to be spent on getting opinions so only facts become important and these often become the vehicles to launch impulsive decisions. Good decisions cannot be hurried; an effective manager knows this and carefully reviews all alternatives. In their haste to make decisions some managers really don't identify what the real problem to the organization is. Therefore lots of decisions are implemented in solving everything, but the truly important issues continue to be neglected.

Today's business world has spotlighted the manager who, through a democratic managerial style, avoids confrontation and offers a leadership form that is often overly heavy with compromise. In some organizations where political relationships dominate management and are the keys to success, it is often taught to and adopted by new managers. In many environments, the aggressive-type manager is being pushed off the stage. As he or she exits, business is losing something valuable for these managers make effective decisions with great courage and imagination. The aggressive manager is a unilateral decision maker who makes things happen. Sometimes the decisions are not right; however, they can be corrected and they are made. When decisions are needed indecisiveness and procrastination soon cause a company to lose momentum and growth with subsequent declines in profits. The aggressive manager uses his or her experiences and abilities and the inputs of committees for insight. Most effective decisions come from self-confident managers who accept leadership responsibility. These aggressive and strong managers are shunned aside in the contemporary scene and are only turned to it times of serious problems. As they often are effective in rescuing the company, wouldn't preventative measures that use his or her skills be less costly and better than the corrective measures?

Industrial nations around the world have developed and grown because of the contributions of authoritarian leadership and the willingness of this type of manager to take risks. Modern managers often forget that they are being paid to take risks and not to avoid them. Society has lost respect for those in positions of authority, and respect is needed for a manager to command and lead people. Failure to have adequate respect further results in a weakened position to secure the accurate and complete information needed to make effective decisions. The result is that the manager becomes surrounded with much worthless data. Having inaccurate and incomplete information leads to ineffective decisions, a loss of esteem and self-assurance, and further decline in respect for the manager.

Contemporary management has replaced the authoritarian and aggressive manager with democracy throughout the organization. When this is effective and management can deliver on its commitments and promises, this should be encouraged. However, often managers are not meeting the goals and objectives and human relationships do not improve. There is an extreme to which a highly democratic leadership can move: That is the point where productivity and profitability falls to unacceptable levels. To turn this situation around requires more-aggressive and authoritarian measures than would ever have been required under a tightly run ship. Excessive democracy in management can result in much indecision and floundering with a loss of self-assurance and neglect of the mission. Dynamic growth for a firm cannot be launched from a weak foundation where decisions are the results of votes and compromise applies to all things. Excessive permissiveness often leads to a loss of control where shareholders, management, and all employees receive less.

For contemporary management to call back the aggressive and authoritarian style of management used in building many of today's great companies would be difficult, for people do not want this strong-type manager. Many people perceive the negative factors as being greater than the positive forces. However, the increasing trend in using the democratic style of management has the potential of leading to increased disorder, and people do not want this. What then is the answer? Perhaps a new management style is needed.

This new management style must be built on a base of high morality, integrity, and sensitivity. Some people within and outside of the organization look at contemporary managers with a high degree of skepticism. The new-style manager must be trustworthy beyond any doubt. Also, the manager's opinions must be expressed without inhibitions while he or she accepts and respects opinions of others. You cannot ask a person to open up with their innermost thoughts and then jump all over him or her if their comments differ from your opinions.

Examples of morality and integrity must be set on the job as well as off the job, and these must be visible to employees as well as all strata of society. Sensitivity is required to blend quantitative measurements with qualitative standards and to match performance to plans. In short, a manager must be able to accomplish his or her goals by persuading those under him or her of the correctness of his or her decisions while at the same time giving due consideration to the opinions of those same people.

Another characteristic of the new-style manager will be an improved ability to examine his or her own weaknesses and strengths. He or she must monitor very closely how each strength is being used to improve people and expand the business. This becomes an ever-more-difficult task, for organizational structures and social structures offer increasing numbers of barriers to effective interpersonal communication. This requires in-depth evaluation of the level of skill possessed for establishing power and influence while managing organizational change. Insight must be acquired as to his or her personal motivations and how they contribute to maturation and growth. As business-world pressures increase, the manager must have a safety zone where he or she can retreat to while regrouping his or her strengths. Unless you understand yourself and have in place strong guiding moral values and principles, you will lack the courage to take dissenting and aggressive positions when they are necessary. Decisions faced by tomorrow's managers will be far more complex and riskier than those in current situations. If you are to be an effective manager, you must have confidence to solve problems and to run with opportunities and challenges.

Bibliography

Berry, Charles H. *Corporate Growth and Diversification.* Princeton, N.J.: Princeton University Press, 1975.

Brown, Courtney C. *Putting the Corporate Board to Work.* New York: Macmillan, 1976.

Drucker, Peter F. *Managing in Turbulent Times.* New York: Harper & Row, 1980.

Glueck, William F. *Business Policy—Strategy Formation and Management Action.* New York: McGraw-Hill, 1976.

Guest, Robert H.; Hersey, Paul; Blanchard, Kenneth H. *Organizational Change through Effective Leadership.* Englewood Cliffs, N.J.: Prentice-Hall, 1977.

Haley, Charles W.; Schall, Lawrence P. *The Theory of Financial Decisions.* New York: McGraw-Hill, 1973.

Herman, Edward S. *Corporate Control, Corporate Power.* Cambridge: Cambridge University Press, 1981.

Johnson, Rodney D.; Siskin, Bernard R. *Quantitative Techniques for Business Decisions.* Englewood Cliffs, N.J.: Prentice-Hall, 1976.

Leontiades, Milton. *Strategies for Diversification and Change.* Boston: Little, Brown, 1980.

Lorange, Peter. *Corporate Planning: An Executive Viewpoint.* Englewood Cliffs, N.J.: Prentice-Hall, 1980.

McSweeney, Edward. *Managing the Manager.* New York: Harper & Row, 1978.

Wheelwright, Stephen C.; and Makridakis, Spyros. *Forecasting Methods for Management*, 3rd ed. New York: Wiley, 1980.

Index

About the Author

Raymond J. Winters received the Ph.D in economics and the M.B.A. in management. Dr. Winters has been active in business management since 1950, and has obtained much practical experience through his association with several major oil and insurance companies. In addition to conducting seminars throughout the world for major multinational corporations, he is teaching graduate-level courses in economics and management at the University of Michigan and Fairleigh Dickinson University. He is currently a senior institute staff member at IBM Corporation's Information Systems Management Institute.